IMISCOE Research Series

This series is the official book series of IMISCOE, the largest network of excellence on migration and diversity in the world. It comprises publications which present empirical and theoretical research on different aspects of international migration. The authors are all specialists, and the publications a rich source of information for researchers and others involved in international migration studies. The series is published under the editorial supervision of the IMISCOE Editorial Committee which includes leading scholars from all over Europe. The series, which contains more than eighty titles already, is internationally peer reviewed which ensures that the book published in this series continue to present excellent academic standards and scholarly quality. Most of the books are available open access.

Roxana Barbulescu • Sara Wallace Goodman
Luicy Pedroza

Editors

Revising the Integration-Citizenship Nexus in Europe

Sites, Policies, and Bureaucracies
of Belonging

 Springer

Editors
Roxana Barbulescu
School of Sociology and Social Policy
University of Leeds
Leeds, UK

Sara Wallace Goodman
Department of Political Science
University of California
Irvine, CA, USA

Luicy Pedroza
Centro de Estudios Internacionales
of El Colegio de México
Mexico City, Mexico

ISSN 2364-4087 ISSN 2364-4095 (electronic)
IMISCOE Research Series
ISBN 978-3-031-25728-5 ISBN 978-3-031-25726-1 (eBook)
https://doi.org/10.1007/978-3-031-25726-1

This work was supported by IMISCOE

This Springer imprint is published by the registered company Springer Nature Switzerland AG
The registered company address is: Gewerbestrasse 11, 6330 Cham, Switzerland

Acknowledgements

First and foremost, we would like to thank the authors for their valuable contributions. We would also like to thank Irina Isaakyan and Anna Triandafyllidou, our editors at the IMISCOE research series, for their helpful feedback and collection of careful reviews. Related, thank you to our anonymous reviewers for your detailed and thoughtful comments.

We thank the IMISCOE Migration, Citizenship, and Political Participation Standing Committee for their generous support in making this volume Open Access. Roxana Barbulescu would like to acknowledge funding from UK Research and Innovation Council grant ES/S007717/1.

Last, the editors would like to thank their families for their support and patience. Assembling an edited volume during a pandemic, across three countries, three time zones, with authors scattered further still, was no small feat. We regret we were never able to assemble together, in-person, but we hold out hope for the future.

Contents

Editors and Contributors

About the Editors

Roxana Barbulescu is Associate Professor in the School of Sociology and Social Policy, University of Leeds. She is the author of *Migrant Integration in a Changing Europe: European Citizens, Co-ethnics and Immigrants in Italy and Spain* (Notre Dame University Press, 2019) and co-author of *Everyday Europe: Social Transformation in an Unsettled Continent*. Her work was also published in *International Migration, Migration Studies, Perspectives on European Societies and Politics, Politique Européenne*, and *Mediterranean Politics*.

Sara Wallace Goodman is Professor of Political Science at the University of California, Irvine (UCI). She is the author of, most recently, *Citizenship in Hard Times: Ordinary Citizens in Democratic Hard Times* (Cambridge University Press, 2022). Her work has also appeared in the *Journal of Politics, International Organization, Comparative Political Studies, World Politics*, and other outlets.

Luicy Pedroza is Research-Professor at the Centro de Estudios Internacionales of El Colegio de México, in Mexico City. She is also an associate fellow at the Institute of Latin American Studies (ILAS) of the German Institute of Global and Regional Studies (GIGA). She has written *Citizenship Beyond Nationality: Immigrants' Right to Vote Across the World* (University of Pennsylvania, 2019), and her works appear journals such as *International Migration, Global Policy, Political Geography*, and *Citizenship Studies*. She co-coordinates the IMISCOE Standing Committee on Migration, Citizenship, and Political Participation (MIGCITPOL).

Contributors

Hannah Alarian University of Florida, Gainesville, FL, USA

Roxana Barbulescu School of Sociology and Social Policy, University of Leeds, Leeds, UK

Vikki Barry Brown Leverhulme Trust Doctoral Scholar, School of Geography, Queen Mary, University of London, London, UK

Alin Croitoru Lucian Blaga University of Sibiu (Romania), Sibiu, Romania

Swantje Falcke Economics and Social History at Utrecht University, Utrecht, The Netherlands

Mariña Fernández-Reino Centre on Migration, Policy and Society (University of Oxford), Oxford, UK

Sara Wallace Goodman Department of Political Science, University of California, Irvine, CA, USA

Marie Godin Refugee Studies Centre, Oxford Department of International Development, University of Oxford, Oxford, UK

Zenia Hellgren Department of Political and Social Sciences, Universitat Pompeu Fabra, Barcelona, Spain

Luicy Pedroza Centro de Estudios Internacionales of El Colegio de México, Mexico City, Mexico

Floris Peters Interdisciplinary Social Sciences at Utrecht University, Utrecht, The Netherlands

Nando Sigona Chair of International Migration and Forced Displacement, Department of Social Policy, Sociology, and Criminology at the University of Birmingham, Birmingham, UK

Djordje Sredanovic Group for Research on Ethnic Relations, Migration & Equality, Université Libre de Bruxelles, Brussels, Belgium

Madeleine Sumption Centre on Migration, Policy and Society (University of Oxford), Oxford, UK

Maarten Vink European University Institute, Fiesole, Italy

Bogdan Voicu Romanian Academy, The Research Institute for Quality of Life, Bucharest, Romania
Lucian Blaga University of Sibiu (Romania), Sibiu, Romania

Verena Wisthaler Eurac Research, Bozen/Bolzano, Italy

Ricard Zapata-Barrero Department of Political and Social Sciences, Universitat Pompeu Fabra, Barcelona, Spain

List of Figures

List of Tables

Chapter 1
Conceptualising the Citizenship-Integration Nexus

Roxana Barbulescu, Sara Wallace Goodman, and Luicy Pedroza

Citizenship is understood and practised as a status that conveys rights, protections, and privileges to an individual vis-à-vis a given state. From voting and standing for office to protections against deportation and access to public funds and welfare, citizenship provides a substantive suite of rights that distinguishes insiders (citizens) from outsiders (noncitizen immigrants). And, by establishing formal institutional ties between an individual and a polity, citizenship also designates national membership, where outsiders become insiders to the national political community. The promise of equality among citizens, a sense of status security akin with that of so-called "native" born citizens and enlarged opportunities in the community (such as better access to the labour market) make citizenship valuable and consequential and persuade thousands of migrants each year to embark on naturalisation journeys.

In linking status and rights to social and cultural inclusion, citizenship goes beyond a status: it is a membership category that denotes "who belongs" to the national political community. Citizens and would be citizens use it to narrate their identities. The question of "Who gets citizenship?" is indivisible from the question of "Who belongs?" The procedure of naturalisation, where a migrant completes a series of requirements to obtain citizenship, thus becomes synonymous with a process of immigrant integration. Sometimes integration is measured as cultural, social, political, and economic advances over time; these advances are, in turn, measured against native-born achievements and attitudes. In either case, the assumption of

R. Barbulescu
School of Sociology and Social Policy, University of Leeds, Leeds, UK
e-mail: r.barbulescu@leeds.ac.uk

S. W. Goodman (✉)
Department of Political Science, University of California, Irvine, CA, USA
e-mail: swgood@uci.edu

L. Pedroza
Centro de Estudios Internacionales of El Colegio de México, Mexico City, Mexico
e-mail: lpedroza@colmex.mx

© The Author(s) 2023
R. Barbulescu et al. (eds.), *Revising the Integration-Citizenship Nexus in Europe*, IMISCOE Research Series, https://doi.org/10.1007/978-3-031-25726-1_1

naturalisation is that it produces belonging and enables incorporation along these dimensions. But by inductively looking beyond the national level where citizenship is granted, we see belonging and incorporation occurs at a multitude of sites, especially in the everyday lives of individuals and communities, where societies are interconnected, share resources locally and where belonging is practiced. Across borders, migrants lead increasingly transnational lives, supported by a bricolage of rights and identities that simultaneously sustain both a 'here' and 'there'.

Interrogating the connection between citizenship and integration is not a new empirical inquiry, nor is it a new theoretical endeavour. Almost two decades ago, researchers convened by the Centre for European Policy Studies (CEPS) and the Centre for Migration Law (Radboud University of Nijmegen) in Brussels, Belgium, to examine the "implications and nature of the nexus." Sergio Carrera (2006, 61) summarized the discussion in noting "[c]urrent national practices and programmes linking integration to immigration and citizenship will negatively impact on the social inclusion of immigrants in European society. An EU framework on integration, if it is to be developed, should not provide a venue for some restrictive national philosophies concerning immigrants to influence the European mainstream."[1]

A lot has changed in the years since. Citizenship has become more materially substantive, but it has also become a significant harder to get. European states have implemented robust and consequential integration requirements for immigration, settlement, and citizenship (Goodman, 2014). If by the mid-2000s the concern was whether citizenship was a meaningful category for promoting incorporation, today, national citizenship has become strengthened as a category of belonging through language and country knowledge integration requirements. It is also harder to obtain because of them (Jensen et al., 2019). Moreover, the European Commission (2020) announced in November 2020 a new action plan on integration and inclusion to encourage and support integration beyond the national level, incorporating regional, and local authorities in the integration process. This builds upon a 2016 action plan by extending integration concerns from third-country nationals (immigrants from outside the EU) to recognize "the challenge of integration and inclusion is particularly relevant for migrants…who might have naturalised and are EU citizens" (Commission, 2020, 1).

Moreover, citizenship rules have also changed in terms of eligibility and retention conditions. Since the early 2000s and concerns about Islamic extremism (including European citizens fleeing to fight for the Islamic State), definitions of what comprises "good behaviour" for naturalisation have changed, and deprivation of citizenship has become more commonplace in countries like the UK and the Netherlands. The conditions for which deprivation of citizenship have proliferated particularly on grounds of threat to national security – and, crucially, the procedures of deprivation – have been simplified with prejudice for naturalised citizens (e.g., UK's Nationality and Borders Bill). Acquiring citizenship has also become more

---

[1] Where Carrera et al. discuss a tripartite nexus of immigration, integration, and citizenship, here we simply the nexus, recognizing that immigration creates the subject group, rendering it implicit but central in our discussion of the integration-citizenship nexus.

expensive for immigrants by raising the costs of application. This makes naturalisation observably more difficult for low-income noncitizens and for large families. Across Europe, fees for naturalisation have doubled in the period between 2000–2014 (Stadlmair, 2018).

Moreover, the context in which citizenship policy is being changes has altered dramatically. Two decades ago, there was an interest and political appetite for the EU to forward a common framework on immigrant integration and for EU citizenship to take on political meaning (McNamara, 2015). Much has also changed in the spirit of EU integration that characterized the wake of Enlargement towards ten new member states in 2004 (including Poland and Hungary), Bulgaria and Romania in 2007, and Croatia in 2013. Exacerbating this waning momentum, the EU has weathered several, successive crises—the eurozone crisis beginning in 2009, the "refugee crisis" in 2015, what some would characterize as the Brexit crisis of 2016, and the Covid-19 pandemic in 2020–22—increasing, with each, its technocracy. Gerhards and Lengfeld (2015) proposed still in 2015 that social integration in Europe was strong enough to withstand crises, more recent studies show heterogeneous public support for immigrant integration across countries (e.g., Dennison & Geddes, 2019; Blatter et al., 2022). Moreover, the enfranchisement of resident non-citizens (mostly at the local level) has expanded significantly in the last fifty years in Europe, further disassociating citizenship status (or nationality) from rights (Pedroza, 2019; Michel & Blatter, 2021). While the force of this trend has ebbed, the citizenship rights status quo has shifted.

For all these reasons, we think it is time to re-examine the citizenship-integration nexus.[2] National citizenship has high integration barriers and EU citizenship is not sufficient for creating integration opportunities—from education and employment to accessing health services or affordable housing. But while existing institutions may be lacking, that is not to say inclusion does not take place in other ways. Not only is the policy landscape completely different today, so too are its demographics. The EU is comprised of over 23 million non-EU citizens. And over a million immigrants come each year, some moving from one EU Member state to another ("second country nationals"), and some from outside the EU, with Ukraine, Morocco, and India topping the list. Refugees from Syria, Afghanistan, Venezuela, Colombia and – again – Ukraine, have also come in unprecedented numbers.[3]

By renewing attention to the nexus, this volume asks a series of new questions about what citizenship does and where integration takes place. Does citizenship produce integration (by which we mean social, cultural, economic, and political incorporation)? Who can acquire citizenship under the conditions, costs and expectations placed on the naturalisation process? What role do bureaucrats play in

---

[2] As a point of clarification, Carrera et al. discuss a tripartite nexus of immigration, citizenship and integration policy, but we largely exclude immigration policy from our volume, including such policies in our study only as they pertain to free movement among EU citizens.

[3] More can be found at https://ec.europa.eu/info/strategy/priorities-2019-2024/promoting-our-european-way-life/statistics-migration-europe_en

determining who accesses the process of naturalisation and how it ends? Moreover, if citizenship through integration is meant to solve the problem of immigrant belonging and membership in a society, how do we evaluate its performance across levels of government, from local to supranational? How does integration take place outside of national citizenship—either above (with EU citizenship) or below (at the regional or municipal level)? How and to what extent do regional governments move these processes of citizenship acquisition away from national *qua* nation state policies and rhetoric? Beyond official jurisdictions and different government levels, how do interactions in public spaces matter for integration and the construction of citizenship beyond formal membership?

This book asks and answers these many questions by curating a series of contributions that span levels of analysis, methodology, country cases, and theory. Each contribution revisits and revises the citizenship-integration nexus by questioning the assumptions built into its theoretical and empirical framework. This includes, at least, three: first, questioning citizenship as a vehicle of incorporation, examining instead lived experiences of belonging of communities of immigrants and EU citizens in Europe. This necessarily includes examining the promises and pitfalls of the EU as a supranational status-conveying institution. Second, examining the policies and processes of citizenship acquisition, including civic integration tests (see Goodman, 2010), language requirements, and other generalized "integration" or assimilation prerequisites. Third, considering the citizenship premium, that is, the boost to income and access to employment which typically follows the formal process of naturalisation. As alternative statuses to citizenship like long-term residence come with increasing political rights and economic mobility—especially in the case of EU citizenship—the question of whether citizenship remains the lodestar of integration is more relevant than ever. Thus, we argue in favour of reuniting the normative conversation of membership with multidisciplinary empirical accounts of belonging.

The diversity of contributions in this volume allows us to marshal a variety of qualitative and quantitative methodologies and data types, from omnibus surveys to open-ended interviews, to provide triangulated evidence on the disjuncture between social and legal integration, that is—integration and citizenship status, as well as to the diverse modes and locations of inclusion. As such, the level of analysis across the chapters moves between national sites and regions, cities and inner urban public spaces, as well as between testimonies of different communities—from Roma in London, to French, English and Italians in Bucharest or the Irish in the UK. That all these spaces contribute to the process of integration may be intuitive and obvious, but the aim of presenting these different tributaries alongside each other is to build an inductive understanding of how public policies may produce integration outcomes alongside – or even outside of – traditional naturalisation routes.

With its diverse contributions, the book demonstrates that concerns about citizenship and integration are both projected and experienced differently depending on the relation between the migrant group and the receiving society. This compels us to also incorporate ethnicity, race, class, and perceived group resources alongside our inductive approach in conceptualising the nexus.

1.1   Conceptualising the Citizenship-Integration Nexus

Most citizens acquire status at birth. There are two modes of acquisition. *Jus sanguinis* is the legal term for how most individuals inherit citizenship – by parentage, that is, directly from one generation to the other, or as the Latin translates, "by blood." A second mode is *jus soli*, which translates from Latin as 'the law of soil', i.e., being born in a given territory. While the United States, Canada, Central and South America exhibit expansive practices of *jus soli,* where even individual born of non-residents obtain citizenship at birth, European practices remain comparatively restrictive (van der Baaren & Vink, 2021). Individuals born into citizenship – regardless of the procedure – are presumed to be integrated. They have automatic ties via family, community networks, social linkages, and other processes of socialization, and these so-called "native born" are automatic insiders. In theory, they define the scale of national belonging. Of course, this is not the case in practice.

On the opposite end of the spectrum from automaticity is the process of naturalisation, a mode of citizenship acquisition for immigrant adults (and oftentimes their spouses and children). This route can be highly discretionary, costly, and require great skill to navigate myriad requirements and respective citizenship bureaucracies. Yet it is by completing this process that outsiders become insiders, or "made natural" as the very term suggests. There is an irony to naturalisation. Overall, only a minority of total citizens in the world get citizenship through naturalisation, yet it is among the more politicized dimensions of immigrant incorporation.

Scholars of global inequality have characterized citizenship as a systemic source of inequality. Ayelet Shachar (2009) has referred to birthright citizenship as a lottery, and Branko Milanovic (2016) has shown that 80% of an individual's wealth stems from where they are born and what passport (citizenship) they hold, rather than one's personal efforts. In this vein and given that citizenship mainly reproduces structural and historical injustices, Kochenov (2019) calls for rethinking citizenship not as emancipatory and democratic but as a repository of hypocrisy and domination, building on Hindess (1998), who denounced citizenship as an imperial project.

We thus recognize that citizenship and integration reproduce colonial orders and exacerbate pre-existing inequalities along gender, race, disability and income. Citizenship has a gendered dimension as historically women tended to lose their citizenship on marriage and automatically take the citizenship of their husbands. In contemporary times, as citizenship continues to have a gendered implications. For example Chap. 6 in this book discusses how political parties take different position vis-a-vis gendered sectors of migration for example highly supportive of women migrant care givers or Chap. 7 sheds new light on the gendered experiences of Muslim women who wear the scarf and how it changes their relationship with the public space in the city.

Citizenship remains the core instrument for immigrant integration, with incorporation goals tailored around milestones for naturalisation. Scholars since the late 1990s have established a cottage industry to study the determinants, effects, and meaning of naturalisation. In particular, the past two decades have seen a boom of policy indices that have made the categorization and comparison of citizenship easier than ever (see GLOBALCIT, 2017; van der Baaren & Vink, 2021; Goodman, 2015; Howard, 2009; Janoski, 2010; Palop-García & Pedroza, 2019; Schmid, 2020), including those that make connections between integration polices and access to citizenship (Ruedin, 2015) not only in Europe but in other regions of the world as well (Solano & Huddleston, 2021; Palop-García & Pedroza, 2021; Acosta 2018). Thus, there is now a significant literature on the empirics at the citizenship-integration nexus, focusing on outcomes including economic (Džankic, 2019; Peters et al., 2018; Hainmueller et al., 2019) and political integration (Hainmueller et al., 2015; Just & Anderson, 2012). There is also a large body of work that examines questions of political theory, preoccupied with questions of justice, (i)liberalism and social theory (Bosniak, 2006; Joppke, 2010; Favell, 2022; Orgad, 2015; Mouritsen, 2011; Modood et al., 2006; Vink & Bauböck, 2013; Kostakopoulou, 2003).

But, we argue, the citizenship-integration nexus has implications not just *at* naturalisation, but also *before* and *beyond* naturalisation. Naturalisation is evidence both *of* assimilation (Fouka, 2019) and a catalyst *for* it (Hainmueller et al., 2017), but there are more muted results for whether it promotes integration (Goodman & Wright, 2015), national attachment among individuals (Simonsen, 2018; Fick, 2016), or social acceptance among the wider public (Alarian & Neureiter, 2021). Then there are the noncitizens that seek citizenship for no integration purpose whatsoever, but rather to leverage the strategic, economic benefits of investment programs (Džankic, 2019; Surak, 2020), which undercuts the citizenship-integration nexus entirely by delinking residency and integration. These individuals may not be immigrants per se; though they are outsiders, they may never even seek or claim residency in the country of their purchased citizenship. Stretching this interpretation to its limit, Joppke (2021) describes citizenship today as neoliberal—harder to get and easier to lose.

If this body of research suggests citizenship performs tasks other than – and sometimes irrespective of – integration, there is also evidence from the integration literature that incorporation goals are often met irrespective of citizenship. With increasingly diverse population, the scholarship examines how states respond to foster participation, such as what types of state policy interventions work and identify obstacles that hinder participation over time (Alba, 2005; Alba & Foner, 2015; Favell, 1998, 2019, 2022; Barbulescu, 2019; Adida et al., 2016; Maxwell, 2012; Givens, 2007; Schinkel, 2017; Hochschild et al., 2013). This vein of work is often focused on access to welfare and structural barriers of discrimination (Koopmans, 2010), as well as multicultural policies, which are explicitly structured around rights recognition and accommodation (Wright et al., 2017; Citrin et al., 2014; Benhabib, 2004). This is not a critique of this scholarship so much as an acknowledgement that integration is a multi-stakeholder process, pluralist in form, manifesting at many sites, and oftentimes irrespective to the process of naturalisation, that is... at the nexus.

Contributing to and combining these scholarly conversations, and considering large-scale empirical change in the last couple of decades, we re-ask: what are the consequences of having citizenship? Does naturalisation establish political, social, economic, or cultural integration? Can we empirically identify cases of integration without citizenship and citizenship without integration?

It is important that we keep asking fundamental questions at the heart of the assumed relation between citizenship and integration, where a series of links—not merely overlaps—are established through policy at the national, supranational/EU level (Hansen, 1998; Maas, 2008, 2017), and local level (Zincone & Caponio, 2006; Adam & Jacobs, 2014; Pedroza, 2019). For instance, as Pedroza (2019) questions citizenship in its understanding as nationality, she compels us to observe the multiple layers of understandings of citizenship in single countries and to question long-assumed relations between citizen rights and nationality. Also, as increased tolerance for dual citizenship has featured as an essential component of citizenship's liberalising turn in the last decades (Baubock & Haller, 2021), holding two or more citizenships formalises multiple parallel memberships. This further challenges the nexus by allowing for strategic positioning of individuals at lower costs (Harpaz, 2019). Finally, in addition to different levels of policy (vertical differentiation) and the rise of dual citizenship, the nexus plays out across policy domains, often in non-migration policy areas such as urban planning and the governance of public spaces because these affect the process of integration and are, oftentimes, regulated through reference to different claims to citizenship (citizenship as status vs. citizenship as practice and/or identity).

Politically, the investigation of the citizenship-integration nexus is perhaps more salient now than ever. Ideals of national membership and belonging are the heart of European politics, influencing and altering not only policies of national citizenship but also practices and everyday interactions between different racial and ethnic communities. For political scientists Norris and Inglehart (2019) 'immigration' and the social transformation it triggers as communities settle and become part of the country is a key driver of what they call 'cultural backlash', or the new populism. And as populist and nationalist parties have made their way into national and European parliaments, they have transformed the politics and rhetoric of 'immigration', staging debates on the borders of identity and belonging to include what it means to be a 'national/citizen'. To wit, the EU Referendum in the UK ("Brexit") was fought on 'taking back control' and, indeed, ending the freedom of movement within the EU (Hobolt, 2016; Sobolewska & Ford, 2020; Favell & Barbulescu, 2018). For all these reasons, immigration plays an outsized, agenda-setting role in national politics and, therefore, citizenship and integration take on a new importance.

1.2 Structure of the Book

Against the rich theoretical and empirical background outlined above from the comparative research on citizenship, integration, and their interconnections, and in the context of prescient political times, the objective of this volume is to provide an up-to-date perspective on how integration and belonging—the everyday "life of citizenship"—are established and achieved alongside, or potentially in spite of, national citizenship rules. Almost two decades after the initial conference on the citizenship-integration nexus, scholars are still asking whether integration as "currently formulated in national policies and laws" coincides with "its more genuine meaning of 'social inclusion' with regard to immigrants" (Carrera et al., 2006, 61)?

This edited book assembles eighteen scholars to investigate the relationship between policies and practices of naturalisation, on the one hand, and – on the other hand – integration as seen from both the policy side and the lived experiences of migrants. Each chapter considers this nexus from the perspective of case-specific contexts. The central, shared contribution of the volume is to show how membership is achieved through, but also around, and sometimes despite formal citizenship requirements in different political and policy arenas. Thus, we consider integration through citizenship, integration below citizenship (that is, beneath the national level) and integration above and around citizenship (specifically, through EU citizenship status).

A second, related contribution is to highlight the *practice* of citizenship, both in the process and procedure of naturalisation itself and in the lived experiences of migrants in Europe. Through this treatment, we expose the fragmented and discretionary nature of citizenship. That is, by proceeding inductively to locate multiple sites of integration and, consequently, dropping the central assumption that naturalisation policy, which for being national, is homogeneously applied because requirements are enunciated in a universal manner, we also observe a far more discretionary process than a deductive approach would allow. There are large differences between procedures and outcomes, as bureaucrats are often located at "street-level" (Jones-Correa, 2001; Lipsky, 2010) and rarely operate with unambiguous guidelines.

The volume's contributions are organised across three thematic sections, to separately investigate the citizenship-integration nexus *through* the process of naturalisation (Part I), *beneath* national citizenship (Part II), and *above or around* national citizenship (Part III). Brexit serves as a particularly useful case study for assessing the before-and-after effects of EU citizenship. As supranational citizenship is the substantive focus of Part III, Brexit and the UK appear as illustrative cases for several chapters therein. As a whole, these chapters are interdisciplinary, multimethod, and consider a variety of case studies and levels of analyses.

Part I – Integration through Citizenship – interrogates how and to what extent naturalisation produces or achieves integration. In other words, it examines the status of the traditional citizenship-integration nexus today. These contributions highlight the differentiated effects of naturalisation, the markedly different interpretation of policies and practices by bureaucracies, and the experience of integration without national status at various sites, including cities. Sredanovic opens the collection with a contribution that looks directly at the procedure of naturalisation, taking us into the back offices of civil servants who decide on naturalisation applications in the UK and Belgium. With unique access, Sredanovic interviews officers on how they navigate and make sense of the evidence people collate for citizenship acquisition. Both the UK and Belgium operate with long lists of requirements including passing tests. Answering in different languages, the civil servants introduce us to how limited the guidance is, where there is flexibility for interpretation in matters of assessing integration but also in areas where one would not expect such as the modalities and reasons for entering the country. Sredanovic also brings an interpretivist perspective into the discussion—centring *ideas* of what integration means, as civil servants question the integration requirements and take clues from the lived experiences of migrants and from what they perceive or expect the economic contribution of the immigrants to be.

Next, Peters, Flacke and Vink focus on the impact of a particular policy change—increases in naturalisation fees—as a prism for understanding the (literal) value of citizenship and in what way it encourages naturalisation – that is, faster and earlier naturalisation – and produces economic returns. An extension of their extensive research program on understanding the effects of citizenship through life course analysis and, specifically, on the relationship between naturalisation and integration (in this case, economic integration), Peters, Flacke and Vink conclude that a change in naturalisation policy has an impact on the propensity to naturalise but also the stratified impact on migrants in low-pay sectors.

Last, Fernandez and Sumption provide an assessment of incentives to naturalise by looking at EU citizens living in the UK before and after Brexit, observing there was little push to naturalise prior to Brexit. However, they document the anticipation of the UK leaving the EU as intensifying the propensity of immigrants to seek British citizenship but to a lower degree for immigrants from non-EU countries, as the latter would get relatively more rights from the status.

What we learn about the citizenship-integration nexus from these studies is that there are several costs and benefits to citizenship, not all of which produce or incentivize integration. The act of becoming a citizen bears expressive and symbolic value, while the meaning attached to it are sometimes related to factors that are external to the cost-benefit calculation. Discretionary practices, high fees, and obscure rights challenge the notion that citizenship reflects, incentivizes, or produces belonging. This was a similar conclusion to the first re-examination of the nexus in 2006, in which Elspeth Guild (2006, 40) remarks "the heart of the nexus is the problem of social exclusion."

In Part II—Integration Below Citizenship—we zoom in on the perspective of the migrant communities, the opportunities of non-citizens and their everyday experiences of citizenship and integration in the absence of nationality. First, Alarian investigates the integration of non-citizens through the lens of access to economic rights. Given tense public debates on migrant eligibility to welfare rights, Alarian examines the effects of access to economic rights before citizenship. While taxed on equal basis but with fewer economic rights, Alarian elegantly poses the question about the kind of incentives that push immigrants to integrate. She shows that in the absence of citizenship, individual integration is achieved through enhanced access to economic rights, opening labour markets to immigrants but also social assistance, so that they can improve their quality of life.

Not only do migrants obtain levels of integration *before* citizenship, but they also find paths of belonging *below* the national level. Wisthaler reminds us that nation states are not the only rule-makers and that regions—particularly in secessionist states, but also autonomous regions and federal states—often define the meaning of belonging instead of centralized political authorities. Integration is rescaled and reframed to align with the collective identity and competing nation-building projects of minority nations. To investigate how regionalists achieve this, Wisthaler collects data on Stateless Nationalist and Regionalist Parties (SNRPs) in five minority regions: Basque Country (Spain), Corsica (France), South Tyrol (Italy), and Scotland and Wales (UK). The findings show that there is wide variation in how parties in minority regions define citizenship and belonging. They constitutionalise membership strategically whilst at the same time create hierarchies of deserving and integrated migrants.

The citizenship-integration nexus can also be challenged from the point of view of everyday interactions. Whilst citizenship offers equality in terms of rights, its impact on the lives of different immigrant communities is limited by and rooted in the resources and perceived characteristics of those different communities in different spaces. Zapata Barrero and Hellgren show how in everyday encounters, perceived integration is anchored in racialised and gendered assumptions rather than in the status of formal citizenship. Collating evidence across multiple years and various research projects, they illustrate how public spaces inhabited and designed by majorities can be discriminatory to minorities *with or without* citizenship, but also how the experiences collected at local scale can help to counteract negative experiences in the broader society, and promote intercultural citizenship, in an understanding beyond the formalism of citizenship-as-nationality.

By looking at integration before and below national citizenship, we see the integral role of communities, employment, and social experiences, as well as regional politics and actors. The lived experiences of immigrant non-citizens may, in the end, look functionally similar to their naturalized equivalent.

Last, Part III examines paths and possibilities of integration above citizenship, looking specifically at the institution of EU citizenship and the variety of experiences of EU citizens. Mobile EU citizens can take their rights further and develop unique transnational lives (Recchi et al., 2019). EU citizenship—the unique membership category fortified by commitment to the non-discrimination principle in Article 18 of the Treaty on the Functioning of the European Union (TFEU) enables separating naturalisation from integration. But this also potentially removes expectations on integration. Whilst integration is explicitly mandated for non-EU citizens, EU citizens are entrusted with the freedom to not integrate and 'let be' (Barbulescu, 2019, 208–225). This third part is particularly important in light of the preoccupations and recommendations of the initial examination of the citizenship-integration nexus in 2006, where the audience was the European Commission and one of the central concerns was the scope for an EU framework of integration. Part III brings into focus precisely the challenges and limitations that EU citizenship, the discourse on integration, political authority, and emerging conflicts when status comes into play.

Sigona and Godin begin this section by focusing on Roma living in London in the wake of Brexit. By focusing on the experiences of a vulnerable, deprived, and racialised community, this chapter sheds light on the emotional landscape of Non-British EU citizens, who often experience discrimination in everyday encounters in a global city that, reminding us that integration is relational and that comparisons of discourses and lived experiences in other societies matter as well.

Next, Voicu and Croitoru keep the focus on EU citizens but look at a group on the other end of the privilege spectrum, focusing on the experiences of high-skilled/ high-wage EU citizens in Bucharest, Romania. Managers and employees of multinational corporations with branches in Southeastern Europe often operate from the capital city, and they make up a unique community of non-citizens which does not perceive its integration to Romanian society to be questioned or required by the native citizens. Voicu and Croitoru's contribution demonstrates how personal resources—actual and perceived—and shared EU citizenship keep pressures and expectations to acquire national citizenship at bay.

Barry Brown brings the analysis back to the UK by looking at a third group of citizens—British citizens with Irish ancestry that are seeking to acquire Irish *qua* EU citizenship in the wake of Brexit. Specifically, this contribution looks at the nexus through the prism of the voting rights of the newly naturalised. The 'Brexit Irish' report mixed feelings as they solder together the two identities while navigating through the changing landscape of Brexit, what Brexit means, and the impact it has for the relationship of Ireland, Northern Ireland and Britain. From this site of observation, the citizenship of Irish abroad is trimmed down by policies of external voting while the Irish EU citizens themselves challenge and debate their belonging vis-à-vis the post-colonial political participation from the UK whilst absent from the Republic.

Finally, Goodman moves the discussion from the individual level and the experience of EU citizens across the continent to the institution of EU citizenship itself, asking "What can EU citizenship do?", "What was it designed to it?" and "What should it do?" This discussion is particularly important given the central role that immigrant integration concerns play in national and supranational politics and the evidence provided in the different previous chapters of the book about the diversity of experiences across individuals in the member states in terms of social, political and economic rights being premised on citizenship or not, depending on class and origin. Goodman's chapter closes the book with a larger picture on EU citizenship, showing how it conveys meaningful rights for promoting political integration, but is an incomplete status, furthering inequalities across the member states. The democratic implications, in areas from Enlargement to Brexit, are disquieting.

This book provides a substantial expansion and advancement on the citizenship-integration nexus. Overall, we show naturalisation is not a foregone pathway to integration and inclusion, local experiences are valuable for building meaningful linkages between migrants and host societies, and EU citizenship is not the panacea it might have been two decades ago. It is rather class and perceived resources that open doors to fluid migration within the EU rather than the EU citizenship as status itself.

Taken as a whole, the contributions in the volume add nuance, interdisciplinarity, and elaboration to studies of politics and policy agendas surrounding the citizenship-integration nexus. These contributions problematize the hierarchies of integration in different levels of political community and look to the different paths of institutional and societal inclusion beyond naturalisation to which migrants assign meaning irrespective of cost-benefit analyses of having a passport (in some cases an additional one) or the right to vote. Moreover, these chapters also take a critical view of the sometimes-implicit logics of deservingness behind what appear to be standard (and standardized) naturalisation rules, as well as the openly discriminatory naturalisation rules and practices and their effect on the incentives of migrants to integrate.

Studies on the citizenship-integration nexus have profited from contributions of sociologists, demographers, political geographers, anthropologists, historians, and political scientists. Today, this field is reverberating with the impulse provided by multilevel analyses that has left behind the assumptions of national homogeneity, tackling the challenges of intra-case and cross-provincial comparisons nested in cross-national comparisons. We hope the insights in this volume push scholars and policymakers alike to similarly push beyond deductive understandings of citizenship-as-integration, and think inductively about potential sites of integration, the utility of national citizenship, and alternative mechanisms to promote incorporation.

References

Acosta, D. (2018). *The national versus the foreigner in South America*. Cambridge University Press.

Adam, I., & Jacobs, D. (2014). Divided on immigration, two models for integration. The multilevel governance of immigration and integration in Belgium. In *The politics of immigration in multi-level states* (pp. 65–85). Springer.

Adida, C. L., Laitin, D. D., & Valfort, M.-A. (2016). *Why Muslim integration fails in Christian-heritage societies*. Harvard University Press.

Alarian, H. M., & Neureiter, M. (2021). Values or origin? Mandatory immigrant integration and immigration attitudes in Europe. *Journal of Ethnic and Migration Studies, 47*(5), 1006–1027.

Alba, R. (2005). Bright vs. blurred boundaries: Second-generation assimilation and exclusion in France, Germany, and the United States. *Ethnic and Racial Studies, 28*(1), 20–49.

Alba, R., & Foner, N. (2015). *Strangers no more: Immigration and the challenges of integration in North America and Western Europe*. Princeton University Press.

Barbulescu, R. (2019). *Migrant integration in a changing Europe: Immigrants, European citizens, and co-ethnics in Italy and Spain*. University of Notre Dame Press.

Baubock, R., & Haller M. (eds) (2021). *Dual Citizenship and Naturalisation. Global, Comparative and Austrian Perspectives*. Austrian Academy of Sciences.

Benhabib, S. (2004). *The Rights of Others. Aliens, Residents and Citizens*. Cambridge University Press.

Blatter, J., Michel, E., & Schmid, S. D. (2022). Enfranchisement regimes beyond de-territorialization and post-nationalism: Definitions, implications, and public support for different electorates. *Democratization, 29*, 1208. https://doi.org/10.1080/13510347.2022.2037567

Bosniak, L. (2006). *The citizen and the alien: Dilemmas of contemporary membership*. Princeton University Press.

Carrera, S., Apap, J., & Besselink, L. F. M. (2006). *The nexus between immigration, integration and citizenship in the EU*. CEPS.

Citrin, J., Levy, M., & Wright, M. (2014). Multicultural policy and political support in European democracies. *Comparative Political Studies, 47*, 1531–1557.

Commission, European. (2020). Action plan on integration and inclusion 2021–2027.

Dennison, J., & Geddes, A. (2019). A rising tide? The salience of immigration and the rise of anti-immigration political parties in Western Europe. *The Political Quarterly, 90*(1), 107–116.

Džankic, J. (2019). *The global market for investor citizenship*. Springer.

Favell, A. (1998). *Philosophies of integration: Immigration and the idea of citizenship in France and Britain*. St. Martin's Press in association with Centre for Research in Ethnic Relations, University of Warwick.

Favell, A. (2019). Integration. Twelfe propositions after Schinkel. *Comparative Migration Studies*, (12), 7.

Favell, A. (2022). *Immigration and colonial power in Liberal democracies*. Polity Press.

Favell, A., & Barbulescu, R. (2018). Brexit, 'Immigration' and anti-discrimination. In P. Diamond, P. Nedergaard, & B. Rosamond (Eds.), *The Routledge handbook of the politics of Brexit* (pp. 118–133). Routledge.

Fick, P. (2016). Does naturalization facilitate integration?: A longitudinal study on the consequences of citizenship Acquisition for Immigrants' identification with Germany. *Zeitschrift für Soziologie, 45*(2), 107–121. https://doi.org/10.1515/zfsoz-2015-1006

Fouka, V. (2019). How do immigrants respond to discrimination? The case of Germans in the US during world war I. *American Political Science Review, 113*(2), 405–422.

Gerhards, J., & Lengfeld, H. (2015). *European citizenship and social integration in the European Union*. Routledge. https://www.routledge.com/European-Citizenship-and-Social-Integration-in-the-European-Union/Gerhards-Lengfeld/p/book/9780815351498

Givens, T. E. (2007). Immigrant integration in Europe: Empirical research. *Annual Review of Political Science, 10*, 67–83.

GLOBALCIT. (2017). Global Database on Modes of Acquisition of Citizenship, version 1.0. Global Citizenship Observatory/Robert Schuman Centre for Advanced Studies/European University Institute. https://globalcit.eu/acquisition-citizenship/

Goodman, S. W. (2010). Integration requirements for Integration's sake? Identifying, Categorising and comparing civic integration policies. *Journal of Ethnic and Migration Studies, 36*(5), 753–772.

Goodman, S. W. (2014). *Immigration and membership politics in Western European*. Cambridge University Press.

Goodman, S. W. (2015). Conceptualizing and measuring citizenship and integration policy past lessons and new approaches. *Comparative Political Studies, 48*(14), 1905–1941.

Goodman, S. W., & Wright, M. (2015). Does mandatory integration matter? Effects of civic requirements on immigrant socioeconomic and political outcomes. *Journal of Ethnic and Migration Studies, 41*(12), 1885–1908. https://doi.org/10.1080/1369183X.2015.1042434

Hainmueller, J., Hangartner, D., & Pietrantuono, G. (2015). Naturalization fosters the long-term political integration of immigrants. *Proceedings of the National Academy of Sciences, 112*(41), 12651–12656.

Hainmueller, J., Hangartner, D., & Pietrantuono, G. (2017). Catalyst or crown: Does naturalization promote the long-term social integration of immigrants? *American Political Science Review, 111*(2), 256–276.

Hainmueller, J., Hangartner, D., & Ward, D. (2019). Citizenship increases the long-term earnings of marginalized immigrants.

Hansen, R. (1998). A European citizenship or a Europe of citizens? Third country nationals in the EU. *Journal of Ethnic and Migration Studies, 24*(4), 751–768.

Harpaz, Y. (2019). *Citizenship 2.0*. Princeton University Press.

Hindess, B. (1998). Divide and rule: The international character of modern citizenship. *European Journal of Social Theory, 1*, 57–70.

Hobolt, S. B. (2016). The Brexit vote: A divided nation, a divided continent. *Journal of European Public Policy, 23*(9), 1259–1277. https://doi.org/10.1080/13501763.2016.1225785

Hochschild, J., Chattopadhyay, J., Gay, C., & Jones-Correa, M. (2013). *Outsiders no more?: Models of immigrant political incorporation*. Oxford University Press.

Howard, M. M. (2009). *The politics of citizenship in Europe*. Cambridge University Press.

Janoski, T. (2010). *The ironies of citizenship. Naturalization and integration in industrialized countries*. Cambridge University Press.

Jensen, K. K., Mouritsen, P., Bech, E. C., & Olsen, T. V. (2019). Roadblocks to citizenship: Selection effects of restrictive naturalisation rules. *Journal of Ethnic and Migration Studies, 47*, 1–19.

Jones-Correa, M. (2001). Institutional and contextual factors in immigrant naturalization and voting. *Citizenship Studies, 5*(1), 41–56.

Joppke, C. (2010). *Citizenship and immigration, immigration & society*. Polity.

Joppke, C. (2021). From liberal to neoliberal citizenship: A commentary on Marion Fourcade. *The British Journal of Sociology, 72*(2), 181–189.

Just, A., & Anderson, C. J. (2012). Immigrants, citizenship and political action in Europe. *British Journal of Political Science, 42*(3), 481–509. https://doi.org/10.2307/23274135

Kochenov, D. (2019). *Citizenship*. MIT Press.

Koopmans, R. (2010). Trade-offs between equality and difference: Immigrant integration, multiculturalism and the welfare state in cross-National Perspective. *Journal of Ethnic and Migration Studies, 36*(1), 1–26. https://doi.org/10.1080/13691830903250881

Kostakopoulou, D. (2003). Why naturalisation? *Perspectives on European Politics and Society, 4*(1), 85–115. https://doi.org/10.1080/15705850308438854

Lipsky, M. (2010). *Street-level bureaucracy: Dilemmas of the individual in public service*. Russell Sage Foundation.

Maas, W. (2008). Migrants, states, and EU citizenship's unfulfilled promise. *Citizenship Studies, 12*(6), 583–596.

Maas, W. (2017). Boundaries of political community in Europe, the US, and Canada. *Journal of European Integration, 39*(5), 575–590.

Maxwell, R. (2012). *Ethnic minority migrants in Britain and France: Integration trade-offs*. Cambridge University Press.

McNamara, K. R. (2015). *The politics of everyday Europe: Constructing authority in the European Union*. Oxford University Press.

Michel, E., & Blatter, J. (2021). Enfranchising immigrants and/or emigrants? Attitudes towards voting rights expansion among sedentary nationals in Europe. *Ethnic and Racial Studies, 44*(11), 1935–1954.

Milanovic, B. (2016). *Global inequality*. Harvard University Press.

Modood, T., Triandafyllidou, A., & Zapata-Barrero, R. (2006). *Multiculturalism, Muslims and citizenship: A European approach*. Routledge.

Mouritsen, P. (2011). Beyond post-national citizenship: Access, consequence, conditionality. In A. Triandafyllidou, T. Modood, & N. Meer (Eds.), *European Multiculturalisms* (pp. 88–115). Edinburgh University Press.

Norris, P., & Inglehart, R. (2019). *Cultural backlash: Trump, Brexit, and authoritarian populism*. Cambridge University Press.

Orgad, L. (2015). *The cultural defense of nations: A Liberal theory of majority rights*. Oxford University Press.

Palop-García, P., & Pedroza, L. (2019). How do we move migration policy datasets and indices further? A proposal to address persisting lacunae and major research imperatives. *Newsletter of the American Political Science Association's Organized Section on Migration and Citizenship, 7*(1), 37–52.

Palop-García, P., & Pedroza, L. (2021). Do diaspora engagement policies endure? An update of the emigrant policies index (EMIX) to 2017. *Global Policy, 12*(3), 361–371.

Pedroza, L. (2019). *Citizenship beyond nationality*. University of Pennsylvania Press.

Peters, F., Vink, M., & Schmeets, H. (2018). Anticipating the citizenship premium: Before and after effects of immigrant naturalisation on employment. *Journal of Ethnic and Migration Studies, 44*(7), 1051–1080.

Recchi, E., Favell, A., Apaydin, F., Barbulescu, R., Braun, M., Ciornei, I., Cunningham, N., Medrano, J. D., Duru, D., Hanquiet, L., Poetzschke, S., Reimer, D., Salamonska, J., Savage,

M., Jensen, J. S., & Varela, A. (2019). *Everyday Europe. Social Transnationalism in an unsettled continent*. Polity Press.

Ruedin, D. (2015). Increasing validity by recombining existing indices: MIPEX as a measure of citizenship models. *Social Science Quarterly, 96*(2), 629–638.

Schinkel, W. (2017). *Imagined societies: A critique of immigrant integration in Western Europe*. Cambridge University Press.

Schmid, S. D. (2020). The architecture of national boundary regimes: Mapping immigration and citizenship policies in 23 democracies 1980–2010. *Comparative Migration Studies, 8*(1), 1–20.

Shachar, A. (2009). *The birthright lottery: Citizenship and global inequality*. Harvard University Press.

Simonsen, K. B. (2018). What it means to (Not) belong: A case study of how boundary perceptions affect second-generation immigrants' attachments to the nation. *Sociological Forum, 33*(1), 118–138.

Sobolewska, M., & Ford, R. (2020). *Brexitland. Identity, diversity and the reshaping of British Politics*. Cambridge University Press.

Solano, G., & Huddleston, T. (2021). Beyond immigration: Moving from Western to global indexes of migration policy. *Global Policy, 12*(3), 327–337.

Stadlmair, J. (2018). Earning citizenship. Economic criteria for naturalisation in nine EU countries. *Journal of Contemporary European Studies, 26*(1), 42–63.

Surak, K. (2020). Who wants to buy a visa? Comparing the uptake of residence by investment programs in the European Union. *Journal of Contemporary European Studies, 30*, 1–19.

van der Baaren, L., & Vink, M. (2021). Modes of acquisition and loss of citizenship around the World-Comparative typology and main patterns in 2020. *Robert Schuman Centre for Advanced Studies Research Paper No.# RSC 90*.

Vink, M. P., & Bauböck, R. (2013). Citizenship configurations: Analysing the multiple purposes of citizenship regimes in Europe. *Comparative European Politics, 11*(5), 621–648.

Wright, M., Johnston, R., Citrin, J., & Soroka, S. (2017). Multiculturalism and Muslim accommodation: Policy and predisposition across three political contexts. *Comparative Political Studies, 50*(1), 102–132.

Zincone, G., & Caponio, T. (2006). 10. The multilevel governance of migration. In *The dynamics of migration and settlement in Europe* (pp. 269–304). Amsterdam University Press.

Part I
Integration Through Citizenship

Chapter 2
Ideas of Integration in Citizenship Laws and Citizenship Acquisition Procedures in Belgium and the UK

Djordje Sredanovic

The sociological study of formal citizenship has been strongly shaped by Brubaker's (1992) analysis of citizenship legislation in France and Germany. Brubaker's intuition was that citizenship laws express the conceptions of membership hold by governments and administrations, if not the society at large (although the author dissociated himself from the simplifications that subdivided nations in "ethnic" and "civic" – Brubaker, 1999).

Subsequent research on everyday citizenship, that is, the study of the conceptions of citizenship of the general population, has shown that the content of the laws does not necessarily match the larger ideas about membership in a society (see e.g. Miller-Idriss, 2006 on Germany and Sredanovic, 2014 on Italy). Further, the study of the bureaucracies of citizenship, while less developed, has shown that the bureaucracies sometimes hold conceptions of membership distinct from those in the law. Hajjat's study of a French prefecture (2012) for example showed that the personnel examining citizenship applications saw the requirements of the law in terms of *integration* despite the letter of the law referring to *assimilation*. Further, the fact that an applicant wore a hijab, officially considered a proof of lack of assimilation both in court judgements and in ministerial circulars, was reinterpreted by the agents interviewed by Hajjat, either refusing to interpret whether the veil worn by the applicant was the "Islamic" hijab proof of lack of assimilation, or following other criteria than those indicated by the ministerial circular (see also Hajjat, 2010).

D. Sredanovic (✉)
Group for Research on Ethnic Relations, Migration & Equality, Université Libre de Bruxelles, Brussels, Belgium
e-mail: djordje.sredanovic@ulb.be

© The Author(s) 2023
R. Barbulescu et al. (eds.), *Revising the Integration-Citizenship Nexus in Europe*, IMISCOE Research Series, https://doi.org/10.1007/978-3-031-25726-1_2

In this chapter I compare the conceptions of integration identifiable in the legislation of Belgium and the UK, and those expressed by the officers of different institutions working on the acquisition of nationality[1] in the two countries. I will largely focus on "ordinary" acquisitions of nationality, that is, the provisions for those not born in the country and not benefitting from reduced requirements. A number of different provisions exist in the laws of the two countries, based on birth in the country, family links, age, disability, "exceptional" merits and, in the UK, on the complex colonial history (on the latter dimension see Sredanovic, 2017). Both Belgium and the UK have seen the introduction of restrictive requirements reflecting a large integrationist tendency in nationality policies across most of Western Europe (cf. Joppke & Morawska, 2003; Goodman, 2010; Rea et al., 2018). It is of interest to examine to what degree the officers working on nationality adhere to such integrationist approach, and whether the visions of integration of the agents are different from those expressed in the policies and in the political debate. Implementation research has shown that bureaucrats tend to apply their own notions of merit when applying policies (Lipsky, 2010). More specifically research on the implementation of migration policies, including residence procedures in France (Spire, 2008) and visa procedures in Belgian consulates (Infantino & Rea, 2012), have shown the tendency of bureaucrats to pursue what they perceive as policy objectives beyond, and even against, the letter of the law. In the cases I present here, the focus on integration in the political debate has left significant traces in the letter of the law, and has filtered down to a degree to the everyday activity of the officers I interviewed. However, the action of the officers seems to be much less oriented by notions of integration that one would expect: with a limited explicit mandate in the letter of the law to verify the integration of the candidates, the interviewees seemed to be more interested in verifying the formal requirements, and in other issues, such as fraud.

In the following pages I first offer some background on the general conditions and procedures for the obtention of nationality in Belgium and the UK, and details about the method of the research. I then discuss the several ways in which integrationist measures have found place in the nationality legislation of the two countries. Focusing on the interview data, I show the ways in which, despite significant space for discretion, the Home Office pursued in a limited ways ideas of integration (although Nationality Checking Services seemed more interested in the concept). I further show how officers working on nationality in Belgium did discuss notions of integration, but mostly within the limits of the formal requirements set in the letter of the law.

---

[1] In UK policy "citizenship" and "nationality" are used interchangeably to indicate the legal status, but in Belgian policy only nationality ("nationalité") is used in this sense. Moreover, while in the UK "naturalisation" indicates the acquisition of citizenship, in Belgium the term is reserved to a special procedure involving the Chamber of Representatives, while the main procedure is called "declaration". In this text I therefore usually use "nationality" and "nationality acquisition" for the context of both countries, except when referring directly to previous literature or to specific provisions in UK law.

2.1   Policies of Naturalization

Here, I present the essential lines of the nationality legislation in Belgium and the UK, before analysing more in detail the integrationist measures present in both countries and the ways in which the concept of integration is managed by the officers implementing the law. In addition to the integrationist orientation present in both the countries, both Belgium and the UK had a two-step procedure at the time of the research, but the UK is an example of a high-discretion citizenship law, while Belgium is characterised by significant limits to the discretion of the officers examining nationality applications. While both the UK and Belgium have decentralised significant domains of policy, including, in Belgium, integration policy (Adam et al., 2018), nationality policy is exclusive domain of the central government in both countries.

In Belgium the nationality application normally requires five years of residence, and has to be submitted to the municipal register of the municipality of residence. The register theoretically should control the presence of all the documents required and transfer the application to the magistrates of the *parquet* – the local office of the *procureur du Roi* ("royal prosecutor"). In practice the municipal registers usually verified whether the applicant meets the requirements and often refused to transfer the application if they consider that some requirements are not met (cf. Sredanovic, 2020, 2022). Once the application reaches the local *parquet* the magistrates verify that it meets the requirements, which, given the "documentary" (Wautelet, 2014) approach of the Belgian law, in which almost all the requirements are expressed by the possession of specific documents, theoretically involves little work of appreciation. If the magistrates consider one of the requirements not to have been met, they can oppose the application, and every opposition can be appealed in the local court. Despite the limited discretion allowed by the law, the decentralised procedure brings to a significant local variation in interpreting aspects of the law such as the definition of employment and the degrees acceptable to fulfil integration requirements, as well as the infractions of the law taken into consideration (Sredanovic, 2020, 2022).

As mentioned, the UK is similar to Belgium in terms of presence of integration requirements and of a potential two-step procedure, but differs in the much larger discretion attributed to officers and in the centralisation of the procedure in a single entity located in Liverpool. In the UK an applicant has first to obtain indefinite leave to remain, which requires five years of residence and completing an English language test and a Life in the UK test. Once this status is obtained, all the applications for nationality are examined by the citizenship team of the UKVI (UK Visas and Integration, a division of the Home Office) in Liverpool. The applicant can choose to send the application directly to Liverpool, but could also choose to use a Nationality Checking Service, a service that local authorities could choose to activate to help with the applications. Starting with the end of 2018, however, the public services of the Nationality Checking Services were transferred to private operators. Differently from Belgium, the UKVI needs to give a formal acceptance of the application, as the procedure is discretionary, and only in limited cases a refusal can be appealed in court.

2.2 Methodology and Research Design

The ethnographic parts of this chapter are based on research conducted between 2016 and 2017 on the implementation of nationality legislation of the UK and Belgium. The main aim of the research was to analyse the discretion and the variation present in the implementation of the laws, but in this chapter I focus in particular on the ways in which integration was discussed (or not) in the interviews collected. The research project included in-depth qualitative interviews with officers working at different institutions linked with nationality acquisition. In Belgium this included 7 interviews with magistrates working in *parquets* and 23 interviews with civil registers across the national territory. In the UK I conducted interviews in 7 Nationality Checking Services in Northern England and Wales, and with 14 officers working on citizenship at UKVI in Liverpool (the latter interviews were conducted together with Émilien Fargues). I contacted most of the institutions involved in the research directly, aiming to represent the territory chosen for the two research projects (the whole national territory for Belgium, Northern England and Wales for the UK), although non-response from several institutions contacted means that, for example, Flemish institutions were under-represented.

The interview guidelines included questions about the organisation of work of each institution (number of employees, routines, volume of work, challenges in their work, formal and informal relations with other institutions), as well as about the interpretation of specific points of the law that emerged as potentially complex from the analysis of the laws and from the first interviews. The participants were asked to describe their own experiences. One important point is that I did not ask the interviewees about their personal opinions about nationality and immigration, as did for example Hajjat (2010) and Andreouli and colleagues (Andreouli & Stockdale, 2009; Andreouli & Dashtipour, 2014). The focus of the research was rather on the practices through which the law is implemented, and the visions analysed here emerged while discussing the everyday operations in applying the law. This means that the interviewees did not express all their opinions, but arguably only those they felt were both legitimate and relevant enough to be mentioned when discussing their work. While the personal opinions are certainly one of the factors that define how laws are implemented, other factors, including the organisation of work, routines, and institutional culture, can be equally or more important (see Sredanovic, 2020, 2022 for a more detailed analysis of the factors in the implementation of nationality law in Belgium and the UK).

The interviews have been conducted in English in the UK and in most institutions in Flanders, and in French in the rest of Belgium. Most interviews have been audio-recorded, always with the authorisation of the interviewees.[2]

2.3 Integrationism in UK and Belgian Nationality Legislation

Citizenship legislation both in the UK and in Belgium has been influenced by the restrictive European tendency toward integrationism in citizenship laws that started in the late 1990s and accelerated after 9/11. Such a tendency requires the applicants for citizenship (but also for permanent residence and, in some cases, for family regroupment) to prove their cultural and linguistic integration, as well as participation in paid work (see e.g. Joppke & Morawska, 2003; Goodman, 2010; Rea et al., 2018). The wave of new requirements reached the UK early, with the New Labour 2002 Nationality, Immigration and Asylum Act introducing formal requirements for applicants to pass both a language and a "Life in the UK" test. Belgium was a relative latecomer, as it has introduced requirements of linguistic, economic and social integration only in 2012, and had a particularly inclusive law between 2000 and 2012 (de Jonghe & Doutrepont, 2013; Wautelet, 2014). Indeed, the 2012 reform has been identified as a shift from nationality as a tool of integration to integration as a requirement of nationality (de Jonghe & Doutrepont, 2013), with some Socialist and Green francophone politicians defending the former approach in the Parliamentary debates around the new law (Sredanovic, 2018). While there has been a clear tendency towards integrationism in Western Europe, cultural requirements existed even before (as noted also by van Oers, 2013): in Belgium cultural and linguistic integration, as well as lack of criminal past, were all examined before 2000 through police interviews. The UK policy was relatively less integrationist, but still formally required knowledge of English (or Welsh or Scottish Gaelic), which was verified only in exceptional cases and through interviews (van Oers, 2013). In other contexts, such as the Swiss one, naturalisation well before the integrationist wave involved procedures that were strongly based on conceptions of merit, and included highly invasive procedures such as circulating a profile of the applicant among all the citizens of the municipality (who often had the right to vote on the individual application), or in some cases the examination of the applicants' high school report cards or bank accounts (Centlivres et al., 1991).

The language and "Life in the UK" tests in UK citizenship law have received extensive attention in literature, being recognised as a form of backlash against multiculturalism, as stigmatisation of the Muslim population in particular, after the 2001 riots in some Northern England cities and then the 2005 London bombings, and as the neoliberal promotion of an "active citizenship" closer to individual

---

[2] With the exception of those conducted at UKVI, for which the author retains extensive notes.

responsabilisation for the failures of the state than to a form of political agency (Kostakopoulou, 2010; van Oers, 2013; Turner, 2014; Puzzo, 2016; Byrne 2017). Not only the tests, but also the ceremonies and the oath have been recognised as part of this design (Byrne, 2012, 2014). A couple of observations could be added to this already substantial literature. While the reform of citizenship in the UK had a clear multicultural backlash content, two of the "autochthonous" minority languages, Welsh and Scottish Gaelic, were legitimated by their inclusion among the languages in which one can take the test (despite the latter having far less speakers in the UK than, for example, Polish or Punjabi). Secondly, while the New Labour reforms of citizenship were clearly inspired by a notion of cultural failure on the part of migrants and their descendants, the policy strived to express requirements in "civic" terms, insisting on learning "everyday" society skills. The "civic" approach of the New Labour government developed in a rather extremist direction with the 2008 Green Paper "The Path to Citizenship" which included plans for provisions such as probationary citizenship, increased residence requirements for those not engaged in volunteering, and barring applicants from obtaining nationality because of infractions committed by their children (Kostakopoulou, 2010). Such civic focus was reversed by the Conservative-Liberal Democratic coalition elected in 2010, which first abandoned the more radical civic plans of the Green Paper, and then explicitly culturalised the Life in the UK test in 2013 by rewriting the official manual to include more references to British history and culture (Turner, 2014; Puzzo, 2016; Byrne, 2017).

In Belgium, with a much higher level of multilingualism than the UK, one of the main issues was defining at what level should migrants integrate culturally. The current Belgian law requires explicitly linguistic *and* social integration, although the two are often linked. Both integration requirements are considered satisfied when the candidate has been in paid work during the qualifying period, recognising an integrative role of work (but see *infra* on contractual requirements). Linguistic integration can also be proved by passing a language test, while having obtained a high school or higher degree in one of the national languages in Belgium also fulfils both the social and the linguistic integration requirement. If the degree was obtained in one of the national languages and in an EU member state, it can be used to prove linguistic integration. The EU limitation is probably linked to issues of common educational frameworks, although it has the effect of othering, for example, francophone education outside Europe (and, presumably, in Switzerland). Both requirements can be further fulfilled by completing an integration course. As integration courses are defined by the three linguistic communities (Dutch-, French- and German-speaking, plus the Brussels Region, which is part both of the French-speaking and the Dutch-speaking communities, and therefore autonomous), this also means that migrants can integrate on a regional level. This was indeed part of the parliamentary debate about the new law. Most French-speaking parties (usually more centralist/unitary) were both sceptical about the integration requirements, and insisted on making the knowledge of any of the national languages the requirement. Most Dutch-speaking parties (usually more localist/autonomist) insisted that migrants should be required to learn the language of the region of residence (see

Sredanovic, 2018). In the end the law requires the knowledge of one of the national languages, making the integration policy not entirely regionalist. One provision of the Belgian law opens theoretically to an integration evaluation on the part of the magistrates of the *parquets*. Candidates who have been resident at least 10 years in Belgium and prove the linguistic integration can have economic and social integration requirements waived if they prove the "participation to the life of the community". Some examples of such "participation" are given in the ministerial circular (8 March 2013) to include formation or work in Belgium or the involvement in associations; the same circular categorically excludes associations linked to the country of origin, showing a fear of "separate societies".

In addition to integrationist measures, the applicant is required to be free of dangerousness, a requirement that is extended in both countries by avoiding legislating in full on the matter. The UK has an extensive and inherently moralising requirement of good character (see Kapoor & Narkowicz, 2019 for an in-depth analysis). The January 2019 Home Office guidance includes among the signs of the lack of good character having been subjected to any sort of police measures, including fines and community sentences (which include court-ordered measures such as alcohol treatment and mental health treatment). Furthermore, such signs include irregularity in the migration history, as well as suspected criminal activity, associations with criminal or extremist organisations and individuals, bankruptcy, and having unpaid taxes or NHS charges. Failure on the part of the applicant to disclose one of these signs is constructed in itself as lack of good character. The officers are called to take in account the time elapsed since the event and disregard minor infractions, but also to identify patterns of "persistent" offences. Moreover, the officers are called to decide whether the sum of different signs suggest a lack of good character, which means that even aspects such as marital status, sexuality and lifestyle, which are defined as normally irrelevant, could be taken in consideration if they become "notorious". In the Belgian legislation the concept of *faits personnels graves* ("serious personal infractions") is used to define a number of factors that can bar from obtaining nationality. The (implementing) Royal decree names explicitly among such impediments for naturalisation crimes punished by a non-suspended prison sentence (as well as procedures that can bring to the same outcome). The decree further mentions explicitly having obtained one's residence through fraud, while the law mentions condemnation for social and fiscal fraud. An explicit definition of crimes barring form naturalisation was a request advanced by the magistrates, who were struggling to implement the law (Apers, 2014). However, the courts' orientation was that those given in legislation were only examples rather than a full list, leaving the situation open (see *infra* on the implementation). An even larger typology of dangerous behaviours included in the Royal decree derives from the reference to security issues as a basis for opposing a nationality application. The security issues are defined through a reference to the Law of 30 November 1998 on intelligence and security services. The latter, giving a large domain of activity to security services, mentions not only links with espionage, terrorism and criminal organisation, but also links with "extremist" organisations (including, among others, nationalist, "totalitarian" and anarchist organisations), and with "sectarian" organisations.

It is clear that such a definition gives extensive discretionary powers regarding nationality policy to security services. While according to my fieldwork security-based oppositions do not seem to be largely used, there are individual cases in which applicants receive an opposition for issues of security, being unable to know the reason of such opposition (and therefore unable to challenge it effectively in court), always for security reasons (Wautelet, 2014).

Another point on which the existing literature on the "integrationist wave" has not focused is the degree to which States want their future citizens to be settled and relatively immobile. The Belgian law requires the qualifying period of five years to be covered by uninterrupted long-term (over three months) legal residence statuses, and limits the toleration of absences from the national territory to periods of six months maximum and/or a maximum one fifth of the residence requirement. The UK similarly tolerates a maximum of 450 days abroad in five years and a maximum of 90 days abroad in the last qualifying year, although some lenience can be discretionally exercised if longer absences are justified by the demands of one's employer. Moreover, if the Belgian law is mostly satisfied with legal residence, in the UK, where legal residence is less clearly defined, candidates have to prove the *physical* presence on the territory, something that can be particularly challenging for candidates less subject to migration controls, such as (at least until the end of 2020) EU27 citizens. Moreover, the UK nationality law has an unusual explicit request that the new citizen makes the UK her or his main residence. While most of the migration literature in the last two decades has insisted on the capacity of migrants to form links with the country of residence despite continued links with the country of origin (e.g. Erdal & Oeppen, 2013) or despite high levels of mobility (e.g. Trenz & Triandafyllidou, 2017), states seem to continue to look at mobile people with suspicion, considering them apparently to lack authentic attachment to the future country of citizenship.

The UK law remains less integrationist than many in Europe by not including employment or income requirements – although such requirements are indirectly enforced through the requirements present in the immigration legislation, as well as through the exceptionally high citizenship fee (cf. Stadlmair, 2018 on how fees and economic requirements stratify by class the applicants). The Belgian law on the other hand explicitly requires most applicants to have spent most of the qualifying period in work, education or training – even profiles that in other countries are exempt from this kind of requirements, such as spouses of citizens, need to fulfil this requirement. While the formulation of the requirement recognises education and (some forms of) training along with work, it still excludes unpaid forms of work from definitions of integration. Further, while work is implicitly recognised as facilitating linguistic and social integration, only applicants that have worked uninterruptedly for the 5 qualifying years are exempted from proving separately linguistic and social integration. While Belgian governments, as most governments in Europe, have spent the last four decades reducing guarantees for workers and promoting temporary forms of work (see e.g. Bouquin, 2006), it is curious that in the nationality legislation candidates in regular, long-term employment are considered to be super-integrated.

2.4   UK: The Routinisation of Integration Requirements

In the the UK, the law does not require officers to verify integration, differently from what happens for example in France (see Hajjat, 2012). Instead, the UK law gives substantial discretionary powers to the Home Secretary: each naturalisation is a concession made by the Home Secretary, who can also decide to waive some requirements, including those relative to physical presence on the territory and absence of irregularities in the immigration history. Such large discretionary powers are largely exercised by the officers of the Home Office.

It is somehow surprising therefore that integration has a limited role in guiding the implementation of the nationality law within the Home Office. None of the case workers interviewed at the UKVI mentioned integration as something that was to be examined or more generally as an issue to be considered. As I discuss immediately below, much more attention was given to ordinary checking of the requirements and to the issue of fraud. Further, in an interview with two managers of the UKVI, direct questions about the role of integration in implementing the law were met with a certain perplexity, as examining the integration of applicants was not perceived to be a part of the mission of the citizenship team, and the integration aims were rather considered to be already fulfilled by the existence and the contents of the Life in the UK test. Upon hearing how "assimilation" was assessed in the procedures in France, the two interviewees further considered the procedure excessively subjective. Curiously, one of the few dimensions of integration mentioned by the two interviewees was that of the intention of remaining in the UK.

Considering the strong emphasis on integration behind the reforms, this could be read as a disjuncture between the policy and the implementation. However, such disjuncture is already present in the letter of the law, which indeed does not include indications to examine the integration of the candidates. The orientation of the officers of the UKVI is part of more general self-limiting approach in nationality questions, in which the ample discretion given by the law is reduced through the routinisation of decisions, aiming to have a relatively uniform treatment of the applications (Sredanovic, 2022).

The few exceptions in which some notions of merit, if not strictly of integration, did emerge, were linked to the discussion of "special" cases. Members of the armed forces, particularly if wounded in combat, were considered difficult to refuse nationality to – which meant that an application that fell short of some requirements was considered difficult to reject, although there were no special formal provisions existing for the naturalisation of the category.

A significant exception to the self-limitation in the use of discretionary powers existed in the examination of potential fraud. I have already underlined how the UK nationality policy is particularly stringent in regards to irregularities in the migratory experiences and to minor infractions. A similar stringency existed around the detection of possible fraud in the application. A number of caseworkers among those interviewed mentioned the importance of identifying fake documents among those submitted with the application – an issue that on the contrary was hardly ever mentioned in the interviews conducted in Belgium. Further issues of fraud were seen in reference to language proficiency. The results of the language test could be considered suspect if the test had been completed in a very short time and with few errors, and at the same time there were doubts about the actual competence of the applicant. However, communications from Nationality Checking Services about the lack of competence of an applicant – which were sent from time to time to Liverpool – could be disregarded if the local registrar spoke English with a strong local accent. The worries linked to suspicion of fraud in language test have been further exacerbated by a reportage of the BBC programme Panorama in 2014, in which some language test centres have been shown to allow sham successful tests in exchange for money. The reportage brought to a tightening of the management of the security of the tests, in order to make any kind of fraud harder (see Harding et al., 2020). This kind of worries had had an impact beyond the increased suspects of fraud, as a large number of foreign students have been expelled from the UK because the English language test necessary for their visa was taken in a language test centre considered to be a sham – although often there are no proofs, or indeed credibility, of an individual fraud (cf. York, 2018; National Audit Office, 2019).

I mentioned in the previous paragraph the abandonment of the 2008 Green Paper and of its radical civic approach to integrationism. The two managers mentioned above explained the abandonment of such plans by referring to doubts about requiring businessmen from other anglophone countries to volunteer in order to naturalise.

The integrationist orientation did however remain significantly inscribed in citizenship ceremonies, which do promote an image of the newly naturalised as integrated and participating to the local community (cf. Byrne, 2012, 2014). The workers of the Nationality Checking Services, who were often involved also in citizenship ceremonies, could therefore be closer to an integrationist approach than the officers working on nationality in the Home Office. An earlier research project conducted between 2007 and 2009, in which the importance of citizenship ceremonies was also noted, also included interviews with Nationality Checking Service workers (Andreouli & Stockdale, 2009; Andreouli & Dashtipour, 2014). In that research project, there was evidence that the officers of Nationality Checking Services expected the applicants to be employed and active in the local society (Andreouli & Dashtipour, 2014) – something that Andreouli and colleagues correctly observe was an official aim of the New Labour citizenship policies of the time, but, as I mentioned, is also something that was never included in the letter of the law. Some of the interviewees in the same research presented xenophobic positions that criticized the migrants as an economic burden or as reproducing separate cultures (Andreouli & Stockdale, 2009).

My interviews with Nationality Checking Service officers did not show a similar interest in integration issues, nor such integrationist attitudes. Such differences could be linked to the time passed between the two research projects, or even to geographical differences (London in the research of Andreouli and colleagues, Northern England and Wales in mine), but most probably the difference is linked to the interview approach. My interviewees arguably did not perceive that their personal opinions were relevant to their job. Indeed, such opinions could have brought

some to decide whether to dissuade specific candidates, but Nationality Checking Service officers did not have a role as determinant as the officers of the Home Office.

When some ideas of merit or integration emerged, it was sometime in reference to marginal details, such as the quality of the filled-in forms

> Officer 1: I mean, some people are so organised, it's perfect, the form is so perfect, immaculate […] other people come and it's a mess, it's scribbled down…
> Officer 2: Certain nationalities tend to be more organised, not always, but generally…
> Officer 1: … yeah, there is a trend.
> [British Nationality Checking Service 1]

Hajjat (2012) has observed how the neatness of the documents presented was a first detail according to which the officers working on nationality in his research in France started to categorize the applicants as integrated or not, but in UK case the impact of the judgement was significantly less. When judgments were made about the linguistic competence of the candidate – which, judging from the interviews conducted in Liverpool, brought some other local registrars to alert the Home Office – some interviewees underlined it was not up to them to evaluate this dimension:

> Officer: … my colleague, she had an awful job, because [the candidate] hadn't been able to complete the form, because his written English wasn't very good, and his spoken English wasn't very good. I don't remember what nationality he was, I think he was Sudanese […]
> Q: But he had passed the test…?
> Officer: [nods] I don't know how. That's not for us to question, he had the certificates.
> [British Nationality Checking Service 2]

This same officer, working in a Nationality Checking Service in Wales, on the other hand showed a particular appreciation of the choice of completing the application in Welsh, although such choice remained a hypothetical one, as she never saw an application of this kind.

The most explicit reference to deservingness emerged in relation to the regularity of the migratory history of the candidates.

> Officer 1: … [migrants likely to have good character problems] mostly coming by lorry, not declared themselves at an official port, got caught by the police getting off a lorry on a motorway. That's an illegal entry, whereas if they arrived at an airport and claimed asylum there, it could be slightly different.
> […]
> Officer 1: … if you ask them [migrants with an unauthorised entry] the question, they don't think they have done anything wrong, at all. Albeit they might have entered illegally, been here illegally. And they don't see a lot of the time that that's a problem. […]
> Officer 2: [The applicant would say] "It's normal". "Does not everybody come on the back of a lorry"?
> Officer 1: Oh we do hear that quite a lot, they [applicants] say that quite a lot.
> Officer 2: "How else might I get in?"
> Officer 1: If one applied for a visa, maybe.
> [British Nationality Checking Service 3]

In the passage quoted the two officers were discussing the fact that unauthorised entries have been redefined as failing the good character requirement around 2014, and specifically the condition of many refugees, who, while obtaining a regular status thanks to a successful asylum procedure, can be still considered to have breached immigration norms through an unauthorised entry for the purpose of a citizenship application. These interviewees were quite knowledgeable of the complexity of different migratory experiences. However, this negative representation of refugees, and migrants more generally, who have entered the UK unauthorised, does not take in account how the visa regime excludes categorically a large proportion of potential migrants, including refugees, from authorised migration (see e.g. Neumayer, 2006).

2.5   Belgium: Integration as the Letter of the Law

In the Belgian context the "documentary" nature of the law (Wautelet, 2014) meant that the different institutions were hardly called to examine the degree of integration of the candidates. To a degree, by linking integration requirements to the possess of specific documents, the legislators have outsourced integration controls to external institutions (integration courses, educational institutions, etc.). The decentred procedure of nationality acquisition left space for significant local variations in the interpretation of the law (Sredanovic, 2020, 2022), but in the interviews I found a rather focus on the letter of the law, rather than on implicit policy objectives.

Visions of integration emerged sporadically in the interviews when discussing specific points of the law – the magistrates were more likely to interpret a specific point as linked to conceptions of integration, while the registrars were less likely to do so.

Some space for specific visions of integration was present when discussing the linguistic competence of the applicants. In one Flemish register, the officers interviewed justified the practice of the local *parquet* to oppose the nationality application of candidates who met the formal requirements but did not convince the police of their language competence during the interview.

> Officer 1: [Some applicants] have the right documents but they don't speak too good, to understand the interview with the police.
> [...]
> Officer 2: Because sometimes you have people who have been working for five years, and then that counts for work, it counts for language, and it counts for integration, but sometimes it's people that just go through their work, are there all day, and then go to their home and don't speak any Dutch, they can't go to the supermarket and explain what they need, because they don't speak the language. They get a letter from someone and they don't know what to do with it. So, that's why they say that you need to speak and understand at least a bit of Dutch to be able to interact with your community.
> [Belgian register 1]

The practice is procedurally problematic, as it means that the explicit requirements present in the letter of the law are disregarded in favour of police interviews, and further there are no guarantees that the candidates lacking competence in Dutch do not speak French or German, which would also mean they meet the formal requirements of the law. In the hypothetical situation mentioned by the second officer of the register, the integration assumption is that such candidates might lack the basic notions of Dutch for everyday interactions, perhaps also because of long working hours that give little opportunities of learning the language. Nevertheless, even such minimal linguistic expectations bring the problem of why the assumptions of integration-through-work of the legislators should be disregarded, and who should examine the actual linguistic ability of the candidates, if the procedures dismiss the more qualified options of integration courses and language tests in favour of police interviews.

Some interviewees on the other hand criticized the norms introduced in the 2012 reform, as in the case of the interviewee of a Walloon local register (Belgian register 2) who considered the migrants in the territory to often be in an economically fragile situation, and resented having to examine the integration of people she already came to knew when they came to the municipality for other procedures (somehow implying that they were already socially integrated and did not have to prove it further). An interviewee in another Walloon register (Belgian register 3) highlighted the situation of those who took early retirement as an alternative measure to being laid off, and could neither prove economic integration nor access the lower requirements reserved for the over-65.

There are some differences along the linguistic divide in Belgium, as in Flanders there is a longer history of integrationist policies (Adam, 2013; Adam et al., 2018), as well as a stronger emphasis on the promotion of Dutch, which is perceived under attack from the increased use in French, especially in some municipalities around the Brussels region. However, this divide is linked only to limited differences, as ideas of integration more restrictive than those of the letter of the law emerged also in interviews with francophone registrars.

The magistrates showed a strong interpretative activity in the definition of *faits personnels graves*. As mentioned, the concept was codified following requests from the magistrates themselves, but the way in which the codification was expressed in legal sources was such that the definition was still considered open. In the parliamentary debate even the far-right Vlaams Belang did not advocate for anything less than a prison sentence to qualify as *fait personnel grave* (Apers, 2014; Sredanovic, 2018). Despite this, a number among the magistrates interviewed followed an extensive definition, including in some cases minor infractions such as traffic violations, and in one case police reports for which there was no decision to prosecute (see Sredanovic, 2020, 2022 for more details), following therefore a line closer to the more restrictive British approach. When deciding where to draw the line, also in relation to infractions that were distant in time, some interviewees seemed to draw from their work outside nationality. There have been critiques of the transfer of the migration portfolio to home affairs, often from ministries of foreign affairs or ministries of employment that formerly held the portfolio in many countries, the latter reflecting a once workforce-centric approach to migration (cf. e.g. Huysmans, 2000 for an EU perspective). The usual focus of home affairs on security and police arguably helps orient migration policies towards securitisation approaches that are less likely to recognise the rights of migrants. The fact that nationality (differently from the rest of the migration portfolio) is held in Belgium by the Ministry of Justice seems to give some guarantees to applicants. Still, the magistrates working on nationality also work as civil, and in some smaller parquets, as penal prosecutors. This seems to be reflected in some answers about the nationality applications that they consider opposing: often the considerations, e.g. whether the fine for the traffic infraction has been promptly paid, seems to follow the concept of "rehabilitation".

Another case in which a number of magistrates included in the research (but not all) explicitly waive the law requirements is language requirements for nationals of confining countries (the Netherlands, France and Germany in particular), as, even when these candidates have no documentary proofs of the knowledge of the language, some magistrates are unwilling to oppose an application for that reason. Except in these cases, while some of the magistrates not included in the research did use police interviews to verify how candidates with documentary proofs speak the language, the magistrates I have interviewed followed more strictly the law. In the two following extracts candidates who do not have a full command of one of the Belgian national languages are partly problematised, but the legal norm, by which such competence has to be examined only documentarily, prevails:

> A couple of weeks ago there was a person who according to his documents should be able to speak Dutch fluently, and who had brought his interpreter to court. Which made the president of the court laugh, but still he didn't feel he could use this information to deny nationality to this person because it's not in the law, if he has his attestation.
> [Belgian magistrate 1]

> I had a case of a Pakistani who works in a late-night shop and does not speak a word of French but works as self-employed since more than five years, and one can't do anything. He is assumed to know the language.
> [Belgian magistrate 2]

Despite doubts raised about the assumptions of integration inscribed in the law the magistrates interviewed prioritised the letter of the law over their visions of integration. It is also worth mentioning that Belgian magistrate 2 mentioned regretting the case of another applicant, unemployed but having worked in Belgium since the 1970s, and unable to pass through the 10-years route for a limited command of the national languages. More generally the 10-year route and the concept of "participation to the life of the community" it includes, while potentially a space for the officers to pursue their conceptions of integration, was largely considered a residual route both by the magistrates and by the registrars. As a consequence, very few kinds of proof of the participation in the life of the community were refused.

Similarly to the language cases of Belgian magistrates 1 and 2, in the interview with Belgian magistrate 3 there was a combination of personal interpretation of integration and priority given to the letter of the law. When discussing having to oppose the application of someone who had lived in Belgium for the qualifying period, but worked outside Belgium, the interviewee first said that "the law is the law" and then further argued the case in this way:

> The meaning of the law is in any case to make one's contribution to the Belgian economy. And so to work elsewhere it's a bit complicated, even if it's true that his life... I can understand the interpretation of [another institution] that said "listen, all his life is in the territory,

and so all his money is spent here", one could think he makes his contribution in this way, but it's clear that the social security [contribution] is zero.
   [Belgian magistrate 3]

While it is easy to consider the economic integration requirement as a duty to contribute to the national economy, in particular through taxation, there is little in the letter of the law that supports explicitly this interpretation. If anything, the economic integration concept seems to aim rather to avoid exclusion from the paid labour market.

Finally, while magistrates, as also the registrars, made mostly reference to the letter of the law when discussing the nationality procedures, there were some critiques of the general approach of the law:

> Trying to put some things in legislation is really not easy; I mean, if you are talking about working, social integration, and such, what is acceptable? Because there are so many facets to a person, and if you come from a system [the pre-2012 one] where nationality was just granted as right, if you happened to meet the formal requirements of law, and you try to go back to more of a merit system... I mean, sometimes a person with all the right documents can have a lot less merit than a person who lacks some documents.
>   [Belgian magistrate 1]

This latter point in a way generalises the more specific critiques of the law advanced in Belgian register 1 and 2 above, pointing to the difficulty of translating complex conceptions of integration into law, and to the necessary mismatch between any conception of merit and the use of documentary proof. However, the question of whether the documentary approach is the real issue in defining access to nationality brings to larger question of implementation that I discuss in the conclusions.

2.6   Conclusions

I have shown how both in the UK and in Belgium the integrationist wave has brought to restrictive norms on nationality acquisition, that demand cultural conformity and lack of any sign of dangerousness from the candidates, that are hostile to highly-mobile lives and, at least in Belgium, privilege long-term forms of paid work. Previous research (Andreouli & Stockdale, 2009; Andreouli & Dashtipour, 2014) has shown some personal adhesion to such visions of integration among at least part of the personnel of Nationality Checking Services. Moreover, the present research has shown instances of following specific conceptions of integration in the implementation of the law, with the particular focus on fraud in the Home Office, and with the extension of the concept of *faits personnels graves* and the waiving of language requirements for candidates from neighbouring countries in some of the *parquets* in Belgium. However, despite the strong focus of the political and policy discourse on integration in both the countries, most of the interviewees in the research showed more interest in the letter of the law than in visions of integration. Most interviewees were likely to prioritise the letter of the law over the definitions of integration they themselves expressed, or to not consider their visions relevant at all to the description of their work. In Belgium such approach was reinforced by a nationality law that leaves limited space of discretion in its implementation. In the UK, the determinant factor seems an organisational preference for routinisation of decisions, despite a law that gives extensive discretional powers in assessing citizenship applications. As the Belgian magistrate 1 mentioned in the last paragraph put it, examining merit is difficult in general, and more so in approaches that attempt to follow uniform procedures. The main issue seems to stem from the will to introduce conceptions of integration, while the documentary approach taken in Belgium seems part of a trade-off inherent in any kind of implementation. Reducing discretion does necessarily make more difficult to waive the norm for "deserving" applicants who cannot match the requirements, but reduces also the space for bias and discrimination unavoidable every time the procedure calls for examining deservingness (a classic trade-off in street-level bureaucracy – see e.g. Lipsky, 2010).

The introduction of tests and formal integration requirements has introduced, both in the UK and in Belgium, new restrictions in the access of nationality that have put migrants at a disadvantage. One positive aspect of such policies is that at least they have codified integration requirements that in an earlier period and in other countries were already applied, sometimes in an even more invasive and arbitrary fashion (cf. Centlivres et al., 1991). Judging from the interviews collected for this research, there is some space in the implementation phase for transforming the integrationist ideology in more routinely applications of the letter of the law, although the mere fact of pursuing a charged and indefinite concept such that of integration introduces both procedural and substantial issues.

References

Adam, I. (2013). *Les entités fédérées belges et l'intégration des immigrés: Politiques publiques comparées.* Éditions de l'Université de Bruxelles.

Adam, I., Martiniello, M., & Rea, A. (2018). Regional divergence in the integration policy in Belgium: One country, three integration programs, one citizenship law. In A. Rea, E. Bribosia, I. Rorive, & D. Sredanovic (Eds.), *Governing diversity: Migrant integration and multiculturalism in North America and Europe* (pp. 235–255). Éditions de l'Université de Bruxelles.

Andreouli, E., & Dashtipour, P. (2014). British citizenship and the 'other': An analysis of the earned citizenship discourse. *Journal of Community & Applied Psychology, 24*(2), 100–110.

Andreouli, E., & Stockdale, J. E. (2009). Earned citizenship: Assumptions and implications. *Tottel's Journal of Immigration, Asylum and Nationality Law, 23*(2), 165–180.

Apers, C. (2014). *La loi du 4 décembre 2012 modifiant le Code de la nationalité.* Kluwer.

Bouquin, S. (2006). Précarités et segmentations sociales, nouveaux facteurs de régulation des marchés du travail? In P. Cours-Salies & S. Le Lay (Eds.), *Le bas de l'échelle: La construction sociale des situations subalternes* (pp. 183–206). Érès.

Brubaker, R. (1992). *Citizenship and nationhood in France and Germany.* Harvard University Press.

Brubaker, R. (1999). The Manichean myth: Rethinking the distinction between «Civic» and «Ethnic» nationalism. In H. Kriesi, K. Arimingeon, H. Siegrist, & A. Wimmer (Eds.), *Nation and National Identity. The European experience in perspective* (pp. 55–72). Rüegger.

Byrne, B. (2012). A local welcome? Narrations of citizenship and nation in UK citizenship ceremonies. *Citizenship Studies, 16*(3–4), 531–544.

Byrne, B. (2014). *Making citizens: Public rituals and personal journeys to citizenship*. Palgrave Macmillan.

Byrne, B. (2017). Testing times: The place of the citizenship test in the UK immigration regime and new citizens' responses to it. *Sociology, 51*(2), 323–338.

Centlivres, P., Cenlivres-Demont, M., Maillard, N., & Ossipow, L. (1991). *Une Seconde Nature. Pluralisme, Naturalisation et Identité en Suisse Romande et au Tessin*. L'Age d'Homme.

de Jonghe, D., & Doutrepont, M. (2013). Le Code de la nationalité belge, version 2013. De « Sois Belge et intègre-toi » à « Intègre toi et sois Belge »…. *Journal des tribunaux*, 6519–6521, 313–319; 329–338; 353–359.

Erdal, M. B., & Oeppen, C. (2013). Migrant balancing acts: Understanding the interactions between integration and transnationalism. *Journal of Ethnic and Migration Studies, 39*(6), 867–884.

Goodman, S. (2010). Integration requirements for Integration's sake? Identifying, Categorising and comparing civic integration policies. *Journal of Ethnic and Migration Studies, 36*(5), 753–772.

Hajjat, A. (2010). Port d'hijab et « défaut d'assimilation ». Étude d'un cas problématique pour l'acquisition de la nationalité française. *Sociologie, 4*(1), 439–455.

Hajjat, A. (2012). *Les frontières de l'«identité nationale»: L'injonction à l'assimilation en France métropolitaine et coloniale*. La Découverte.

Harding, L., Brunfaut, T., & Unger, J. W. (2020). Language testing in the 'hostile environment': The discursive construction of 'secure English language testing' in the UK. *Applied Linguistics, 41*(5), 662–687.

Huysmans, J. (2000). The European Union and the securitization of migration. *Journal of Common Market Studies, 38*(5), 751–777.

Infantino, F., & Rea, A. (2012). La mobilisation d'un savoir pratique local: attribution des visas Schengen au Consulat général de Belgique à Casablanca. *Sociologies Pratiques, 24*, 67–78.

Joppke, C., & Morawska, E. (Eds.). (2003). *Toward assimilation and citizenship: Immigrants in Liberal nation-states*. Palgrave Macmillan.

Kapoor, N., & Narkowicz, K. (2019). Characterising citizenship: Race, criminalisation and the extension of internal borders. *Sociology, 53*(4), 652–670.

Kostakopoulou, D. (2010). Matters of control: Integration tests, naturalisation reform and probationary citizenship in the United Kingdom. *Journal of Ethnic and Migration Studies, 36*(5), 829–846.

Lipsky, M. (2010[1980]). *Street-level bureaucracy. Dilemmas of the individual in public services*. Russell Sage Foundation.

Miller-Idriss, C. (2006). Everyday understandings of citizenship in Germany. *Citizenship Studies, 10*(5), 541–570.

National Audit Office. (2019). Investigation into the response to cheating in English language tests. Report.

Neumayer, E. (2006). Unequal access to foreign spaces: How states use visa restrictions to regulate mobility in a globalized world. *Transactions of the Institute of British Geographers, 31*(1), 72–84.

Puzzo, C. (2016). UK citizenship in the early 21st century: Earning and losing the right to stay. *Revue Française de Civilisation Britannique, 21*(1).

Rea, A., Bribosia, E., Rorive, I., & Sredanovic, D. (Eds.). (2018). *Governing diversity: Migrant integration and multiculturalism in North America and Europe*. Éditions de l'Université de Bruxelles.

Spire, A. (2008). *Accueillir ou reconduire: Enquête sur les guichets de l'immigration*. Raisons d'agir.

Sredanovic, D. (2014). Culture or taxes? The conceptions of citizenship of migrants and local factory workers in Italy. *Citizenship Studies, 18*(6–7), 676–689.

Sredanovic, D. (2017). Was citizenship bord with the enlightenment? Developments of citizenship between Britain and France and "everyday citizenship" implications. *Miranda, 15*.

Sredanovic, D. (2018). Mérite et conformité culturelle aux marges de la loi: le cas de la nationalité en Belgique. In A. Garnier, L. Pignolo, & G. Saint-Laurent (Eds.), *Gérer les migrations face aux défis identitaires et sécuritaires* (pp. 97–108). Université de Genève.

Sredanovic, D. (2020). Barriers to the equal treatment of (aspirant) citizens: The case of the application of nationality law in Belgium. *International Migration, 58*(2), 15–29.

Sredanovic, D. (2022). *Implementing citizenship, nationality and integration policies: The UK and Belgium in comparative perspective*. Bristol University Press.

Stadlmair, J. (2018). Earning citizenship. Economic criteria for naturalisation in nine EU countries. *Journal of Contemporary European Studies, 26*(1), 42–63.

Trenz, H.-J., & Triandafyllidou, A. (2017). Complex and dynamic integration processes in Europe: Intra EU mobility and international migration in times of recession. *Journal of Ethnic and Migration Studies, 43*(4), 546–559.

Turner, J. (2014). Testing the liberal subject: (in)security, responsibility and 'self-improvement' in the UK citizenship test. *Citizenship Studies, 18*(3–4), 332–348.

van Oers, R. (2013). *Deserving citizenship: Citizenship tests in Germany, the Netherlands and the United Kingdom*. Martinus Nijhoff.

Wautelet, P. (2014). La nationalité belge en 2014 – l'équilibre enfin trouvé ? In I. P. Wautelet & F. Collienne (Eds.), *Droit de l'immigration et de la nationalité: fondamentaux et actualités* (pp. 274–382). Larcier.

York, S. (2018). The 'Hostile Environment' – How Home Office immigration policies and practices create and perpetuate illegality. *Tottel's Journal of Immigration, Asylum and Nationality Law, 32*(4), 363–384.

Chapter 3
Becoming Dutch at What Cost? Increasing Application Fees and Naturalisation Rates of EU Immigrants in the Netherlands

Floris Peters, Swantje Falcke, and Maarten Vink

3.1 Introduction[1]

Citizenship policies in Europe have been characterized by contrasting trends over the past decade with reforms such as dual citizenship acceptance or shorter residency requirements making citizenship more accessible to immigrants (Vink & de Groot, 2010; Vink et al., 2019). In contrast, the introduction of civic integration and economic requirements have provided new obstacles to immigrants' naturalisation (Goodman, 2012). Economic requirements can take different forms. They can either be direct, such as proof of economic self-sufficiency, or indirect, such as the payment of substantial application fees. In the European context, especially the United Kingdom and the Netherlands have witnessed significant increases of application fees in the past decade (Stadlmair, 2018). This increase may well prejudice the changes of immigrants of becoming a citizen of the destination country.

While the overall impact of naturalisation requirements on citizenship acquisition rates is well understood (Huddleston, 2020; Huddleston & Falcke, 2020; Vink et al., 2013, 2021), the relevance of economic requirement remains largely understudied in Europe. Administrative fees contribute to the costs of naturalisation and may therefore impact the propensity to naturalise (Goodman, 2010). Existing

[1] **Funding**: research for this paper has received funding from the European Research Council (ERC) under the European Union's Horizon 2020 research and innovation programme (grant agreement No 682626). See for more information: https://www.milifestatus.com

F. Peters (✉) · S. Falcke
Utrecht University, Utrecht, Netherlands
e-mail: f.w.c.peters@uu.nl; s.falcke@uu.nl

M. Vink
European University Institute, Fiesole, Italy
e-mail: maarten.vink@eui.eu

research in the United States indicates that fees are a substantial barrier for low-income immigrants (Hainmueller et al., 2018; Hotard et al., 2019; Yasenov et al., 2019). However, in the European context the impact of fees on naturalisation propensities remains an open question.

To investigate the role of application fees in the naturalisation decision of immigrants in Europe, in this chapter we look at the case of the Netherlands, where fees have increased from 336 euro in 2003 to 901 euro in 2020 – an increase of 168% points – for a single application, with significant hikes in the fee in 2010 and 2011. Simultaneous changes in the civic integration requirements for permanent residence likely had a positive effect on naturalisation rates among non-EU immigrants and consequently may have obfuscated the impact of the higher fees. As EU immigrants can move freely within the EU and are thus not affected by requirements for permanent residence, we expect that for this group of immigrants, increased fees directly affected the cost-benefit calculation of applying for citizenship. Hence, in this chapter, we analyse naturalisation rates among EU immigrants in the context of increasing application fees by using longitudinal microdata from administrative registers on the complete immigrant population between 2007 and 2014. We use a two-step identification strategy. First, we apply a single-difference regression, based on a fixed-effects model, to investigate immigrant naturalisation rates in conjunction with increased application costs. We subsequently explore impact heterogeneity by household income and use a double-difference regression, based on a difference-in-differences model, to test whether the relevance of the fee increase is conditioned by income groups.

The remainder of the chapter is organised as follows: the next section provides an overview of the increased naturalisation fees in the Netherlands and discusses simultaneous changes in the context of civic integration policy that affect immigrants' cost-benefit calculations. In the third section we provide a description of the dataset and the empirical strategy to estimate the impact of the fee increase on naturalisation propensities. In Sect. 3.4, we discuss the main results, and end the chapter with a summary of our main results and reflection on the wider implications of these findings.

3.2 Naturalisation Fees in the Netherlands

Access to citizenship in the Netherlands is regulated by the 1985 Dutch Nationality Act which defines immigrants as eligible for independent naturalisation if they are at least 18 years of age, in possession of a permanent resident permit, legally and uninterruptedly reside in the Netherlands for 5 years (or 3 years if married to a Dutch national) and have made an effort to renounce the citizenship of their country of origin, if they do not lose this automatically (van Oers et al., 2013). Since 2003, immigrants need to demonstrate that they are sufficiently integrated into Dutch society. They have to pass the civic integration exam which tests sufficient Dutch language capabilities (currently level A2, in the Common European Framework of

Reference for Languages) and knowledge of Dutch society (see IND (2021a) for more information on current requirements).

In order to naturalise in the Netherlands there is no direct economic requirement, such as economic self-sufficiency. However, besides the costs for the naturalisation exam (which amount to 350 euro in 2020, increased from 260 euro when the exam was introduced in 2003, cf. van Oers, 2006, p. 30) and costs for preparatory courses, immigrants have to pay an application fee. This fee needs to be paid when submitting the application and is not reimbursed when an application is rejected or the applicant withdraws her or his application. In 2020, the fee for an individual naturalisation request in the Netherlands stood at 901 euro (see IND, 2021b for currently applicable fees). Reduced tariffs apply to stateless persons or holders of a residence permit asylum (670 euro in 2020) and for applicants submitting an application together with their partner (1150 euro in total).

As Fig. 3.1 shows, the application fee for naturalisation requests has increased dramatically from 336 euro in 2003 to 901 euro in 2020 for a single application, with significant hikes in the fee in 2010 and 2011. A similar trend applies to reduced fees

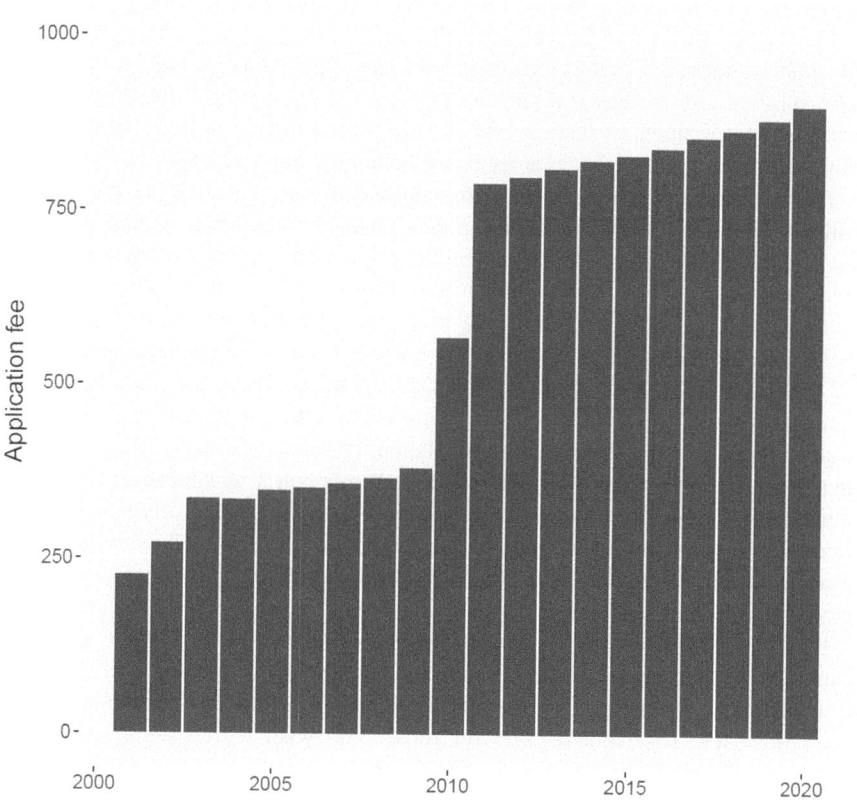

Fig. 3.1 Application fee for a single naturalisation request in the Netherlands over time. (Source: Government Gazette of the Kingdom of the Netherlands)

and to the fees for joint applications.[2] This trend of increased costs for naturalisation applications is part of a longer trend of increased restriction of Dutch naturalisation policy. During the early ninetees, Christian Democrats (CDA) and Conservative Liberals (VVD) developed an assimilationalist perspective on naturalisation. Where requirements previously had been relatively liberal, reflecting the notion of naturalisation as a stepping stone for integration (Heijs, 1995), this gradually shifted towards a view of naturalisation as the social, legal and emotional completion of the integration process (de Hart, 2007, p. 91). From that perspective, responsibility for successful integration increasingly fell to immigrants, whose integration would be tested rather than facilitated. This is evident in the (re)introduction of the renunciation requirement in 1997 and a language and civic integration test in 2003.

This restrictive turn in naturalisation policy is also characterised by a broader neoliberal trend in Dutch immigration and integration policy (van Houdt et al., 2011; Suvarierol & Kirk, 2015). This includes the notion that public services need to be 'cost efficient', which has gained increasing ground (IND, 2004). As a result, the Netherlands has witnessed growing marketisation regarding the implementation of integration policy where the government sets norms for exams, but the implementation of preparatory courses is left to private actors. In 2009, the government concluded that the costs of processing all naturalisation applications were higher than what was covered by the received income from fees. As a result, the fees needed to be substantially increased to ensure a closer approximation of the costs of the procedure (Department of Justice, 2009). After substantial jumps in 2010 and 2011, subsequent incremental increases are based on annual indexed wages.

These restrictions in requirements for naturalisation are mirrored in a decreasing number of naturalisations. While the policy changes were implemented with the aim of encouraging immigrants to integrate, it has been argued that these requirements in practice have led to exclusion (Groenendijk, 2003; van Oers et al., 2013, p. 46). Indeed, in particular vulnerable immigrants from economically less developed countries (Peters et al., 2016) or with lower levels of education (Vink et al., 2021) were deterred by restrictive citizenship policies. These are also the immigrants who stand to benefit most from naturalisation to mitigate their structurally disadvantaged position in for instance the labour (Peters et al., 2018, 2019) or housing market (Leclerc et al., 2022; Peters, 2020). While policy makers never explicitly intended these policies to serve a selective purpose, they paradoxically may hamper integration by obstructing a realistic pathway to citizenship for those immigrants who need it most. Whether the fee increase also had this stratifying impact remains an open question, however.

The fee increase coincided with a number of other policy changes. First, in January 2010, passing a civic integration exam became a requirement to receive a permanent residence permit for immigrants with an integration obligation under the Integration Act. The same is true for those who wish to receive a temporary

---

[2] Joint applications, together with a partner, increased from 316 euro in 2001 to 1150 euro in 2020. Reduced fees increased at a slower rate between 2002 and 2020 from 110 to 191 euro.

residence permit for family reunification purposes. This requirement applied to most non-EU immigrants, but not to EU immigrants and their non-EU partners and neither to citizens from Norway, Iceland and Switzerland (Besselsen & de Hart, 2014, p. 16). Whether immigrants from Turkey could be obliged to do the civic integration exam as a condition for permanent residence was disputed. Initially, they were included in the new obligatory civic integration policy; yet in 2011 this was rejected in court with reference to the free movement rights of Turkish citizens under the Association Agreement between Turkey and the EU. Second, funded opportunities to prepare for the exams were offered, which was not the case previously (van Oers et al., 2013, pp. 31–32).

The cost-benefit calculation for naturalisation is likely affected by these changes because the impact of the increase in the application fees is offset by the financial support that was made available to prepare for the civic integration tests from 2010. Since then civic integration courses were offered locally and financially covered from the 'participation budget' allocated by the State to municipalities as part of a so-called 'Deltaplan' to ensure greater participation in language and integration courses (Algemene Rekenkamer, 2017, p. 16). The assumption that offering free participation changed the cost-benefit calculation of naturalisation decisions is supported by the observation that, after the funded training opportunities were introduced, the number of participants in preparatory courses and naturalisation tests increased (van Oers et al., 2013, p. 32). Moreover, since passing the now-required tests is also a pre-condition for naturalisation, 'skipping the permanent residence stage in favour of naturalisation seems rather self-evident' (van Oers et al., 2013, p. 31). For both reasons, for non-EU immigrants we may expect an increase in the propensity to naturalise, in contrast to an expected decrease due to the fee increase for EU immigrants.

In the next section, we introduce our data sources, clarify the empirical focus on EU immigrants and discuss our empirical strategy to identify how naturalisation rates may have changed for this group in the context of increased application fees.

3.3 Data and Methodology

3.3.1 Data

To study the impact of the increase in application fees for naturalisation in the Netherlands in 2010, this paper draws on administrative register data from Statistics Netherlands. These data include all legally registered individuals in the Netherlands over time, allowing for a comparative analysis of immigrant naturalisation rates before and after an increase in the application fees in 2010.

As outlined above, for most non-EU immigrants the fee increase coincided with simultaneous policy changes implying, on the one hand, that taking the civic integration test became obligatory for continued residence in the Netherlands and financial support for taking preparatory courses became available, on the other. Hence, these changes are expected to offset possible effects of higher application fees and likely increase the propensity to naturalise (van Oers et al., 2013, p. 31; Besselsen & de Hart, 2014, p. 31). To disentangle the impact of the application fee from simultaneous policy changes in civic integration policy, we focus on immigrants from EU countries, as well as those from associated states Iceland, Norway and Switzerland with which the EU shares a freedom of movement regime (hereafter we refer to both citizens of the European Union and from associated states as EU immigrants). These immigrants are exempted from the integration requirement for residence because this would violate their right to freedom of movement within the EU. Moreover, the application fee for naturalisation likely plays a relatively important role for these immigrants. Indeed, since EU immigrants already enjoy many of the rights that Dutch citizenship would provide, the benefits of naturalisation are few (e.g. voting rights at the national level, or the symbolic value of being a citizen of the country in which you reside). On balance, a high application fee may thus be particularly relevant to EU immigrants, whereas this is less likely to dissuade immigrants for whom the benefits of naturalisation are larger. In sum, we focus on EU immigrants to ensure that our estimation is not biased by coinciding integration policy changes that affect the naturalisation cost-benefit decision, and because application fees are likely to play an important role in their cost-benefit calculation for naturalisation.

In light of these considerations, the research population consists of all foreign-born EU citizens registered at a Dutch municipality between 2007 and 2014 (observations = 1,230,925; N = 203,962). We select this observation window to facilitate a comparison of the period before and after the increase of the application fees for naturalisation in 2010 and avoid confounding period shocks due to new origin countries entering the research population as a result of EU enlargement, which may interfere with our identification strategy (outlined below). To ensure stability in the sample, the observation window includes member states that joined in 2007 (Bulgaria and Romania) from the start. For the same reason, we exclude immigrants from Croatia (which joined in 2013) from our analysis (6134 observations). Note that the sample size grows over the observation period due to a substantial increase in the number of EU migrants in the Netherlands from 2005 onwards (CBS, 2020). Furthermore, we focus on immigrants who are born abroad and whose parents were born abroad, are 18 years or older and not a Dutch citizen at the moment of arrival in the Netherlands, and are eligible for naturalisation. These immigrants are observed annually on the first of January of each year.

3.3.2 Identification Strategy

Our identification strategy is based on a two-step approach: a single-difference and double-difference regression. The single-difference regression analyses the effect of the fee increase for the immigrant population overall, as well as in sub-group analyses for immigrants from low and high-income households separately. The double-difference regression then provides a more robust test of the differential impact of the fee increase for immigrants from low-income households versus those from high-income households.

The single-difference regression is based on a fixed-effects model, and is formalized as follows:

$$Y_{icmt} = \alpha + Post2010_t + X_{icmt} + \gamma_c + d_{ct} + p_t + \delta_m + \varepsilon_{icmt} \tag{3.1}$$

where Y_{icmt} indicates whether an immigrant i from origin country c and municipality m is a Dutch citizen in year t. $Post2010$ is a dummy that is set to unity in 2010 and all subsequent years, which is used to identify the impact of the fee increase. X_{icmt} is a vector of control variables at the individual level, including gender, age at migration, age at migration squared, the partner status (including whether the potential partner is a native-born, a naturalised or non-naturalised citizen), having minor children, employment, household income and the highest level of education. The model also includes origin country fixed-effects (γ_c), as well as a further control for dual citizenship toleration of origin country c at time t (d_{ct}). We include municipality fixed effects (δ_m) to account for local differences, in particular regarding potential differences in the coverage of fees from special welfare budgets. Finally, the model has two period controls: the share of votes for far-right parties and the annual employment rate (p_t) (Alarian, 2017; Graeber, 2016). α denotes the intercept and ε_{icmt} the error term. We account for potential heteroskedasticity by calculating robust standard errors clustered at the individual level.

As outlined above, we expect the relevance of the fee increase (as identified by $Post2010_t$) to be particularly strong among households with lower levels of income. To test that expectation, we perform subgroup analyses for immigrants with below or equal to/above modal household income (€37,500 in 2010).

To test the robustness of the differential impact of the fee increase by household income group, we formulate a double-difference regression. This model draws on the logic of a Difference-in-Differences (DiD) design, and is formulated as formalized:

$$Y_{icmt} = \alpha + HHinc_{icmt} * t + t + X_{icmt} + d_{ct} + \gamma_c + \delta_m + \varepsilon_{icmt} \tag{3.2a}$$

$$Y_{icmt} = \alpha + HHinc_{icmt} * Post2010_t + Post2010_t + X_{icmt} + d_{ct} + \gamma_c + \delta_m + \varepsilon_{icmt} \tag{3.2b}$$

Model (3.2a) tests the parallel trend assumption. More specifically, it draws on the expectation that if $Post2010_t$ indeed captures the relevance of the fee increase, and this matters in particular to low income households, then we should only observe a difference in the naturalisation rate between immigrants with below/above modal household income ($HHinc_{icmt}$) in the years 2010 and after (when the fee increased), all else constant. This is measured through the interaction term $HHinc_{icmt} * t$ (note that a control for $HHinc_{icmt}$ is included in vector X_{icmt}). Statistically insignificant coefficients prior to 2010, and negative coefficients from 2010 onwards, are consistent with our expectation. This would indicate that the naturalisation rate prior to 2020 followed the same trends whereas it dropped more strongly among below modal income household from 2010 onwards. Model (3.2b) then estimates the overall DiD coefficient by replacing the individual year dummies in the interaction term (*t*) with a post 2010 dummy (*Post*2010*ᵢ*).

3.4   Analysis

3.4.1   Trends

Figure 3.2 shows naturalisation rates within the observation period for EU immigrants with below/above modal household income. The former group has a higher cumulative naturalisation rate than the latter (between 39 and 33 compared to 31 to 27%). This can be explained in part by the fact that immigrants with lower levels of income originate more often from countries with lower levels of economic development. It is well established that these immigrants have a higher propensity to naturalise (Graeber, 2016; Vink et al., 2021), although note that the discrepancy is

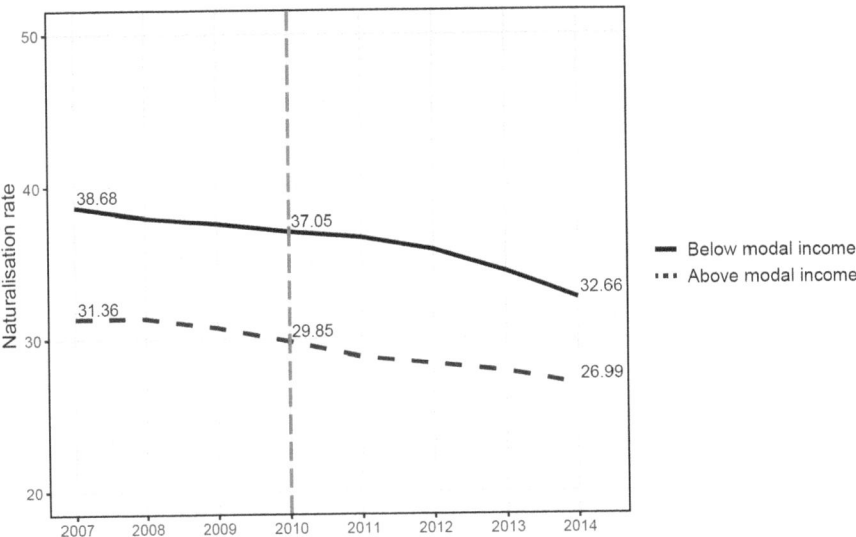

Fig. 3.2 Cumulative naturalisation rate of immigrants from the EU (incl. CH, IS and NO but excl. HR) in the Netherlands between 2007–2014 by modal household income. (Source: Statistics Netherlands)

limited here because levels of economic development are generally high within the EU. While we observe a drop in the naturalisation rate, this is gradual over time rather than concentrated around the year 2010. However, the downward trend is stronger among immigrants from below modal income households, in particular after 2010. This is consistent with the notion that the fee increase particularly affected immigrants who would have difficulty meeting those requirements. The decrease in the naturalisation rate of immigrants with lower household incomes is especially strong during the last observation years (2013 and 2014). A possible reason for this is that immigrants who wish to naturalise need to pass a number of language and civic integration tests. The decision to naturalise thus precedes the moment of naturalisation by several years, as immigrants prepare for the formal requirements. An increase in the application fee is less likely to dissuade immigrants who have already decided to naturalise in the past, and have started to prepare for the tests. The impact of the application fee is thus expected to be particularly visible among later observation years, as these contain more immigrants who had not yet decided to naturalise before the fee was increased.

3.5 Single-Difference Regression: Main Effect and Impact Heterogeneity

While the trends are consistent with our expectations, no firm conclusions can be drawn about the specific impact of the fee increase due to potential compositional, regional or period confounders. To account for this, we perform a single-difference regression for the full sample based on Model specification (1). As outlined above, we interpret the post-2010 dummy as the impact of the fee increase by holding all other variation at the individual, municipal and origin level constant (see Sect. 3.2 for a list of controls). Results in Fig. 3.3 show that the naturalisation rate decreased by 6.9% points from 2010 onwards compared to the preceding period, all else constant (see Table 3.1 for details). In other words, the general downward trend observed in Fig. 3.2 cannot be fully attributed to variation at the individual, municipal and origin level, or by period effects that we control for in our model.

To test our expectation that an increase in the application fee for naturalisation in particular affects immigrants with limited financial means, we perform subgroup analyses for those with a household income below/above modal household income. Results in Fig. 3.3 confirm that expectation (Table 3.1). More specifically, while the naturalisation rate among those with high household incomes decreases by 5.6% points after 2010, it drops by 7.2% points among those with lower incomes. In other words, the negative coefficient in the main model is predominantly driven by those with below modal household incomes.

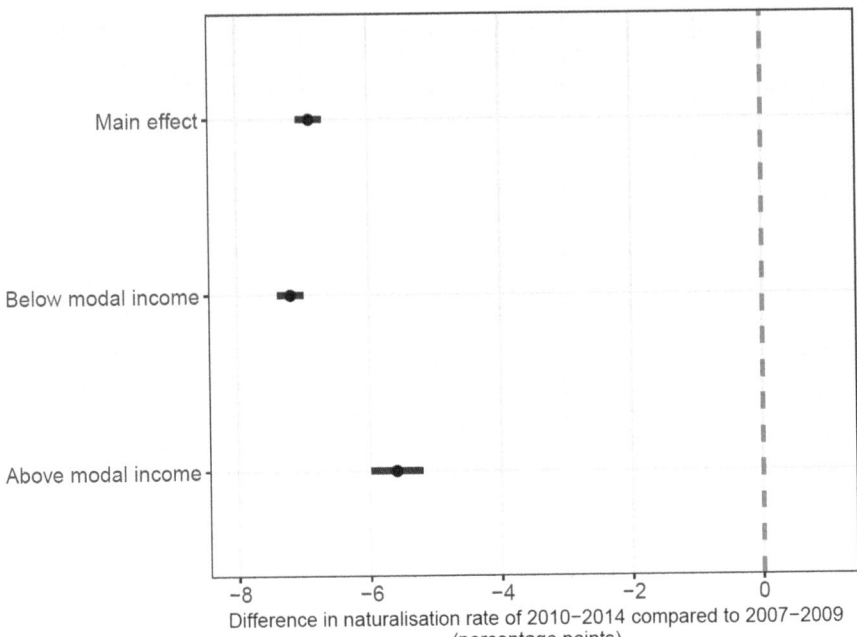

Fig. 3.3 Linear fixed-effects regression on the heterogeneous effect of the increase in application fees for naturalisation in the Netherlands in 2010 on naturalisation rates (immigrants from the EU, incl. CH, IS and NO but excl. HR; 2007–2014). Dots denote point estimates and horizontal lines correspond to 95% confidence intervals. (Source: Table 3.1; Statistics Netherlands)

Table 3.1 Linear fixed-effects regression on the heterogeneous effect of the increase in application fees for naturalisation in the Netherlands in 2010 on naturalisation rates (immigrants from the EU, incl. CH, IS and NO but excl. HR; 2007–2014)[a]

Year	F.E. regression		F.E. regression - below modal household income		F.E. regression - above modal household income	
	B	Std. error	B	Std. error	B	Std. error
2010–2014	−0.069***	0.001	−0.072***	0.001	−0.056***	0.002
2007–2009	ref.	ref.	ref.	ref.	ref.	ref.
***: $p < 0.001$	N = 203,962		N = 176,806		N = 77,796	
	Obs = 1,230,925		Obs = 925,502		Obs = 305,423	
	R² = 0.3418		R² = 0.3468		R² = 0.3344	

Source: Statistics Netherlands
[a]results include controls for gender, years since migration, years since migration squared, age at migration, age at migration squared, partner status, having minor children, employment, household income, highest level of education, dual citizenship toleration, municipality fixed-effects, origin country fixed-effects, and the annual employment rate and vote share for far-right parties. Standard errors clustered by individuals

3.6 Double-Difference Regression: Conditioned Relevance of the Fee Increase

To delve deeper into the conditioned relevance of the fee increase, we next perform a double-difference regression based on Model (3.2a) and (3.2b), which has two advantages. First, we include a control for the annual employment rate and share of votes for far-right parties in our single-difference model to disentangle the fee increase from coinciding period shocks. This still leaves open the possibility that other such confounders for which we do not control are picked up by our period dummy, and thus bias our estimation of the impact of the application fee. The most robust approach would be to include a control for year fixed-effects, but this is not possible because of collinearity with the period dummy we rely on for impact identification. The double-difference model addresses this problem by drawing on the assumption (as confirmed in Fig. 3.3) that the fee increase mattered in particular to immigrants with lower household incomes. More specifically, it identifies the impact of the fee increase not through a period dummy but with an interaction between time and a 'treatment group'. While strictly speaking, we do not have a treatment group because the entire sample was subject to the fee increase, our findings in the subgroup single-difference regression confirms that the fee increase mattered in particular to immigrants from below modal income households. By interacting time with a dummy indicating below modal household income, we are free to include year fixed-effects as a control. Second, while the subgroup single-difference models show that the naturalisation rate decreased more post-2010 *within* the group of immigrants from below modal income households compared to immigrants with higher household incomes, it is difficult to identify the relative difference *between* these two groups post-2010. Since the double-difference model is based on the full sample, the interaction terms tell us more about how the impact of the fee increase differed between income groups.

Results in Fig. 3.4 based on Model (3.2a) which tests the parallel trend assumption, confirm our expectation: there is no statistically significant difference in the naturalisation rate between immigrants from below or above modal income households prior to 2010 (see Table 3.2). Only after the introduction of the fee increase does the difference appear, from 0.7% points in 2010 to 3.1% points in 2014. Overall, according to our estimates from Model (3.2b), the naturalisation gap between both income groups during the post-2010 period increases with 1.5% points. Two conclusions can be drawn from these results. First, the findings from the single-difference regression models cannot be fully attributed to confounding period effects. Second, the impact of the increase in application fees for naturalisation is indeed stronger for immigrants from households with below modal levels of income, as the single-difference models suggested.

To get a sense of the impact magnitude of the fee increase, consider the year 2014. In that year, 81,042 individuals from below modal income households were eligible for naturalisation in the sample. If we multiply the DiD coefficient of that year from the double-difference regression to the affected population, we obtain the

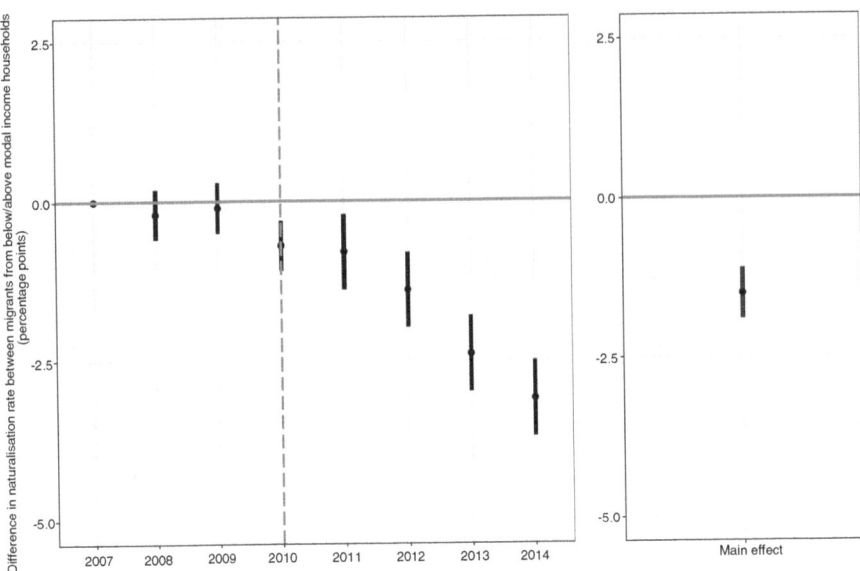

Fig. 3.4 Linear difference-in-differences regression on the effect of the increase in application fees for naturalisation in the Netherlands in 2010 on naturalisation rates among immigrants from below modal income households relative to immigrants from above modal income households (immigrants from the EU, incl. CH, IS and NO but excl. HR; 2007–2014). The left panel shows the analysis of the parallel trend assumption, and the right panel shows the overall difference-in-differences coefficient. Dots denote point estimates and vertical lines correspond to 95% confidence intervals

Table 3.2 Linear difference-in-differences regression on the effect of the increase in application fees for naturalisation in the Netherlands in 2010 on naturalisation rates among immigrants from below modal income households relative to immigrants from above modal income households (immigrants from the EU, incl. CH, IS and NO but excl. HR; 2007–2014)[a]

	Main model		Parallel trend assumption	
Year * household income	B	Std. error	B	Std. error
post * < modal household income	−0.015***	0.002		
2007 * < modal household income			ref.	ref.
2008 * < modal household income			−0.002	0.002
2009 * < modal household income			−0.001	0.002
2010 * < modal household income			−0.007**	0.002
2011 * < modal household income			−0.008**	0.003
2012 * < modal household income			−0.014***	0.003
2013 * < modal household income			−0.024***	0.003
2014 * < modal household income			−0.031***	0.003
***: $p < 0.001$	N = 203,962		N = 203,962	
**: $p < 0.01$	Obs = 1,230,925		Obs = 1,230,925	
	R^2 0.3411		R^2 0.3411	

Source: Statistics Netherlands
[a]results include controls for gender, years since migration, years since migration squared, age at migration, age at migration squared, partner status, having minor children, employment, household income, highest level of education, dual citizenship toleration, municipality fixed-effects, origin country fixed-effects and year fixed-effects. Standard errors clustered by individuals

number of immigrants from below modal income households who decided not to naturalise in 2014 because of the fee increase, based on EU immigrants' propensity to naturalise in 2007 (the reference category). This calculation suggests that an estimated 2512 immigrants from below modal income households (81,042 * −0.031) did not naturalise because of the policy change. More generally, if we contrast the overall DiD coefficient to the covariates in the same model (Table 3.3), then the impact of the fee increase is slightly smaller than the difference between having a low rather than high level of education.

Table 3.3 Linear fixed-effects regression on the heterogeneous effect of the increase in application fees for naturalisation in the Netherlands in 2010 on naturalisation rates, including coefficients for covariates (immigrants from the EU, incl. CH, IS and NO but excl. HR)[a]

Covariates			B	Std. error
Post * < modal household income			−0.015***	0.002
Post			−0.041***	0.001
< Modal household income			0.016***	0.002
Gender	Male		0.119***	0.002
	Female		ref.	ref.
Years since migration			0.021***	0.000
Years since migration ^ 2			−0.000***	0.000
Age at migration			−0.011***	0.001
Age at migration ^ 2			0.000***	0.000
Partner	No partner		ref.	ref.
	Foreign-born foreign partner		−0.209***	0.002
	Foreign-born naturalised partner		0.121***	0.006
	Native partner		−0.006	0.005
Minor children	Yes		0.006**	0.002
	No		ref.	ref.
Paid employment	Yes		−0.001	0.002
	No		ref.	ref.
Household income			0.000*	0.000
Highest level of education	High		ref.	ref.
	Middle		−0.005	0.004
	Low		−0.021***	0.004
	Unknown		−0.020***	0.003
Dual citizenship toleration	Yes		0.007	0.005
	No		ref.	ref.
***: $p < 0.001$			N = 203,962	
**: $p < 0.01$			Obs = 1,230,925	
*: $p < 0.05$			$R^2 = 0.3411$	

Source: Statistics Netherlands

[a]Includes municipality fixed-effects and origin country fixed-effects. Standard errors clustered by individuals

3.7 Conclusion

Substantial variation in citizenship policies across Europe (Goodman, 2010; Vink & de Groot, 2010) has given rise to a large field of literature analysing the impact of these institutional conditions for immigrants' propensity to naturalise. Over the last decade, scholars have increasingly drawn on panel data and quasi-experimental methodologies for that purpose. Although robust identification strategies often place limits on the comparative scope of such studies, there is a growing understanding of the relevance of requirements for naturalisation, including language and integration tests (Vink et al., 2021), nationality procedures (Huddleston & Falcke, 2020) and residence or renunciation requirements (Mazzolari, 2009; Vink et al., 2021). What has remained understudied in the European context, however, are economic requirements, varying from demands on self-sufficiency to application fees. In this chapter, we focus on the latter in the Dutch context, where the application fee has risen markedly over the last decades. We exploit a significant increase of the fee in 2010 to analyse whether, and if so for whom, such requirements matter for the propensity to naturalise. We use Dutch administrative data between 2007 and 2014 on immigrants from the EU and associated states with whom the EU shares a freedom of movement regime. These immigrants were exempted from integration requirements that were implemented in parallel with the fee increase. Moreover, the application fee for naturalisation likely plays an important role for these immigrants given the relatively limited added benefit of a Dutch passport compared to their EU citizenship.

We use a two-step identification strategy, formulating a single-difference and double-difference regression model based on the logic of a fixed-effects and DiD regression respectively. Results from our single-difference models reveal a decrease in EU immigrants' naturalisation rate after the fee increase in 2010, all else constant. Consistent with our expectation that economic requirements matter particularly to immigrants with limited financial means, subgroup analyses show a stronger decrease among those with below modal household incomes compared to immigrants with higher incomes. To delve deeper into the conditioned relevance of the fee increase, we exploit the observed impact heterogeneity in double-difference models, which confirm that the main findings cannot be fully attributed to unmeasured period shocks, and that there is indeed a statistically significant difference in the relevance of the fee increase by household income. Our tentative interpretation of the stronger impact in later observation years is that application fees in the context of restrictive requirements for naturalisation are particularly relevant early in the decision-making process, resulting in a delayed effect. Immigrants who were already preparing for language and civic integration requirements were less likely to be dissuaded by an increase in the fees than those who still had to decide whether they would invest in becoming a citizen in the future. From that perspective, the impact of the fee increase should be less visible in the initial years after the fee increase, as many migrants will have decided to naturalise before then. The individual year-coefficients in the double-difference regression are consistent with that expectation, but more specific analyses need to confirm the presumed mechanism.

These findings align with conclusions from existing research on the relevance of economic requirements for naturalisation in the United States (Hainmueller et al., 2018; Hotard et al., 2019; Yasenov et al., 2019). They also present several avenues for further research into the impact of economic requirements for naturalisation in Europe. First, future research can investigate the role of different types of economic requirements on naturalisation propensities. While some countries, like the Netherlands and the United Kingdom, have high application fees, other countries, such as Belgium, Denmark, Finland and Germany, demand economic activity, a minimum level of income or no reliance on welfare benefits over a given period prior to the application for citizenship. These requirements are not mutually exclusive, as is evident in the case of Austria which combines strict economic naturalisation criteria with high fees (Stadlmair, 2018). To what extent and for whom specific economic requirements matter for the propensity to naturalise remains an open question. Second, given that economic requirements are only one aspect of citizenship policies governing access to nationality, the question remains how various requirements interact. For instance, immigrants with lower levels of education or from less developed countries of origin are most deterred by restrictive language and civic integration tests (Vink et al., 2021). Since these are typically also immigrants with limited financial means, is the impact of economic requirements in countries with demanding naturalisation tests nullified by selection into naturalisation? In other words, do economic requirements matter more in countries whose overall citizenship policies are relatively liberal? Third, due to the coinciding policy changes for non-EU immigrants, our analysis focused on EU immigrants residing in the Netherlands. This raises the question whether the findings can be generalized to the immigrant population more broadly. Naturalisation rates in the Netherlands are average in the EU (Eurostat, 2021) due to relatively accessible citizenship policies. However, EU immigrants show generally lower propensities to naturalise, and this is particularly true in the Netherlands, where the renunciation requirement is an important deterrent for these immigrants (Vink et al., 2021, p. 11). Similar to the differential impact of restrictive dual citizenship regulations, which affect EU migrants more strongly than non-EU migrants, we expect that due to the limited benefits citizenship acquisition provides to EU immigrants, the costs associated with naturalisation (such as application fees) will weigh relatively heavy in the decision to naturalise. In other words, if we did not observe an impact of the application fees among EU immigrants, it is unlikely that we would observe such an effect for non-EU immigrants. Whether this expectation holds empirically remains to be tested in other studies, in the Netherlands or elsewhere, given that the design of our study that is set around the specific policy context of 2010 only allows a focus on EU migrants. Future research should assess whether application fees have a depressing effect on naturalisation rates for immigrants in general, or whether fees matter most to those who stand to gain least from citizenship acquisition.

References

Alarian, H. M. (2017). Citizenship in hard times: Intra-EU naturalisation and the Euro crisis. *Journal of Ethnic and Migration Studies, 43*(13), 2149–2168.

Algemene Rekenkamer. (2017). Inburgering: Eerste resultaten van de Wet Inburgering 2013. Available at https://www.rekenkamer.nl/publicaties/rapporten/2017/01/24/inburgering

Besselsen, E., & de Hart, B. (2014). *Verblijfsrechtelijke consequenties van de Wet inburgering. Een onderzoek naar de ervaringen van migranten in Amsterdam.* Wolf Legal Publishers.

CBS. (2020). Bevolkingsontwikkeling: migratieachtergrond en generatie. Centraal Bureau voor de Statistiek: Statline.

de Hart, B. (2007). The end of multiculturalism: The end of dual citizenship? Political and public debates on dual citizenship in the Netherlands (1980–2004). In T. Faist (Ed.), *Dual citizenship in Europe* (pp. 77–103). Ashgate Publishing.

Department of Justice. (2009). Besluit van 15 september 2009, houdende wijziging van het besluit optie- en naturalisatiegelden 2002. *Staatsblad van het Koninkrijk der Nederlanden, 2009*(388).

Eurostat. (2021, July 15). Acquisition of citizenship: Number of acquisitions. https://ec.europa.eu/eurostat/databrowser/view/tps00024/default/bar?lang=en

Goodman, S. W. (2010). Naturalisation policies in Europe: Exploring patterns of inclusion and exclusion. Robert Schuman Centre for Advanced Studies: EUDO Citizenship Observatory.

Goodman, S. W. (2012). Fortifying citizenship: Policy strategies for civic integration in Western Europe. *World Politics, 64*(04), 659–698.

Graeber, J. (2016). Citizenship in the shadow of the euro crisis: Explaining changing patterns in naturalisation among intra-EU migrants. *Journal of Ethnic and Migration Studies, 42*(10), 1670–1692.

Groenendijk, K. (2003). De toegenomen koppeling van de RwNed aan de Vw: meer barrieres en minder integratie. *Migrantenrecht, 4*(5), 148–157.

Hainmueller, J., Lawrence, D., Gest, J., Hotard, M., Koslowski, R., & Laitin, D. D. (2018). A randomized controlled design reveals barriers to citizenship for low-income immigrants. *PNAS, 115*(5), 939–944.

Heijs, E. (1995). *Van vreemdeling tot Nederlander: de verlening van het Nederlanderschap aan vreemdelingen 1913–1992.* Het Spinhuis.

Hotard, M., Lawrence, D., Laitin, D. D., & Hainmueller, J. (2019). A low-cost information nudge increases citizenship application rates among low-income immigrants. *Nature Human Behaviour, 3*(7), 678–683.

Huddleston, T. (2020). Naturalisation in context: How nationality laws and procedures shape immigrants' interest and ability to acquire nationality in six European countries. *Comparative Migration Studies, 8*(1), 18.

Huddleston, T., & Falcke, S. (2020). Nationality policies in the books and in practice: Comparing immigrant naturalisation across Europe. *International Migration, 58*(2), 255–271.

IND. (2004). *Nieuwe legessystematiek IND 2004: Eindrapport van het projectteam legessystematiek IND.* Immigration and Naturalisation Service.

IND. (2021a, January 13). Naturalisation. Immigration and Naturalisation Service. https://ind.nl/en/dutch-citizenship/Pages/Naturalisation.aspx

IND. (2021b, January 13). Fees: Costs of an application. Immigration and Naturalisation Service. https://ind.nl/en/Pages/Costs.aspx#Becoming_a_Dutch_citizen

Leclerc, C., Vink, M., & Schmeets, H. (2022). Citizenship acquisition and spatial stratification: Analysing immigrant residential mobility in the Netherlands. *Urban Studies, 59*(7), 1406–1423.

Mazzolari, F. (2009). Dual citizenship rights: Do they make for more and richer citizens? *Demography, 46*(1), 169–191.

Peters, F. (2020). Naturalization and the transition to homeownership: An analysis of signalling in the Dutch housing market. *Housing Studies, 35*(7), 1239–1268.

Peters, F., Vink, M., & Schmeets, H. (2016). The ecology of immigrant naturalisation: A life course approach in the context of institutional conditions. *Journal of Ethnic and Migration Studies, 42*(3), 359–381.

Peters, F., Vink, M., & Schmeets, H. (2018). Anticipating the citizenship premium: Before and after effects of immigrant naturalisation on employment. *Journal of Ethnic and Migration Studies, 44*(7), 1051–1080.

Peters, F., Schmeets, H., & Vink, M. (2019). Naturalisation and immigrant earnings: Why and to whom citizenship matters. *European Journal of Population, 36*, 511–545.

Stadlmair, J. (2018). Earning citizenship: Economic criteria for naturalisation in nine EU countries. *Journal of Contemporary European Studies, 26*(1), 42–63.

Suvarierol, S., & Kirk, K. (2015). Dutch civic integration courses as neoliberal citizenship rituals. *Citizenship Studies, 19*(3–4), 248–266.

van Houdt, F., Suvarierol, S., & Schinkel, W. (2011). Neoliberal communitarian citizenship: Current trends towards 'earned citizenship' in the United Kingdom, France and the Netherlands. *International Sociology, 26*(3), 408–432.

van Oers, R. (2006). *De naturalisatietoets geslaagd? Een onderzoek naar de totstandkoming en effecten van de naturalisatietoets.* Wolf Legal Publishers.

van Oers, R., de Hart, B., & Groenendijk, K. (2013). Country report: The Netherlands. Robert Schuman Centre for Advanced Studies: EUDO Citizenship Observatory.

Vink, M., & de Groot, G. (2010). Citizenship attribution in Western Europe: International framework and domestic trends. *Journal of Ethnic and Migration Studies, 36*(5), 713–734.

Vink, M. P., Prokic-Breuer, T., & Dronkers, J. (2013). Immigrant naturalization in the context of institutional diversity: Policy matters, but to whom? *International Migration, 51*(5), 1–20.

Vink, M., Schakel, A. H., Reichel, D., Luk, N. C., & de Groot, G.-R. (2019). The international diffusion of expatriate dual citizenship. *Migration Studies, 7*(3), 362–383.

Vink, M., Tegunimataka, A., Peters, F., & Bevelander, P. (2021). Long-term heterogeneity in immigrant naturalisation: The conditional relevance of civic integration and dual citizenship. *European Sociological Review, 37*, 751. https://doi.org/10.1093/esr/jcaa068

Yasenov, V., Hotard, M., Lawrence, D., Hainmueller, J., & Laitin, D. D. (2019). Standardizing the fee-waiver application increased naturalization rates of low-income immigrants. *Proceedings of the National Academy of Sciences, 116*(34), 16768–16772.

Chapter 4
Citizenship and Naturalisation for Migrants in the UK After Brexit

Mariña Fernández-Reino and Madeleine Sumption

While immigration has played a major role in public debate in the UK over the past twenty years, citizenship and naturalisation have received much less attention. Polling data have suggested that the UK public is broadly supportive of the idea of giving long-term migrants the opportunity to become UK citizens (British Future, 2020). The UK Home Office, in its 2019 Indicators of Integration Framework, described citizenship as an "important bedrock to the integration of any individual in a society" (Ndofor-Tah et al., 2019: 18). Indeed, there is some evidence that becoming a citizen has a positive impact on economic and social integration. For example, the OECD (2011) found that naturalisation was associated with labour market outcomes of many groups of foreign nationals in France, Germany, Sweden and the United States, particularly for the most disadvantaged. Studies from Switzerland and Germany have also shown positive social and economic impacts of naturalisation (Hainmueller et al., 2017; Gathmann & Keller, 2018; but see also Bartram, 2019); and that those who naturalise increase their attachment to British Identity (Bartram, 2021).

In practice, however, there are wide variations in the extent to which different groups of migrants in the UK choose to take up UK citizenship and some migrant groups face important obstacles to naturalisation. In this chapter, we analyse these patterns and look at the facilitators of and barriers to becoming a citizen in UK post Brexit. In doing so, we examine how naturalisation propensities in the UK are conditioned by a range of factors including country of origin, age at migration, visa status at migration, and administrative barriers and costs. Finally, we also show that despite increasing numbers of EU citizens applying to become UK citizens, EU migrants are still less likely to naturalise than those from outside of the EU.

M. Fernández-Reino · M. Sumption (✉)
Centre on Migration, Policy and Society (University of Oxford), Oxford, UK
e-mail: marina.fernandez-reino@compas.ox.ac.uk; madeleine.sumption@compas.ox.ac.uk

© The Author(s) 2023
R. Barbulescu et al. (eds.), *Revising the Integration-Citizenship Nexus in Europe*, IMISCOE Research Series, https://doi.org/10.1007/978-3-031-25726-1_4

4.1 British Nationality Law

Migrants in the UK who are foreign nationals can acquire the right to live in the UK permanently without becoming British citizens. Non-UK citizens who have permanent residence or settlement (*Indefinite Leave to Remain* [ILR] or EU *settled status* for those who acquired their residence under the EU Settlement Scheme) have extensive rights similar to those of UK citizens. However, becoming a British citizen brings certain additional rights, such as the the right to vote and to stand as a candidate in general elections. In addition, it is much harder for the government to deport UK citizens, and citizenship cannot be lost as a result of long absences from the country.

British nationality law is complex and different rules apply depending on people's date of birth (before 1 January 1983, between 1 January 1983 and 1 July 2006, and after 1 July 2006)[1]. There are three main ways of becoming a UK citizen: automatic acquisition at birth, registration (usually for children), and naturalisation (usually for adults). Almost all migrant adults without a British parent will have to naturalise in order to become UK citizens. Adult migrants who apply for citizenship must usually have lived in the UK for at least five or six years and must already have the permanent right to live in the UK (i.e. ILR or EU settled status). They must meet an English language requirement and pass the 'Life in the UK' test, which is designed to evaluate their knowledge of UK institutions, history and culture. The level of English language required for adult applicants is 'intermediate', which is considered sufficient to have conversations about a range of familiar topics, but not necessarily enough to function fully in an English-speaking workplace. Applicants must also have 'good character,' which includes paying taxes and not having a recent criminal record. The 'good character' requirement was first introduced in 1981 and it is subject to change, as it is not defined in law but regularly revised in the Home Office guidance. In 2006, it was extended to include children aged 10 and over who register as UK citizens. Applicants must also have been physically present in the UK for most of the previous three to five years. For a more detailed overview of naturalisation requirements in the UK, see Halliday (2019) and Prabhat (2018).

Since the British Nationality Act 1981, children who are born in the UK no longer automatically acquire British citizenship in all cases. They need at least one of their parents to be either a UK national or a settled or permanent resident in order to acquire automatic British citizenship at birth. UK-born children are eligible to *register* for citizenship if they have lived in the UK until the age of 10 and their parents receive ILR or EU settled status. Children will need to pay a registration fee of

---

[1] *Current rules are set out in the British Nationality Act 1981, which was amended in 2002 and 2006. The Nationality and Borders Bill 2021–22 was published on 6 July 2021 and proposed some changes to the current law, including an additional requirement for citizenship applications of UK-born stateless children* (Gower, 2021).

£1012, although their parents can apply for a fee waiver if they can demonstrate that they cannot afford it. Unlike for adults, there are some circumstances in which children can become citizens without first applying for ILR; this includes certain children without legal residence status, if they meet the conditions (e.g. if they have lived in the UK for a long time).

While Brexit had a major impact on immigration policy by bringing decades of free movement to an end, it did not directly affect nationality law. Naturalisation requirements are also similar for EU and non-EU citizens, at least on paper. However, there are additional complexities for certain EU citizens as a result of how free movement rules were implemented in the UK. In particular, under free movement, some EU citizens becoming permanent residents—namely students and self-sufficient people such as non-working partners of British citizens—faced a little-known requirement to hold private health insurance. This meant that many EU citizens were rejected for permanent residence as a consequence. This requirement was removed for the EU Settlement Scheme, but citizenship applications still require caseworkers to consider whether EU citizens who were students or self-sufficient people had health insurance in the ten years prior to their application, and then consider whether to exercise discretion in their favour (Vassiliou, 2020). This means that some EU applicants may be rejected on this basis, and others may be deterred for fear of losing their substantial application fee if they are rejected.

4.2   Who Becomes a UK Citizen? Differences Between EU-born and Non-EU Born Migrants

There were an estimated 6.2 milion foreign citizens living in the UK in the year 2019 (authors' calculations based on the APS 2019). Eight of the top ten foreign nationalities that year were from EU countries despite the fact that the EU-born population represented a minority (38 per cent) of the foreign born (authors' calculation based on the Annual Population Survey [APS] 2019).[2] This is because EU citizens have been less likely to naturalise than non-EU citizens in the last decades. For example, in 2019, among migrants who moved to the UK at least 10 years ago, only 24 per cent of the EU born said they were UK nationals, while this percentage was 72 per cent among migrants born outside the EU (authors' calculation based on the APS 2019).

---

[2] *The Annual Population Survey (APS) is the most comprehensive data source on migrants in the UK and has been used by the Office of National Statistics to estimate the UK population by country of birth and nationality. The APS is, however, likely to understate rates of citizenship acquisition among the foreign-born population due to its failure to capture dual nationality.*

Among the top fifteen migrant communities in the UK that year, the share of UK citizens among long-term residents (i.e. those who migrated at least 10 years ago) was particularly low for those born in Romania (14 per cent) Portugal (11 per cent), Poland (7 per cent) or Lithuania (4 per cent) (author's calculations based on the APS 2019). By contrast, the share of British citizens was considerably higher among long-term residents from non-EU countries such as Bangladesh (84 per cent), Pakistan (78 per cent), India (78 per cent) or South Africa (73 per cent) (author's calculations based on the APS 2019). A consequence of the difference naturalisation rates between EU and non-EU migrants is that non-EU born migrants make up the majority of the population born overseas (62 per cent or 5.8 million in 2019), but EU citizens represent the majority of foreign nationals living in the UK (61 per cent or 3.9 million).

4.3 Factors Affecting the Acquisition of Citizenship Among EU and Non-EU citizens, and the Role of Brexit

Both instrumental and non-instrumental factors affect migrants' decision to become citizens of the country they have moved to. Naturalisation has instrumental value if migrants perceive that it provides them with opportunities and rights that they would otherwise lack (Bauböck, 2019: 1022), e.g. right to vote in general elections, legal certainty about their residence and work rights, exemption for immigration controls, protection from potential discrimination, or the ability to travel and spend time in the country of origin without restrictions (see e.g. Aptekar, 2016; Birkvad, 2019; Rutter et al., 2008; Sigona & Godin, 2019). Migrants may also decide to naturalise for non-instrumental reasons, such as the desire to be recognised as a full member of society or because they feel a strong sense of belonging to the country where they wish to naturalise (Bauböck, 2019). The relevance of instrumental motivations in migrants' decision to naturalise has been linked to the increasing number of states accepting dual nationality since the 1990s (Harpaz & Mateos, 2019). In the UK, dual citizenship has been allowed since the British Nationality Act 1948.

4.3.1 Origin Countries

There are large disparities in naturalisation rates between EU and non-EU citizens (see Table 4.1), but also across nationals from non-EU countries, which ranged in 2019 from 5 per cent among Japanese nationals to 90 per cent among Afghans ten after their entry visa (Fig. 4.1). These disparities partially reflect the different instrumental value that the acquisition of British citizenship has for migrants depending on their nationality. For example, migrants from developing or politically unstable non-EU countries are more likely to naturalise than those from higher-income non-EU countries. As shown in Fig. 4.1, among non-EU citizens who had ILR 10 years

Table 4.1 Share of UK nationals among migrant residents born in the top 15 countries of birth, 2019

Country of birth	Time since migration 0–9 years	Time since migration 10+ years	Total	Share of UK citizens among those who migrated 10+ years ago
India	301,000	561,000	863,000	77.7
Poland	315,000	503,000	818,000	7.3
Pakistan	152,000	395,000	547,000	78.2
Romania	343,000	84,000	427,000	13.9
Ireland	59,000	301,000	360,000	20.6
Germany	58,000	231,000	289,000	69.9
Bangladesh	55,000	205,000	260,000	83.8
South Africa	70,000	182,000	252,000	73.5
Italy	138,000	95,000	233,000	21.8
Nigeria	62,000	153,000	215,000	68.3
France	89,000	93,000	182,000	26.4
Lithuania	85,000	82,000	168,000	4.3
Portugal	95,000	71,000	165,000	10.9
United States	72,000	88,000	160,000	52.9
Australia	58,000	95,000	153,000	59.3
EU countries	1,660,000	1,920,000	3,580,000	24.4
Non-EU countries	1,832,000	3,880,000	5,713,000	72.0
Total	3,492,000	5,801,000	9,293,000	56.2

Source: Annual Population Survey, January–December, 2019 (Office for National Statistics, Social Survey Division, 2022)

after migrating to the UK, over 80 per cent of those from the Philippines, Russia, Somalia and Afghanistan became UK citizens, compared to less than 40 per cent of migrants from the United States, Canada or South Korea. This is consistent with trends found across other EU countries (Dronkers & Vink, 2012), and is thought to be because migrants from lower- and middle-income countries perceive the relative benefits of taking on nationality from a Western country such as the UK to be higher (Milanovic, 2013; Kochenov & Lindeboom, 2017; Harpaz & Mateos, 2019).

As mentioned earlier, EU citizens have historically been less likely to naturalise than non-EU citizens and this is reflected in their citizenship application rates (Fig. 4.2). While the UK was part of the EU, nationals from other EU states (in addition to those from Norway, Iceland, Lichtenstein and Switzerland) had fewer incentives to naturalise given that their citizenship allowed them be exempt from immigration control and enjoy the same rights as UK nationals in terms of employment, taxation or access to public services and benefits (Moreh et al., 2018). While many EU countries are wealthy and thus their citizens might be expected to have a lower naturalisation rate than citizens from some non-EU countries (as discussed above), the share of UK citizens among migrants born in high-income non-EU countries like the United States and Australia are nonetheless substantially higher than for most EU countries (Table 4.1).

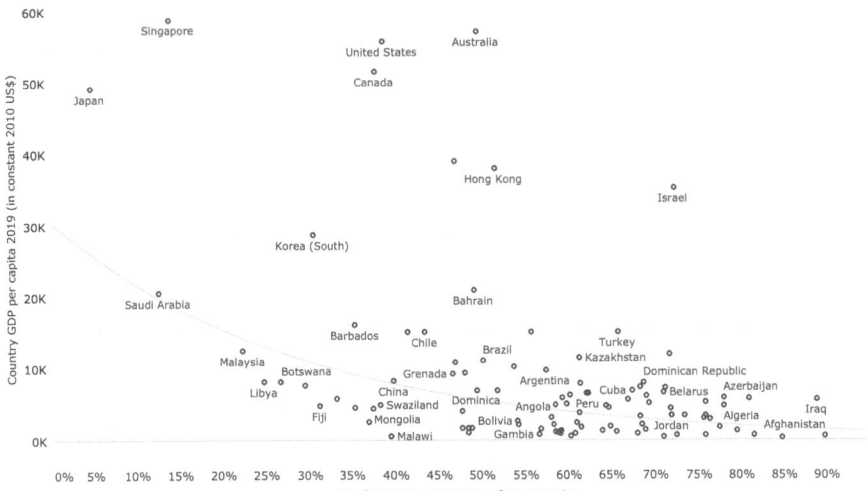

Fig. 4.1 Relationship between country of origin GDP per capital and UK citizenship acquisition, 2019

Sources: Home Office (2020) Migrant Journey: 2019 report, table D01. World Band data 2019 (GDP per capita in constant 2010 US$)

Note: Home Office data refers to all non-EU citizens who were granted an entry visa for work, family or study between 2005and 2009. Expired visas are excluded from the count

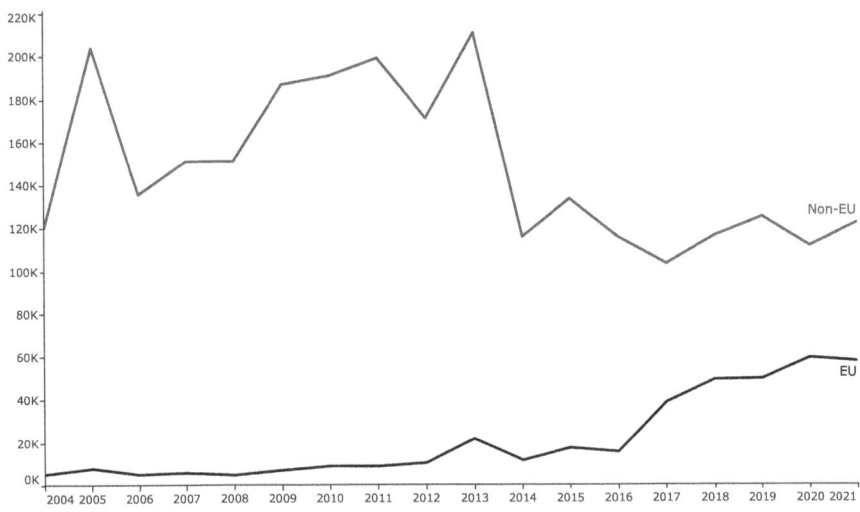

Fig. 4.2 Applications for UK Citizenship among EU and non-EU citizens, 2004–2020

Source: Home Office (2021). Immigration statistics, year ending June 2021, table cit D01

Barriers in the process may have also played a role in the low naturalisation rates of EU citizens: all people applying for UK citizenship must already have proof of their permanent status, but until recently the process for most EU citizens to get such a document was quite complex (Migration Observatory, 2016). Most EU citizens will also not have had any contact with the immigration system, whereas non-EU citizens will generally have already had to submit multiple applications (e.g. for entry visas, renewals and indefinite leave to remain), making them more familiar with the process and perhaps more aware of the benefits of securing status for the long term by acquiring citizenship.

Scholars have argued that political and economic instability in the last ten years have made EU citizens living in other EU states more likely to become citizens than before (Graeber, 2016; Moreh et al., 2018; Sredanovic, 2020). Becoming British may have also been perceived as a way to 'escape the negative stigma' EU citizens felt was attached to being a migrant in the UK (Sigona & Godin, 2019). Concerns about immigration were an important driver of the UK public's vote to leave the European Union in 2016, and recent studies have shown that EU citizens' trust in UK institutions decreased after the vote (Sigona & Godin, 2019) while their perceptions of hostility increased.

After the Brexit referendum in 2016, the number of EU citizens applying for UK citizenship increased sharply from previously low levels (Fig. 4.2). From 2010 to 2014, an average of 10,800 EU citizens became UK citizens each year, and by 2020 this had increased to around 59,000. This upward trend in British citizenship acquisition among EU citizens is not surprising; naturalisations are expected to increase in response to legislative change that reduces the rights of non-citizens (Sredanovic, 2020: 3). EU citizens are thus choosing to naturalise as a way to protect their rights and avoid becoming subject to immigration control after 30 June 2021, when the Brexit transition period ended (O'Brien, 2021). Despite this trend, however, EU citizens made up only 35% of all successful applications in 2020.

4.3.2 Age at Migration and Years of Residence

Age at migration and years of residence are also factors affecting the propensity to naturalise (Peters et al., 2016). People who moved to the UK as children are more likely to be British citizens, and this trend is particularly clear among the EU born (Fig. 4.3). Both EU- and non-EU-born migrants who moved to the UK when they were children, especially those who moved at age 5 or younger, are more likely to be UK citizens than people who moved later. This is partly because people who moved to the UK when they were younger are more likely to have been in the UK for longer than those who moved at older ages. This confirms previous research showing that migrants who migrate at younger ages are more likely to become citizens (Peters et al., 2016; Chiswick & Miller, 2009). Among people who moved to the UK as adults, however, the likelihood of being a UK citizen is unrelated to their age of migration.

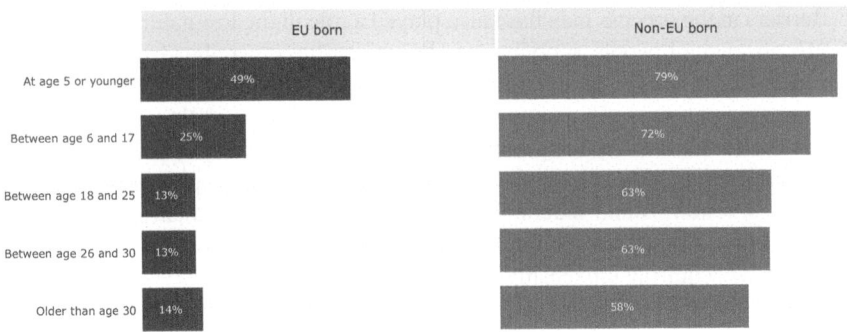

Fig. 4.3 Estimated share of foreign born who are UK nationals, by age at migration and controlling for years of residency in the UK, 2019
Source: Annual Population Survey, January–December, 2019 (Office for National Statistics, Social Survey Division, 2020)

4.3.3   Citizenship Policy in the Origin and Destination Countries: Dual Nationality Policies, Visa Type and Citizenship Fees

Citizenship policies of the origin and destination country are also thought to play a role in migrants' propensity to naturalise. The recognition of dual nationality in both origin and destination countries, birthright citizenship, and the implementation of easy and inexpensive legal and procedural requirements to naturalise have been considered particularly important (Labussière & Vink, 2020; Solano & Huddleston, 2020). For example, destination countries with more liberal citizenship polices that facilitate citizenship acquisition tend to have a higher share of naturalised migrants (Dronkers & Vink, 2012). In the UK, dual nationality is recognised since the British Nationality Law 1948. Birthright citizenship–by which UK citizenship is acquired by being born in the UK – was restricted in the British Nationality Law 1981 and currently UK-born children are automatically British only if one of their parents was British or had permanent immigration status at the time of children's birth. In 2019, there were an estimated 474,000 UK-born residents without UK citizenship, 90 per cent of whom were under age 18 (authors' calculation based on the APS 2019).

The type of visa on which migrants move to the UK also conditions their path to citizenship. This is visible in data on the amount of time it takes for people who came to the UK on different visa types to become citizens, provided they are still in the UK. In particular, students (and, to some extent, work visa holders) have a much longer path to permanent status than family visa holders, and thus are likely to contribute substantially to the non-citizen population. This is because the time spent in the UK under a youth mobility visa or a student visa does not count towards the 5 year period that is usually required to apply for permanent residence (ILR or EU settled status), which is a requirement before applying for citizenship. On the other hand, migrants who naturalise as British citizens by marriage are required to have

Migrants whose entry visa was issued in 2006

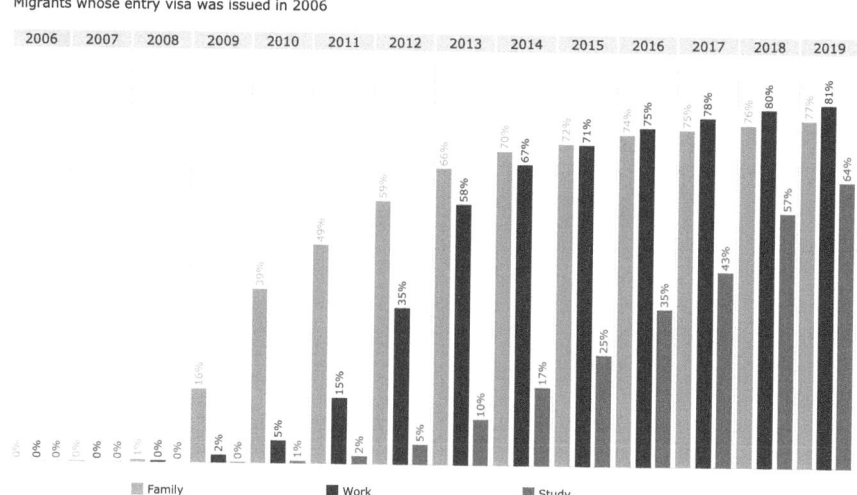

| 2006 | 2007 | 2008 | 2009 | 2010 | 2011 | 2012 | 2013 | 2014 | 2015 | 2016 | 2017 | 2018 | 2019 |

■ Family   ■ Work   ■ Study

Fig. 4.4 Successful applications for British citizenship among non-EU citizens, by entry visa category

Sources: Home Office Migrant Journey: 2019 report, table D01

lived in the UK for at least three years. As shown in Fig. 4.4, among people granted entry visas in 2006, those on family visas tended to become UK citizens the fastest, with 56 per cent already UK citizens by the end of 2012 (i.e. after 6–7 years). International students took longer to become British citizens, but the gap narrowed significantly after 10 years since arrival—so by 2019 the overall the share of UK citizens was only slightly lower for migrants with student entry visas than for those with family entry visas (Fig. 4.4).

Citizenship fees in the UK are substantially high compared to other Western countries. According to the Migrant Integration Policy Index (2020), non-EU citizens in the UK who want to settle permanently or become British citizens face among the highest costs in the developed world. Since 2018, the cost of an adult citizenship application was £1330, up from £268 in 2005 (Fig. 4.5). This compares to an estimated marginal cost of £372 to process each application (Home Office, 2019a, b), and the 'surplus' is used to make the immigration system 'self-funding', e.g. covering overhead costs.

The effect of fees on the citizenship application rate is hard to measure, although a 2019 report by the Independent Chief Inspector of Borders and Immigration (a public appointee independent from government who is responsible for monitoring and reporting on the efficiency and effectiveness of the immigration, asylum and nationality system) documented concerns among lawyers, civil society and applicants about the impacts of high costs of citizenship registration for children in particular (ICIBI, 2019; see also Ealing Law Centre, 2014). In February 2021, the Court of Appeal ruled that children citizenship fees were unlawful and in 2022 the Home Office introduced a fee waiver for children whose families can demonstrate

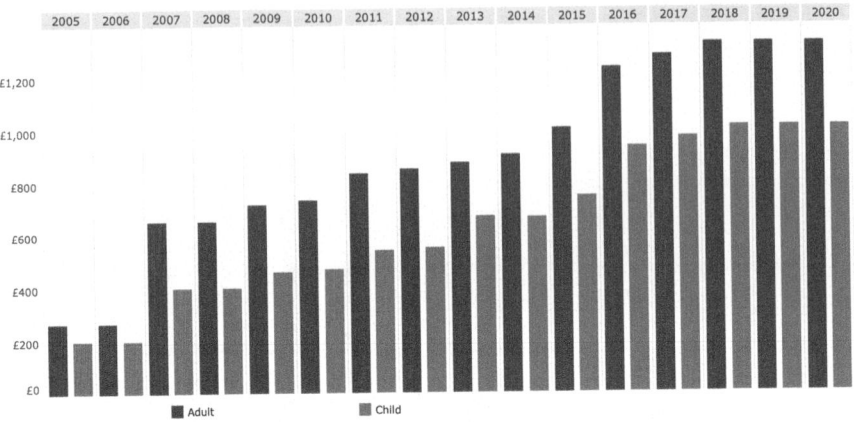

Fig. 4.5 Naturalisation fees, 2005–2020
Source: Home Office immigration and nationality Fees: 1 July 2021
Note: includes £80 citizenship ceremony fee for adults

that they cannot afford the fee. EU citizens in the UK have cited the fee as a significant deterrent (Sigona & Godin, 2019), and evidence from the United States, where
fees are lower, has found that fee subsidies significantly increased application rates
(Hainmueller et al., 2018).

Previous research has identified various other barriers to becoming a UK citizen
in addition to fees, including the 'Life in the UK' test, which was implemented in
2005 in response to the Nationality, Immigration and Asylum Act 2002 (see e.g.
Valdez-Symonds, 2019; van Oers, 2014; Byrne, 2014; Monforte et al., 2018).
So-called 'civic integration' tests such as 'Life in the UK' and other mandatory
integration requirements have become common in Europe since the early 2000s,
though there are notable variations across countries (Goodman, 2010, 2011, 2012).
In the UK and other Western states, civic integration and language tests were introduced in response to public opinion concerns about the lack of integration of some
migrant communities and its impact on social cohesion (Byrne, 2016). The pass
rates of 'Life in the UK' test vary widely across nationalities; for example, in the
year 2013 (the last full year on which there is available data on pass rates by applicants' nationality), the pass rates for nationalities with at least a hundred applicants
sitting the test range from above 95 per cent among Australians, New Zelanders,
Irish, Singaporeans and Americans to below 60 per cent among Afghans, Albanians,
Bangladeshis, Iraquis and Jamaicans (Home Office, 2014).

In total, around 6623 or 4 per cent of citizenship applications were refused in
2019, excluding withdrawn applications. The most common reason for refusal was
not passing the 'good character' test. According to the Home Office, applicants for
citizenship aged 10 or older will not be considered of good character if they have
been involved in crime, have not paid their taxes, have been deliberately dishonest
or deceptive in their dealings with the UK government, have breached immigration
law or have been deprived of their citizenship before (Home Office, 2019a, b). In

other words, refusals do not appear to be the major driver of non-citizenship in the UK. Rather, it is decisions not to apply or barriers to applying, among the eligible population and particularly among EU citizens.

4.4 Conclusions and Gaps in the Data

Overall, the data suggest that there are multiple barriers to becoming a UK citizen, but that differences in demand to become a citizen also play a role. These factors are difficult to disentangle, and may affect different people in different ways. For example, it is possible that the cost of naturalisation has in the past been more of a deterrent for EU citizens who felt secure in their current citizenship and immigration status, compared to non-EU citizens who have more experience of navigating visa processes. Nonetheless, the gaps in citizenship acquisition between EU and non-EU citizens are sufficiently large that it is likely that motivation to become a citizen also plays a strong role. Holding EU citizenship appears to have been a deterrent to applying for UK citizenship; now that the rights associated with EU citizenship have been greatly reduced, this has changed to some extent. However, even despite the increase in EU citizens' naturalisation applications, they are still underrepresented among applicants. It remains to be seen whether and how this will change over the coming years, as EU citizens adjust to life under the post-Brexit rules.

Acknowledgments This work was produced using statistical data from Office for National Statistics (ONS). The use of the ONS statistical data in this work does not imply the endorsement of the ONS in relation to the interpretation or analysis of the statistical data. This work uses research datasets which may not exactly reproduce National Statistics aggregates.

References

Aptekar, S. (2016). Making sense of naturalization: What citizenship means to naturalizing immigrants in Canada and the USA. *Journal of International Migration and Integration, 17,* 1143–1161. Available online.

Bartram, D. (2019). The UK Citizenship process: Political integration or marginalization? *Sociology, 53*(4), 671–688. https://doi.org/10.1177/0038038518813842

Bartram, D. (2021). Does the UK 'citizenship process' lead immigrants to reject British identity? A panel data analysis. *Ethnicities, 21*(2), 375–394. https://doi.org/10.1177/1468796820963963

Bauböck, R. (2019). Genuine links and useful passports: evaluating strategic uses of citizenship. *Journal of Ethnic and Migration Studies, 45*(6), 1015–1026.

Birkvad, S. R. (2019). Immigrant meanings of citizenship: mobility, stability, and recognition. *Citizenship Studies, 23*(8), 798–814. Available online.

British Future. (2020). *Barriers to Britishness.* Report of the Alberto Costa Inquiry into Citizenship Policy. Available online.

Byrne, B. (2014). *Making Citizens: Public Rituals and Personal Journeys to Citizenship.* Palgrave.

Chiswick, B., & Miller, P. W. (2009). Citizenship in the United States: The roles of immigrant characteristics and country of origin. *Research in Labor Economics, 29*(2009), 91–130.

Dronkers, J., & Vink, M. P. (2012). Explaining access to citizenship in Europe: How citizenship policies affect naturalization rates. *European Union Politics, 13*(3), 390–412.

Ealing Law Centre. (2014). *Systemic obstacles to children's registration as British citizens*. Ealing Law Centre.

Gathmann, C., & Keller, N. (2018). Access to citizenship and the economic assimilation of immigrants. *The Economic Journal, 128*(616), 3141–3181.

Goodman, S. W. (2010). Integration requirements for integration's sake? Identifying, categorising and comparing civic integration policies. *Journal of Ethnic and Migration Studies, 36*(5), 753–772.

Goodman, S. W. (2011). Controlling immigration through language and country knowledge requirements. *West European Politics, 34*(2), 235–255. https://doi.org/10.1080/0140238 2.2011.546569

Goodman, S. W. (2012). Fortifying citizenship: Policy strategies for civic integration in Western Europe. *World Politics, 64*(4), 659–698.

Gower, M. (2021). Nationality and borders bill. *House of Commons Library*, 1–61. Retrieved from https://researchbriefings.files.parliament.uk/documents/CBP-9275/CBP-9275.pdf

Graeber, J. (2016). Citizenship in the shadow of the Euro crisis: explaining changing patterns in naturalisation among intra-EU migrants. *Journal of Ethnic and Migration Studies, 42*(10), 1670–1692.

Hainmueller, J., Hangartner, D., & Pietrantuono, G. (2017). Catalyst or crown: Does naturalization promote the long-term social integration of immigrants? *American Political Science Review, 111*(2), 256–276.

Hainmueller, J., Lawrence, D., Gest, J., Hotard, M., Koslowski, R., & Laitin, D. (2018). A randomized controlled design reveals barriers to citizenship for low-income immigrants. *Proceedings of the National Academy of Sciences, 115*(5), 939–944.

Halliday, I. (2019). The pathway to British citizenship for European nationals in the UK. *Free Movement*. Available online.

Harpaz, Y., & Mateos, P. (2019). Strategic citizenship: negotiating membership in the age of dual nationality. *Journal of Ethnic and Migration Studies, 45*(6), 843–857.

Home Office. (2014). Knowledge of langague and life in the UK test processed fro British citizenship, 2009 to 2014, FOI release 30799. https://www.gov.uk/government/publications/knowledge-of-language-and-life-in-the-uk-test-results-2009-to-2014

Home Office. (2019a). Nationality: good character requirement. Available online.

Home Office. (2019b). Visa fees transparency data. Available online.

Home Office (2020). Migrant Journey: 2019 report. Retrieved 31 January 2021, from https://www.gov.uk/government/statistics/migrant-journey-2019-report

Home Office (2021). Immigration statistics, year ending June 2021. Retrieved 1 September 2021 from https://www.gov.uk/government/statistics/immigration-statistics-year-ending-june-2021

ICIBI. (2019). *An inspection of the policies and practices of the Home Office's Borders*. Immigration and Citizenship Systems relating to charging and fees.

Kochenov, D., & Lindeboom, J. (2017). Empirical assessment of the quality of nationalities: the quality of nationality index (QNI). *European Journal of Comparative Law and Governance, 4*(4), 314–336.

Labussière, M., & Vink, M. (2020). The intergenerational impact of naturalisation reforms: the citizenship status of children of immigrants in the Netherlands, 1995–2016. *Journal of Ethnic and Migration Studies, 46*(13), 2742–2763.

Migration Observatory. (2016). *Here today, gone tomorrow? The Status of EU citizens already living in the UK*. Migration Observatory. Available online.

Milanovic, B. (2013). Global income inequality in numbers: in history and now. *Global Policy, 4*(2), 198–208.

Monforte, P., Bassel, L., & Khan, K. (2018). Deserving citizenship? Exploring migrants' experiences of the 'citizenship test' process in the United Kingdom. *British Journal of Sociology.* https://doi.org/10.1111/1468-4446.12351

Moreh, C., McGhee, D., & Vlachantoni, A. (2018). The return of citizenship? An empirical assessment of legal integration in times of radical sociolegal transformation. *International Migration Review, 0197918318809924.*

Ndofor-Tah, C., Strang, A., Phillimore, J., Morrice, L., Michael, L., Wood, P., & Simmons, J. (2019). *Home Office Indicators of Integration framework 2019* (3rd ed.). Home Office.

O'Brien, C. (2021). Between the devil and the deep blue sea: vulnerable EU citizens cast adrift in the UK post-Brexit. *Common Market Law Review, 58*(2).

OECD. (2011). Naturalisation: A passport for the better integration of immigrants? *OECD Publishing, Paris.* https://doi.org/10.1787/9789264099104-en

Office for National Statistics, Social Survey Division. (2020). Annual population survey, January–December, 2019. [data collection] (4th ed.). UK Data Service. SN: 8632. https://doi.org/10.5255/UKDA-SN-8632-4

Office for National Statistics, Social Survey Division. (2022). Annual population survey, 2004–2022: Secure Access. [data collection] (25th ed.). UK Data Service. SN: 6721. https://doi.org/10.5255/UKDA-SN-6721-24

Peters, F., Vink, M., & Schmeets, H. (2016). The ecology of immigrant naturalisation: a life course approach in the context of institutional conditions. *Journal of Ethnic and Migration Studies, 42*(3), 359–381.

Prabhat, D. (2018). *Britishness, Belonging and Citizenship Experiencing Nationality Law Bristol.* Polity Press.

Rutter, J., Latorre, M., & Sriskandarajah, D. (2008). *Beyond Naturalisation: Citizenship policy in an age of super mobility.* Institute for Public Policy Research.

Sigona, N., & Godin, M. (2019). Naturalisation and (dis)integration. *Eurochildren Brief Series, 6.*

Solano, G., & Huddleston, T. (2020). Migrant Integration Policy Index 2020.

Sredanovic, D. (2020). The tactics and strategies of naturalisation: UK and EU27 citizens in the context of Brexit. *Journal of Ethnic and Migration Studies.* https://doi.org/10.1080/1369183X.2020.1844003

Valdez-Symonds, S. (2019). Children's rights to British citizenship. In D. Prabat (Ed.), *Citizenship in Times of Turmoil.* Edward Elgar Press.

Van Oers, R. (2014). *Deserving citizenship: citizenship tests in Germany, the Netherlands and the United Kingdom.* Martinus Nijhoff Publishers.

Vassiliou, J. (2020). It just got even more difficult for EU nationals to get British citizenship. *Free Movement.*

Part II
Integration from Below

Chapter 5
Immigrant Economic Rights in the European Union

Hannah M. Alarian

EU member states, over the course of two decades, have steadily extended economic rights once reserved for citizens to non-EU immigrants. Since 2007 alone, twenty-one EU countries have increased non-EU immigrant access to economic benefits including employment access, educational grants, housing assistance, social security, and broader welfare benefits (Solano & Huddleston, 2020). Although EU citizens benefit from economic rights in virtue of the non-discrimination principle,[1] the decision to provide non-EU citizens with economic entitlements is largely left up to individual member-states, generating substantial variation where non-EU immigrants can make economic claims on their state of residence.[2] How do these non-EU immigrants respond to expansive economic rights? Can providing non-EU immigrants with rights below citizenship foster political, psychological, and legal inclusion?

This chapter addresses these questions, advancing our understanding of non-EU immigrant[3] incorporation as occurring both above and below citizenship. Immigrant integration contains multiple facets, assessing a wide range of experiences and abilities immigrants possess within their new society (see e.g. Harder et al., 2018). To wit, this chapter brings evidence to bear on the effects of economic rights on immigrant integration from both the institutional and migrant perspective, specifically addressing the psychological, political, and social aspects of immigrant integration. First, I explore how immigrant economic rights shape individual perceptions of

---

[1] Treaty on the Functioning of the European Union (TFEU) Art 18.

[2] It should be noted, however, that EU Directive 2003/109/EC on Long Term-Resident (LTR) Third Country Nationals prohibits discrimination against non-EU immigrants who have acquired EU LTR status.

[3] Henceforth, the term immigrant or non-citizen refers only to non-EU citizen migrants.

H. M. Alarian (✉)
University of Florida, Gainesville, FL, USA

© The Author(s) 2023
R. Barbulescu et al. (eds.), *Revising the Integration-Citizenship Nexus in Europe*, IMISCOE Research Series, https://doi.org/10.1007/978-3-031-25726-1_5

one's political and social lives. Second, I consider how these same rights predict integration at the institutional level via naturalization.

The sum total of the results reveal that economic rights enhance the psychological, political, and social lives of non-EU immigrants within the EU. Earlier access to the labour market, for example, corresponds with greater satisfaction with democracy, government, and life overall. Further although welfare appears in some instances negatively associated with integration, I find strong evidence this relationship is moderated by citizenship policy. That is, immigrants who can receive social assistance without incurring additional barriers to integration (i.e. policies which prolong or prohibit the naturalisation of immigrant welfare recipients), are more likely to enjoy the formal benefits of citizenship status. Moreover, this collective evidence provides a clear agenda for EU member states committed to enhancing immigrant integration: provide immigrants with economic rights.

The chapter proceeds as follows. First, I offer a brief discussion of immigrant economic rights within EU member states. Next, I discuss these policies in relation to immigrant integration from both individual and institutional perspectives. I take care here to outline the varied perspectives of immigrant integration below and above citizenship and their relationship to economic rights. After describing the theoretical expectations, I introduce my analytical strategy, describing the data, identifying the measures, and presenting the results for my two studies independently. The chapter concludes with a discussion of the policy implications and suggestions for future scholarship.

5.1   The Economic Rights of Migrants

What economic rights are granted to third country immigrants in the EU? Although the EU can advocate, promote, or ensure EU citizens are provided equality of economic rights, no such formal protections exist for much of their non-EU migrant communities.[4] This consequently leaves decisions of the type, kind, and scope of economic rights for third country nationals regardless of long-term resident status up to the discretion of national governments, causing considerable variation across the continent (Könönen, 2018).[5] Some states, for example, ensure non-EU citizens have immediate access to labour market sectors (e.g. Spain, Czechia), where others preserve employment sectors or the labour market as a whole for their citizens (e.g. Slovakia, France). Others too offer non-citizens equality of access to welfare and

---

[4] As mentioned previously, EU law regulates a range of socio-economic rights of LTR third country nationals (eligible after five years of residence). This bundling of socio-economic rights has led to the characterization of an EU denizenship or quasi-citizenship for long-term resident third country nationals (see e.g. Hammar, 1990).

[5] It is neither the purpose nor the scope of this chapter to explain the myriad motivations for the permission or prohibition of such rights to non-EU citizens. See e.g. Ruhs, 2013 for a discussion of the trade-offs between recruitment and settlement rights within and outside the EU.

social security assistance – ensuring non-citizens are awarded with the same social safety net as citizens (e.g. Portugal, Greece). Other EU member states alternatively take a targeted approach to migrants, giving these immigrants equal access to resources to improve socio-economic mobility (e.g. Estonia, Belgium). Finally, some offer very little in the way of providing non-EU migrants with any economic rights or protections (e.g. Latvia).

Given the variation in type of economic entitlements granted to immigrants, three specific categories of rights are most relevant to immigrant integration: (1) employment access; (2) welfare and social security rights and; (3) socio-economic mobility. The first category represents immigrant access to various aspects of the labour market, including public, private, and self-employment options. Welfare and social security rights, on the other hand, relegate immigrant access to a wealth of social security benefits, including unemployment benefits, pension, invalidity benefits, maternity leave, family benefits, and social assistance. The final type of economic rights — socio-economic mobility — represents an immigrant's access to benefits aimed at improving their social and economic position including access to public sector employment services, training, and study grants.

Exactly how varied are EU member state approaches to non-citizen economic rights? Although EU law has harmonized some national provisions with respect to socio-economic rights for long-term resident third country nationals,[6] Fig. 5.1 reveals these policies remain nationally distinct. Overall, these policies over time range from hostile (i.e. 0) to extremely welcoming (i.e. 10), with the average policies scoring as rather inclusive (i.e. 7.03).[7] Further, countries do not appear to be either universally accepting nor restrictive in their approach to immigrant economic rights. Austria, Estonia, and Greece, for example, possess relatively closed labour markets despite allowing some non-citizen access to welfare and socio-economic mobility rights. Denmark, Poland, and the United Kingdom, however, present the opposite policy environment whereby employment access is more regulated than welfare or mobility. And while some of the included countries certainly offer relatively similar access across economic rights (e.g. Portugal), the vast majority of the included countries appear to favour providing welfare rights over those associated with equality in employment or socio-economic mobility. France is an exemplar of this trend, on average offering its non-citizen population near equal access to social assistance (i.e. 10) despite being one of the most restrictive with respect to granting migrant access to the labour market (i.e. 1.33).

Despite this variance, all EU member-states share a practical interest in providing immigrants with economic rights. Enabling access to employment opportunities for migrant communities can advance economic growth and native prosperity

---

[6] EU Directive 2003/109/EC lifted discriminatory provisions in several EU member-states with regard to access to employment; social security, social assistance and social protection; and provision of public services in areas such as social housing (see Art. 11 of the Directive).

[7] Re-aggregation of Migration Policy Indices (Solano & Huddleston, 2020). A detailed discussion of the coding, indexing, and data source for these polices appears below (see Empirical Approach).

Fig. 5.1 Comparative
Economic Rights in
Reference Year (2009)

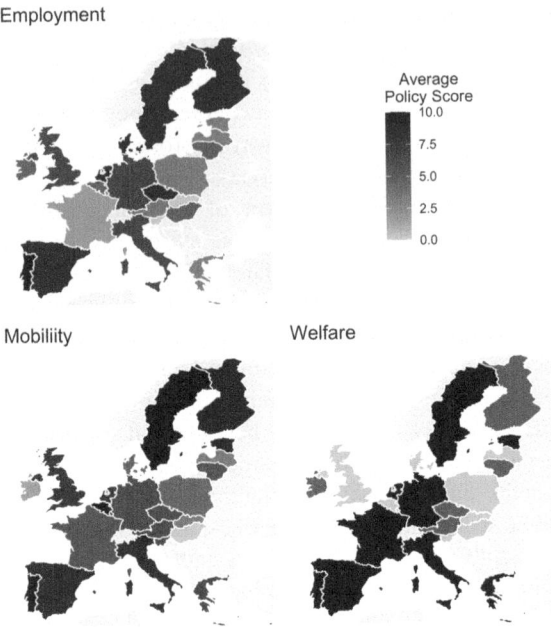

(Borjas, 1994; Dancygier & Laitin, 2014) whereas protecting employment opportunities for citizens alone can enable immigrant marginalization, depression, and depreciate overall life satisfaction (Clark et al., 2001; Lelkes, 2006). Beyond such instrumental state concerns, economic rights may be crucial to promoting migrant societal incorporation. As alienation and marginalization expand through unemployment, so may pathways to violent extremism and radical policies (Dancygier, 2010; Eatwell, 2006; Falk et al., 2011; Sobolewska, 2010). Former UK Prime Minister David Cameron's statement in response to the 7/7 bombings that, "We have failed to provide a vision of society to which they feel they want to belong" is further indication of the state's pressing desire to decrease exclusion as a means to prevent radicalization (Cameron, 2011). Former French Interior Minister Manuel Valls conversely suggested inclusion may beget inclusion across immigrant communities, proclaiming that divorcing citizenship status from economic preconditions would ensure "French nationality should not be sold off or reserved for the elite" (France to make it easier to become French, 2012).

Insights as to whether economic rights affect integration, however, require first the broader discussion of immigrant integration itself. Immigrant integration is a multi-dimensional concept, encompassing a vast array of relationships between an individual immigrant and their host society (Harder et al., 2018). This intricacy is often lost however, within the extant literature (Schinkel, 2018), partially due to an overemphasis on the naturalised as objects of inquiry or a focus on problematizing the immigration-diversity nexus (see e.g. Bloemraad, 2006; Hainmueller et al., 2015; Yang, 1994). Although citizen-migrants are clearly important in their own right, this singular focus omits not only any experience between arrival and naturalisation but also reduces integration to a phenomenon which either only begins or ends after citizenship acquisition. This is particularly problematic as states continuously promote policies treating the two in reverse: integration as the finish line and citizenship as the ultimate prize (Van Hook et al., 2006). This focus too also ignores the power relationships inherent between the state and the final markers of immigrant integration — again, often measured as citizenship acquisition.

To reframe this integration conversation, I therefore aim to take a holistic approach to the concept of immigrant integration: considering both individual and institutional markers of integration of non-citizen immigrants. Of the former, I specifically consider psychological and social facets of integration which captures an individual's general satisfaction with their personal and political life in their country of residence. Of the latter, I examine citizenship acquisition as an institutional marker of immigrant integration.

Integration within this broader understanding is a clear obligation of the state. To this end, states may extend economic rights with the goal of facilitating broader integration (Huddleston & Vink, 2015). Such inclusion would therefore be path dependent — whereby early inclusive experiences enable immigrants to actively view themselves within the national identity, increasing the likelihood of citizenship acquisition. Provided inclusion is in fact habit-forming (Cho & Tam., 1999; Ferwerda et al., 2020; Street, 2017), allowing immigrants to access economic environments prior to citizenship would provide the conditions necessary for their naturalisation. As citizenship itself is unlikely to foster complete inclusion (Bevelander & Veenman, 2006; Levin, 2013), these early inclusive experiences constitute a meaningful step toward rather than hurdle to integration.

In addition to the possibility of economic inclusion's path dependence, research reveals inclusion broadly and within the economic realm specifically engenders connections to the democracy and the state. For one, research in the United States reveals the lives and subsequent integration of immigrants and their families improve when welfare and other economic benefits expand to include non-citizens (Bitler & Hoynes, 2011; Perreira & Pedroza, 2019). Policies geared toward increasing equality across the public — such as expanding equality in economic rights to non-citizens — improve social and political trust and perceptions of governmental quality (Sirovátka et al., 2019; Ziller & Helbling, 2019). Alternatively, immigrants are less satisfied with democracy when residing within environments of exclusion or welfare retrenchment (Just, 2017; Larsen, 2018). Employment access specifically is likely to possess a unique role in immigrant lives, enhancing non-citizen political participation and civic belonging (Alarian, 2017b). These rights are core components of embedded structured mobilization where inclusive policies move beyond mere bureaucratic tools and additionally act as normative signals broadcasting an inclusive, tolerant citizenship to the wider national community (Bloemraad, 2006; Cort, 2012; Tankard & Paluck, 2017). Through this inclusion, immigrants appear to be more trusting of, satisfied with, engaged in, and accepted by their destination – all conditions which are critical in an individual's quality of life and a state's decision to facilitate citizenship acquisition.

Still, others contend that immigrant economic rights specifically harm immigrants by increasing dependency on the state and depreciating participatory citizenship (Mohanty & Tandon, 2006). Koopmans (2010) exemplifies this argument, relying on relative deprivation theory (cf. Gurr, 1970) to conclude "unrestricted access to the full panoply of welfare-state benefits without demanding much in return ... have often turned [immigrants] into passive welfare state clients" (Koopmans, 2010, pp.22). More practically, it is likely that political opposition factors may prevent polices from reaching their intended integration goal. States may counterbalance liberal economic rights with exceptions for those applying for citizenship, effectively prohibiting or prolonging the naturalisation of those who received the provided economic benefits. In other words, the integration benefits of immigrant economic rights may be constrained by a state's political will to formally incorporate immigrants within society.

By way of summary, I theorize inclusion via economic rights encourages immigrant integration. States doing such would actively treat economic rights as a pathway to citizenship and improving the daily lives of immigrants, signalling to majority and minority members alike that immigrants are permanent, valued fixtures within the national community. Conversely, states systematically excluding migrants from economic benefits risk regularising immigrant segregation in perpetuity. As such, I test the following hypotheses:

Hypothesis 1: Immigrant economic rights increases social and psychological integration.
Hypothesis 2: Immigrant economic rights increase citizenship acquisition.

5.2 Empirical Approach

I examine the relationship between economic rights and immigrant integration in two steps: first individually (i.e. social and psychological integration) and second institutionally (i.e. citizenship acquisition). Below, I describe the data, measurement, and results for each of these steps separately.

5.2.1 Integration below Citizenship: Social and Psychological Integration in the EU

I first address the question of how economic rights affect individual social and psychological integration within the EU. The assessment of such individual experiences therefore requires the use of survey-level data across a variety of economic right settings. To do such, I rely on the cumulative European Social Survey (ESS) — a biennial cross-national survey of European countries (European Social Survey Cumulative File, 2020). This data allows for a test of a wide range of individual perceptions of the quality and satisfaction with one's experience across a collection of democracies with varied economic rights policies. I identify non-EU citizens within the ESS as any respondent who indicated both that they are not a citizen of the survey country and do not hold a citizenship with an EU member state. To further account for the possibility of including either immigrant citizens or EU citizens in my sample, I exclude any individual who reported voting in the last national election.[8] In total, the sample includes 11,451 adult non-EU immigrant respondents across 23 EU countries and 14 years.[9]

5.3 Measurement

I first assess social and psychological integration as satisfaction with one's life within their country of residence with four survey items. The first three assess individual satisfaction with (1) democracy, (2) government,[10] and (3) life[11] and the fourth measures an immigrant's overall happiness.[12] All items are recoded to range from 0 to 1, with higher scores indicating greater satisfaction, happiness, or interest in politics.[13] All items are chosen for their ability to triangulate both across integration experiences and over time — including only those variables which are asked of survey respondents across all relevant survey waves. Further, these items possess nearly identical response options, which allow for a meaningful interpretation and comparison of the resulting coefficients. Together, these items allow me to capture a broad understanding of the relationships between non-citizen economic rights and integration across time.

---

[8] I assess this population through ESS items ctzcntr, ctzshipc, and vote.

[9] Austria, Belgium, Czechia, Denmark, Estonia, Finland, France, Germany, Greece, Hungary, Ireland, Italy, Lithuania, Latvia, the Netherlands, Poland, Portugal, Slovakia, Slovenia, Spain, Sweden, and the United Kingdom. Years include 2007–2019. The following study, as described below, does not capture the same set of countries due to data reliability. To ensure the ensuing results are not an artefact of said data inclusion or exclusion, I also conduct the same analyses limiting to the same sample of countries included within study two (e.g. excluding Greece, Lithuania, Latvia, and Slovakia), yielding a similar pattern of results.

[10] Item phrasing: On the whole, how satisfied are you with the way democracy works in [country]? and Now thinking about the [country] government, how satisfied are you with the way it is doing its job? Response options for both from Extremely dissatisfied to Extremely satisfied.

[11] All things considered, how satisfied are you with your life as a whole nowadays? Options range from Extremely dissatisfied to Extremely satisfied.

[12] Taking all things together, how happy would you say you are? Options range from Extremely unhappy to Extremely happy.

[13] Interested readers can find these items listed directly within the ESS codebook as: stfdem; stfgov; polintr; stflife; and happy.

5.3.1 Economic Rights

I measure employment access, welfare and social security, and socio-economic mobility rights using re-aggregated policy scores from the Migrant Integration Policy Index (MIPEX, Solano & Huddleston, 2020). MIPEX is a useful tool for this endeavour, compiling annual policy experts' assessments on integration and citizenship policies across the EU between 2007 and 2020. Once scored, these policies are categorised into policy indices with scores reflecting unfavourable (i.e. 0) to highly favourable policies toward migrants (i.e. 10).[14] In other words, values closer to zero reflect policies limiting non-citizen access to economic rights whereas scores closer to 10 indicate non-citizens have relatively equal rights compared to natives.

Rather than using these aggregated, curated indices, I use individual policy indicators on the Labour Market Mobility index to create my own precise indicator of interest (see e.g. Goodman, 2015). For employment rights, I take the average of a country's annual policies regulating non-citizen access to: (1) the labour market overall; (2) public sector employment; and (3) self-employment.[15] Welfare and social security rights scores come from a single measure assessing the degree of immigrant access to social security, including unemployment benefits, pension, invalidity benefits, maternity leave, family benefits, and social assistance.[16] The final economic rights indicator — socio-economic mobility — is represented by the average equality in access to (1) public sector employment services; and (2) training and study grants.[17] These three policy indices are used to separate the policy effects of various economic rights that migrants enjoy.

Finally, I include individual demographic variables within the analysis which may account for any relationship between economic rights and the key integration components of interest. These demographic indicators include gender identity, age, marital status, religious affiliation, and employment status.[18] Similarly, I consider several immigrant-specific variables including how long an individual has resided within the destination country, immigrant heritage, and speaking any of the

---

[14] MIPEX scores are originally coded in units of 100 and are recoded in units of ten for ease of interpretation in all analyses.

[15] Items aa1, aa3, and aa5 in the Solano and Huddleston (2020) and 1, 3, 5 in prior MIPEX iterations. Wherever data is missing in the most current dataset, I supplement with scores from the 2015 MIPEX iteration and cross-reference to GLOBALCit (née EUDO Cit) country reports (e.g. Ersbøll, 2013; Marín-Rubio et al., 2015).

[16] Item ad18 or 18 in the corresponding MIPEX database.

[17] MIPEX 2020 items ab6, and ab7ab8. To combine with MIPEX 2015 for missing data in Austria, items 7 and 8 were averaged prior to being averaged with item 6.

[18] In order, these items are: male (recoded as a Female dummy), edvula, and agea, marsts (recoded as a married dummy), and rlgblb (recoded as a religious denomination dummy). Employment status is a dummy reflecting a positive response to pdwrk, excluding those who answered not applicable, don't know, or refused response to the set of employment items.

destination country official languages at home.[19] Models also include year fixed effects calculated as the year of survey completion.[20]

5.4 Analysis

All analyses are conducted using ordinary least squares regression estimation with post-stratification weights and include year fixed effects with clustered robust standard errors by destination country.[21] Figure 5.2 below reveals the unstandardized

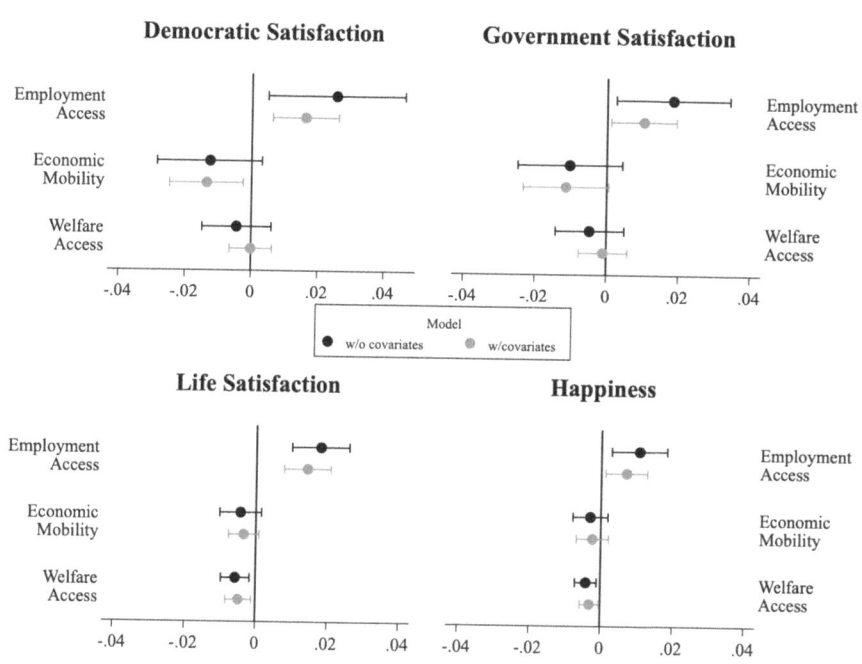

Fig. 5.2 Predicting Social and Psychological Immigrant Integration by Economic Rights. Unstandardized Beta Coefficients with 90 and 95 percent confidence intervals

---

[19] Years in country calculated using interview year (inwyee) and item liveccnta. Immigrant heritage reflects a dummy indicating whether any parent was born outside the destination country (facntr and mocntr). Destination countries were hand coded to reflect whether an individual reported speaking any related official language most or second most at home (lnghoma, lnghom1, lnghomb, or lnghom2).

[20] Although the ESS survey waves are organized by years, this often does not correspond to the year the respondent completed the survey within a given country or survey wave. In the interest of increasing precision as much as possible, I therefore calculate year from ESS item inwyye.

[21] I point interested readers to the ESS for detailed information about the calculation of these weights by survey round (see e.g. European Social Survey Cumulative File, 2020).

beta coefficients for these models with and without covariates by the dependent variable of interest.[22] Within these figures, I present the main effects of these policies with and without all relevant covariates.

Regarding rights regulating immigrant access to employment, I find immigrant social and psychological integration is significantly improved when granted equal access to the labour market. Specifically, liberalisation in employment rights from restriction (i.e. 0) to even moderate access (i.e. 5) corresponds with an approximate increase of 8% increase in democratic satisfaction, controlling for all covariates. Individuals similarly report greater satisfaction in life and with one's government, similarly representing an approximate increase of 7% and 5% respectively. Non-EU citizens also report an increase in happiness when employment rights reach equality between native and migrant communities. These findings suggest that when states provide migrants with employment rights, immigrants are more supportive of democracy, satisfied with the government, and report living happier lives. Conversely, when states tie employment access to citizenship status, non-EU immigrant experience within and support of one's country of residence declines. This finding mirrors well with those of refugee employment status, finding that blocking refugee access to the labour market has a marked decline on their subsequent integration (e.g. Hainmueller et al., 2015). In conversation with this work, these findings should act as a call to action for states to reduce restrictions to ensure refugee and immigrant populations are included socially, economically, and democratically regardless of citizenship.

Socio-economic mobility, however, largely appears unrelated to immigrant social and psychological integration. Practically, this suggests that targeted socio-economic support (i.e. educational grants, public employment assistance) may not alter an immigrant's evaluation of their political or private lives in the EU. Although one can observe a negative relationship between these socio-economic mobility rights and democratic satisfaction when including all covariates in the model, this finding is not present within the basic model suggesting this finding may be spurious. Employment access consequently appears distinct in its apparent inclusive effect on individual integration.

Yet more puzzling is the mixed depiction of social welfare access on immigrant integration. Such access is unrelated to democratic or governmental evaluations and negatively, albeit meagrely, associated with individual life satisfaction and happiness. Although these findings may on face value appear in line with other research suggesting welfare negatively affects immigrant lives (Koopmans, 2010), this relationship should not be interpreted, as a negative relationship between actual welfare reception and individual integration within society. Specifically, this indicator only measures the possibility of welfare access as opposed to actual welfare reception. Thus, the messaging surrounding dissemination of these welfare rights may account for this decline in self-reported life satisfaction and happiness. Moreover, these coefficients are small and inconsistent across all key dependent variables of interest

---

[22] See Online Appendix B.1 and B.2 for regression tables.

which suggests this relationship may tell us little substantively. Including all covariates, moving from complete exclusion from (i.e. 0) to access to (i.e. 10) social welfare benefits corresponds with a 3% and 5% decline in self-reported happiness and life satisfaction respectively. Still even when accounting for all economic rights and individual covariates, employment rights far exceed this negative effect — with a positive effect size more than double that of welfare access in either domain. Put simply, the meagre effect size across the EU suggests a more nuanced examination of the relationship between welfare access and immigrant integration is required.

I wish to pause here to reflect on the collective findings in relation to the extent literature advocating that economic rights diminishes 'pushes' to integrate. These findings fail to support such claims, revealing instead that opening up labour markets to immigrants can improve immigrant lives — both normatively and practically. Hence outside of harming immigrant economic lives, restricting access to economic rights also likely damages immigrant social and psychological well-being. These findings behove scholars to engage with the unique importance of such economic belonging. More importantly, this conclusion provides a clear path forward for European states to foster immigrant integration: simply remove barriers to immigrant employment.

5.4.1 Integration at Citizenship: Naturalisation Within the EU

Although economic rights — specifically employment access — appears positively correlated to immigrant social and psychological integration, questions remain as to whether these rights also affect state recognition of integration via citizenship acquisition. In this second component of my analysis, I use administrative-level naturalisation data compiled from OECD (2020), Eurostat (2020), World Bank (2020), and national census estimates. It is necessary for this cross-validation across sources to ensure reliability and supplement missing data if possible from official sources. Cases were only excluded if data could not be validated across these primary and secondary sources for a given year and country pairs. In what follows, I describe this measurement and modelling strategy in more detail to assist in the interpretation of the ensuing results. After merging across these data sources, this second study includes a total of 14,680 citizenship acquisitions of 133 non-EU origins[23] within 19 EU destinations[24] between 2009 and 2018.

---

[23] See Online Appendix A.1 for a list of the included origin countries

[24] Austria, Belgium, Czechia, Denmark, Estonia, Finland, France, Germany, Hungary, Ireland, Italy, Luxembourg, the Netherlands, Poland, Portugal, Slovenia, Spain, Sweden, and the United Kingdom

5.5   Measurement

Naturalisation, the central variable of interest, is measured as the annual number of citizenship acquisitions of an origin group within a destination. As a simple example, one data point could represent the number of naturalisations in the United Kingdom from migrants with Moroccan descent for the year 2017. Consequently, I adopt pseudo-gravity modelling approach (see e.g. Alarian & Goodman, 2017; Fitzgerald et al., 2014). This modelling strategy allows for the consideration of both origin and destination elements which may also account for the relationship between economic rights and naturalisation annually. Importantly, I opt to use count of acquisitions as opposed to a rate for each origin group. This is accordance with the EU's statistical office warnings against using naturalisation rates (see Eurostat, 2020) in addition to methodological concerns of introducing error in predicting naturalisation outcomes (e.g. Alarian, 2017a).[25] To ensure accurate estimates, I also include indicators of the immigrant population as necessary independent controls within each model. Regardless of the measurement, however, it is crucial to note the results cannot be interpreted as estimating individual desire for citizenship. Although the dyadic approach does estimate naturalisation patterns between an origin and destination, citizenship acquisition itself is beholden to destination bureaucracy, policy, and discretion.

Although the independent variable measurement remains the same as the first study, I include a one- year policy lag within this second study to represent the time delay for these policies to affect year-end reported citizenship acquisitions. Again, all models include the requisite measures of citizenship policy and naturalisation social assistance penalties. In addition, I include a variety of control variables known to affect the relationship between naturalisation and economic rights including historical legacies, democratic quality, and economic health. In the interest of clarity, these variables, coding schemes, and sources are found in Table 5.1. As stated above, after merging across these data sources yields a total sample of 14,680 citizenship acquisition dyads between 133 non-EU sending and 19 EU receiving countries over ten years.

5.6   Analysis

To estimate the effect of economic rights on immigrant integration through naturalisation, I conduct a series of mixed-effects models estimated through ordinary least squares regression.[26] Each model includes a random origin-destination dyad intercept and clusters the robust error term by origin-destination dyad. The results of

---

[25] As the outcome of interest is a count variable, I use the inverse hyperbolic sine transformation. See Bellemare et al. (2013) or Bellemare and Wichman (2020) for applications of this approach.

[26] Online Appendix B.3 contains full regression tables.

Table 5.1 Covariate Predictors of Naturalisation in the EU

Variable	Definition	Source
Immigrant stock[a]	Natural log of the annual foreign-born population	OECD, 2020; World Bank 2020a; Eurostat, 2020
Immigration flow[a]	Natural log of the annual total inflow of immigrants	OECD, 2020; World Bank 2020a; Eurostat, 2020
Unemployment	Annual population share experiencing un-employment in origin and destination, lagged one year	World Bank, 2020a, b
GDP	Natural log of 2011 USD GDP per capita in origin and destination, lagged one year	World Bank, 2020a, 2020b
Origin democratic regime	VDem electoral democracy scale	Coppedge et al., 2020
Colonial relationship	1 if colonial legacy exists, 0 otherwise	Mayer & Zignago, 2011
Common language	1 if a language spoken by at least 9% of both populations, 0 otherwise	Mayer & Zignago, 2011
Citizenship access[b]	MIPEX citizenship strand[b], 0–10	Solano & Huddleston, 2020

[a] Includes cross-validation with World Bank, Eurostat, and national census estimates when possible (see e.g. Alarian & Goodman, 2017; Fitzgerald et al., 2014)
[b] Re-aggregated index excludes conditions for citizenship for immigrant children

these models — found in Fig. 5.3 below — represent the unstandardized beta coefficients with their respective 90% and 95% confidence intervals.[27] Similar to the first analysis, the figures first present the main effects of these policies without any relevant covariates. The subsequent model includes all relevant covariates of interest (see Table 5.1) as well as fixed effects accounting for year and region of origin. These fixed effects therefore subsume any unchanging attributes of the place or time that may be unaccounted for with the included covariates.

First, similar to the individual integration findings, states appear to award citizenship more often when immigrants also possess more freedom to access the labour market. This finding, however, is not robust to the inclusion of origin and destination covariates. Unlike the previous study, however, this study suggests citizenship acquisitions increase alongside socio-economic mobility policies. Moving one point toward policy liberalisation, for example, would predict an approximate 8% increase in citizenship acquisitions from a given origin. Given the disconnect between individual and institutional integration arrangements, this relationship may be attributed directly to state interest. In other words, states may reach out to assist migrant socio-economic mobility when they also have an interest in making these immigrants into citizens.

Potentially most surprising, however, is the negative relationship between welfare access and citizenship. Although this finding again may appear conform to the

---

[27] I remind the reader that the outcome variable is IHS transformed when interpreting coefficients from all models.

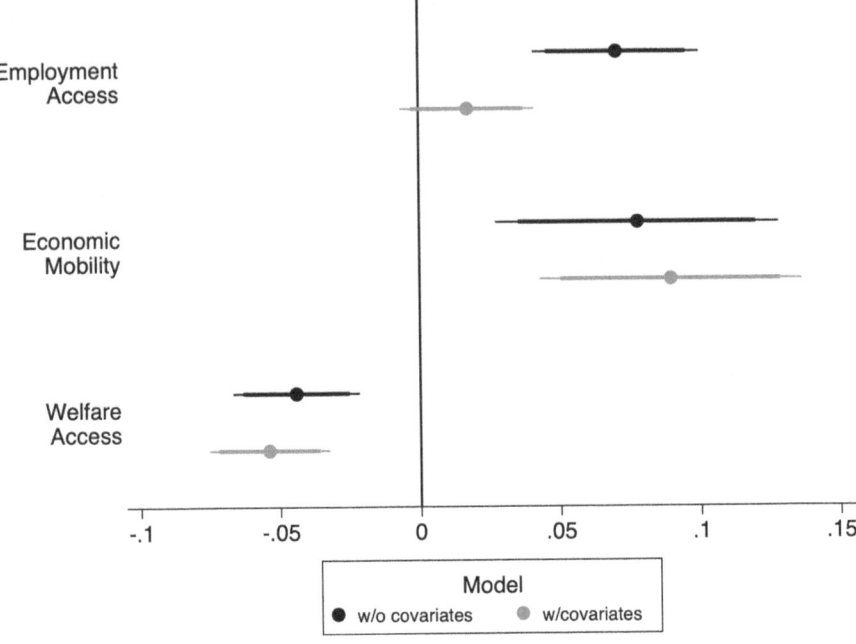

Fig. 5.3 Predicting Citizenship Acquisition by Economic Rights. Unstandardized Beta Coefficients with 90 and 95 per cent confidence intervals

expectations of the 'penalty of welfare', a deeper consideration of the relationship reveals a nuanced relationship between the two. Despite offering welfare access, many of the included states penalise migrants for accessing such welfare or social assistance. Denmark, for example, explicitly prohibits naturalisation for migrants who have accessed social benefits in the past year (Ersbøll, 2013; Stadlmair, 2018). Even Slovenia, who generally does not permit non-EU citizens to access full social assistance, additionally disqualifies any individual from acquiring citizenship if they receive welfare. In total, nearly half of the sample countries restrict immigrants who wish to naturalise from accessing welfare or social assistance. Hence this negative relationship obfuscates a complex story, whereby states may grant rights as a means to exclude — rather than integrate — migrant communities (cf. Huddleston & Vink, 2015). Should this be the case, it may also partially explain the negative relationship between such rights and life satisfaction found above in study one.

To test for this possibility, I code each country over time within the sample as to whether they expressly penalise welfare access within the naturalisation process. In doing so, I rely on primary and secondary sources including official government policies and GlobalCit country reports (see e.g. Ersbøll, 2013). Importantly, I code only those policies with specific welfare penalties as opposed to other existing policy coding of economic resource or employment requirements for naturalisation (cf. Solano & Huddleston, 2020). Once coded, I interact this policy with the measure of

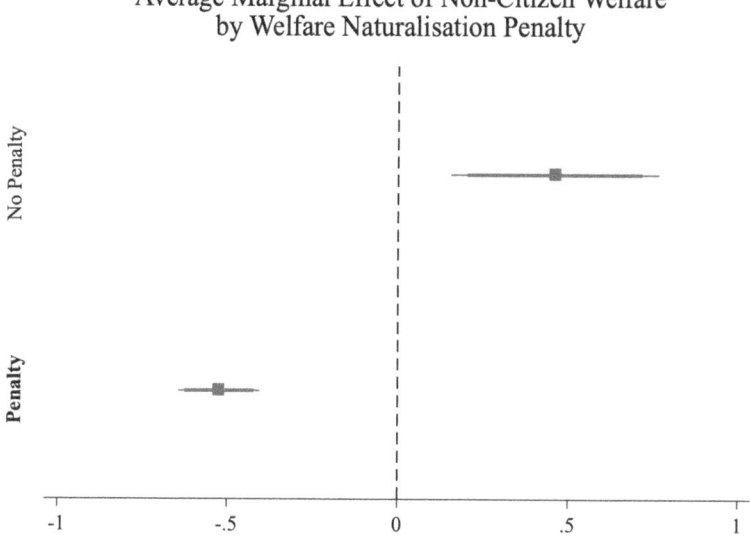

Fig. 5.4 Average Marginal Effects of Non-EU Citizen Welfare Access on Citizenship Acquisitions by Welfare Naturalisation Penalty

welfare access as described above. Fig. 5.4 above represents the average marginal effects of this significant interaction.[28]

The evidence from this analysis is clear. Despite a negative main effect of welfare access, such rights are associated with a decline in citizenship acquisitions only when welfare in penalised within the naturalisation process. Even more, citizenship acquisition significantly increases when such penalties are not codified within state citizenship policy. As such, the degree to which welfare access is truly a policy of inclusion and integration depends not only on its existence but also its omission as a hurdle to permanent membership. Where welfare policy exists with strings attached to permanent membership, the policy serves as a tool of prolonged exclusion. Hence the sum total of results across these two studies suggest that policies of economic inclusion — labour market access and social assistance — can be powerful tools for immigrant integration both above and below citizenship.

5.7   Conclusion

In late 2016, the International Monetary Fund made a stark declaration of the state of EU member states. Europe's economic growth, the IMF concluded, will "depend on the speed of newcomers' integration in the labour market" (Aiyar et al., 2016,

---

[28] See Online Appendix B.3 for OLS results.

pp.12). Can the expansion of non-citizen economic rights rise to the challenge and integrate immigrant communities in Europe? To what degree does such inclusion truly cultivate political and social belonging? The answer, I find, depends on the policy domain of inclusion. Specifically, states providing immigrants with equal access to employment —regardless of their citizenship or long-term residence status—are more likely to yield immigrants with higher regard for and satisfaction with their lives. Despite this measurable increase in the social and psychological lives of immigrants personally, this relationship is noticeably absent institutionally, as citizenship appears unmoved by employment rights. And although exclusion from economic protections vis-à-vis the welfare state heightens rather than deters citizenship acquisition, this relationship appears driven by state citizenship policy.

The conflicting evidence presented here still directly conflicts with the theoretical expectations of 'citizenship light' (Joppke, 2010) and equality trade-offs (Koopmans, 2010), revealing instances in which expansive economic rights can encourage rather than deter immigrant commitments to their countries of residence. This evidence further suggests the observed path dependency of non-citizen inclusion is not confined to political participation alone (see e.g. Coppock & Green, 2016; Ferwerda et al., 2020; Meredith, 2009). In short, destinations which grant immigrants access to the economic community appear to successfully cultivate individual inclusion. Consequently, destinations excluding immigrants from their political and economic communities may be more likely to face the costs associated with heightened return migration and marginalised migrant communities.

These conclusions further compel scholars to grapple with these puzzles of integration, inclusion, and rights below citizenship. These analyses, for one, are unable to address how immigrants without access to rights or citizenship interact with their political and social world. Perhaps these policies coincide with return migration, bleeding into larger rates emigration as migrants opt to exit when denied economic opportunities or political voice. On the other hand, immigrants may seek alternative status – namely permanent residence – when excluded from economic rights. In addition to destination encouragement, migrants themselves may be more inclined to acquire permanent residence in lieu of formal inclusion provided rights are comparable. And as nowhere is permanent residence more present as a secondary level of membership and often requirement prior to obtaining citizenship status than in Europe (Goodman, 2014), future scholarship in the EU would be wise to shift focus toward such experiences of permanent residence.

Moreover, within an era and region often examined from the context of exclusion, I encourage others to continue to advance our understanding of inclusion via public policy. Future research could too expand the boundaries of inclusion to include claims made of one's origin. Doing so would consider both internal and external modes in affecting political, economic, and social behaviour. Such focus will require new methods and approaches to citizenship and immigrant behaviour, pushing scholars of policy, immigration, and behaviour broadly to think creatively and holistically about the theoretical and empirical processes of inclusion and consequently exclusion. The conclusions here, however, are merely the first step in a long journey of unearthing the role of non-citizen rights to immigrant lives. As these integration debates endure, these conclusions implore future policy and scholarship to expand the approach of immigrant inclusion as a path dependent process – one that has the power to perpetuate exclusion or create communities of new citizens.

References

Aiyar, S., Barkbu, B., Batini, N., Berger, H., Detragiache, E., Dizioli, A., Ebeke, C., et al. (2016). *The refugee surge in Europe*. International Monetary Fund.

Alarian, H. M. (2017a). Citizenship in hard times: Intra-EU naturalisation and the euro crisis. *Journal of Ethnic and Migration Studies, 43*(13), 2149–2168.

Alarian, H. M. (2017b). *Migrant employment and the foundations of integration: A multimethod approach*. PhD diss., UC Irvine.

Alarian, H. M., & Goodman, S. W. (2017). Dual citizenship allowance and migration flow: An origin story. *Comparative Political Studies, 50*(1), 133–167.

Bellemare, M. F., & Wichman, C. J. (2020). Elasticities and the inverse hyperbolic sine transformation. *Oxford Bulletin of Economics and Statistics, 82*(1), 50–61.

Bellemare, M. F., Barrett, C. B., & Just, D. R. (2013). The welfare impacts of commodity Price volatility: Evidence from rural Ethiopia. *American Journal of Agricultural Economics, 95*(4), 877–899.

Bevelander, P., & Veenman, J. (2006). Naturalization and employment integration of Turkish and Moroccan immigrants in the Netherlands. *Journal of International Migration and Integration/ Revue de l'integration et de la migration internationale, 7*(3), 327–349.

Bitler, M., & Hoynes, H. W. (2011). *Immigrants, welfare reform, and the US safety net* (Vol. w17667). National Bureau of Economic Research.

Bloemraad, I. (2006). Becoming a citizen in the United States and Canada: Structured mobilization and immigrant political incorporation. *Social Forces, 85*(2), 667–695.

Borjas, G. J. (1994). *Ethnicity, Neighborhoods, and Human Capital Externalities* (Vol. w4912). National Bureau of Economic Research.

Cameron, D. (2011). "Speech at Munich security conference". National Archives. https://www.gov.uk/government/speeches/pms-speech-at-munich-security-conference

Cho, W. K., & Tam. (1999). Naturalization, socialization, participation: Immigrants and (non-) voting. *The Journal of Politics, 61*(4), 1140–1155.

Clark, A., Georgellis, Y., & Sanfey, P. (2001). Scarring: The psychological impact of past unemployment. *Economica, 68*(270), 221–241.

Coppedge, M., Gerring, J., Carl, H. K., Lindberg, S. I., Teorell, J., Altman, D., Bernhard, M., et al. (2020). *V-Dem codebook* (Vol. 10).

Coppock, A., & Green, D. P. (2016). Is voting habit forming? New evidence from experiments and regression discontinuities. *American Journal of Political Science, 60*(4), 1044–1062.

Cort, D. A. (2012). Spurred to action or retreat? the effects of reception contexts on naturalization decisions in los angeles. *International Migration Review, 46*(2), 483–516.

Dancygier, R. M. (2010). *Immigration and conflict in Europe*. Cambridge University Press.

Dancygier, R. M., & Laitin, D. D. (2014). Immigration into Europe: Economic discrimination, violence, and public policy. *Annual Review of Political Science, 17*(2014), 43–64.

Eatwell, R. (2006). Community cohesion and Cumulative extremism in contemporary Britain. *The Political Quarterly, 77*(2), 204–216.

Ersbøll, E. (2013). *Naturalisations procedures for immigrants: Denmark*. GLOBALCIT.

European Social Survey Cumulative File. (2020). ESS 1-9, Data file edition 1.0. In *NSD – Norwegian Centre for Research Data, Norway - data archive and distributor of ESS data for ESS ERIC*. ESS-CUMULATIVE. https://doi.org/10.21338/NSD-

Eurostat. Acquisition of loss and citizenship (migr acqn), Statistical Office of the European Union. 2020. Accessed December 18, 2020.

Falk, A., Kuhn, A., & Zweimüller, J. (2011). Unemployment and right-wing extremist crime. *Scandinavian Journal of Economics, 113*(2), 260–285.

Ferwerda, J., Finseraas, H., & Bergh, J. (2020). Voting RIghts and immigrant incorporation: Evidence from Norway. *British Journal of Political Science, 50*(2), 713–730.

Fitzgerald, J., Leblang, D., & Teets, J. C. (2014). Defying the law of gravity: The political economy of international migration. *World Politics, 66*(3), 406–445.

France to make it easier to become French. (2012). France24. 18 Oct. https://www.france24.com/en/20121018-france-make-it-easier-become-french-citizeship-nationality-valls-foreigners-passport

Goodman, S. W. (2014). *Immigration and membership politics in Western Europe*. Cambridge University Press.

Goodman, S. W. (2015). Conceptualizing and measuring citizenship and integration policy: Past lessons and new approaches. *Comparative Political Studies, 48*(14), 1905–1941.

Gurr, T. R. (1970). *Why men rebel*. Princeton University Press.

Hainmueller, J., Hangartner, D., & Pietrantuono, G. (2015). Naturalization fosters the long-term political integration of immigrants. *Proceedings of the National Academy of Sciences, 112*(41), 12651–12656.

Hammar, T. (1990). *Democracy and the nation state. Aliens, denizens and citizens in a world of international migration*. Avbury.

Harder, N., Figueroa, L., Gillum, R. M., Hangartner, D., Laitin, D. D., & Hainmueller, J. (2018). Multidimensional measure of immigrant integration. *Proceedings of the National Academy of Sciences, 115*(45), 11483–11488.

Hook, V., Jennifer, S. K., & Brown, and Frank D. Bean. (2006). For love or money? Welfare reform and immigrant naturalization. *Social Forces, 85*(2), 643–666.

Huddleston, T., & Vink, M. P. (2015). Full membership or equal rights? The link between naturalisation and integration policies for immigrants in 29 European states. *Comparative Migration Studies, 3*(1), 1–19.

Joppke, Christian. Citizenship and immigration, . 2010.

Just, A. (2017). The far-right, immigrants, and the prospects of democracy satisfaction in Europe. *Party Politics, 23*(5), 507–525.

Könönen, J. (2018). Differential inclusion of non-citizens in a universalistic welfare state. *Citizenship Studies, 22*(1), 53–69.

Koopmans, R. (2010). Trade-offs between equality and difference: Immigrant integration, multiculturalism and the welfare state in cross-National Perspective. *Journal of Ethnic and Migration Studies, 36*(1), 1–26.

Larsen, E. G. (2018). Welfare retrenchments and government support: Evidence from a natural experiment. *European Sociological Review, 34*(1), 40–51.

Lelkes, O. (2006). Tasting freedom: Happiness, religion and economic transition. *Journal of Economic Behavior & Organization, 59*(2), 173–194.

Levin, I. (2013). Political inclusion of Latino immigrants: Becoming a citizen and political participation. *American Politics Research, 41*(4), 535–568.

Marín-Rubio, R., Sobrino, I., Martín-Pérez, A., & Moreno-Fuentes, F. J. (2015). *Country report on citizenship law*. EUDO Citizenship Observatory.

Mayer, Thierry, and Soledad Zignago. "Notes on CEPII's distances measures: The GeoDist database." (2011).

Meredith, M. (2009). Persistence in political participation. *Quarterly Journal of Political Science, 4*(3), 187–209.

Mohanty, R., & Tandon, R. (Eds.). (2006). *Participatory citizenship: Identity*. Exclusion.

OECD. International migration database. 2020. Accessed December 18, 2020. URL: http://stats.oecd.org/Index.aspx?DataSetCode=MIG

Perreira, K. M., & Pedroza, J. M. (2019). Policies of exclusion: Implications for the health of immigrants and their children. *Annual Review of Public Health, 40*, 147–166.

Ruhs, M. (2013). *The Price of rights: Regulating international labor migration*. Princeton University Press.

Schinkel, W. (2018). Against 'immigrant integration': For an end to Neocolonial knowledge production. *Comparative Migration Studies, 6*(1), 1–17.

Sirovátka, T., Guzi, M., & Saxonberg, S. (2019). Satisfaction with democracy and perceived performance of the welfare state in Europe. *Journal of European Social Policy, 29*(2), 241–256.

Sobolewska, M. (2010). Religious extremisim in britain and British muslims. *The New Extremism in 21st Century Britain, 5*, 23.

Solano, G. & Huddleston, T. (2020). Migrant integration policy index. ISBN: 978-84-92511-83-9.

Stadlmair, J. (2018). Earning citizenship. Economic criteria for naturalisation in nine EU countries. *Journal of Contemporary European Studies, 26*(1), 42–63.

Street, A. (2017). The political effects of immigrant naturalization. *International Migration Review, 51*(2), 323–343.

Tankard, M. E., & Paluck, E. L. (2017). The effect of a supreme court decision regarding gay marriage on social norms and personal attitudes. *Psychological Science, 28*(9), 1334–1344.

World Bank. United Nations Population Division. World Population Prospects, http://databank.worldbank.org/data/. 2020a. Accessed December 10, 2020.

World Bank. International Labour Organization, ilostat database, http://databank.worldbank.org/data/. 2020b. Accessed December 10, 2020.

Yang, P. Q. (1994). Explaining immigrant naturalization. *International Migration Review, 28*(3), 449–477.

Ziller, C., & Helbling, M. (2019). Antidiscrimination Laws, policy knowledge and political support. *British Journal of Political Science, 49*(3), 1027–1044.

Chapter 6
Migrants, New Citizens, Co-Citizens and Citizens by Adoption – Regionalist Parties' Framing of Immigrants in the Basque Country, Corsica, South Tyrol, Scotland and Wales

Verena Wisthaler

6.1 Introduction

At different times and in different places, immigration has been perceived and framed as a challenge or a benefit, with migrants being conceptualized as 'social parasites' and 'criminals' threatening the established way of life and stealing the jobs of 'native' citizens, as sources of necessary labour to counterbalance demographic decline in Europe, or as new citizens, contributing to the framing of the receiving territory as open, tolerant and modern. Political elites have reinforced the binary categorizations of insider and outsider, establishing an immigration hierarchy of those who are 'like us', those who are 'wanted' and those who are 'unwanted', based chiefly on the incomers' perceived added value to a territory and its society.

Such underlying discursive frames affect the politics of immigration and have institutional, legal, and policy implications (Korkut et al., 2013), and the construction of immigrant population as 'others' or as 'new citizens' has an impact on, and is reflected in, policies of integration (Schneider & Ingram, 1993; Verkuyten, 1997). These shifting frames also show how boundaries between natives and newcomers evolve, and how citizenship at the substate level, and hence the collective identity of the in-group, is constructed in relation to an out-group. While research on immigrant integration policies and the various actors involved is, by now, an established line of research, we know little about underlying discursive frames, and how they evolve and shift over time. This aspect is the primary focus of the article: How are migrants discursively constructed in minority regions? Are they referred to as 'migrant workers' contributing to the economy, as 'welfare tourists' taking advantage of the welfare system, or as 'new citizens' and hence symbolically belonging to the community?

V. Wisthaler (✉)
Eurac Research, Bozen/Bolzano, Italy
e-mail: Verena.Wisthaler@eurac.edu

© The Author(s) 2023
R. Barbulescu et al. (eds.), *Revising the Integration-Citizenship Nexus in Europe*, IMISCOE Research Series, https://doi.org/10.1007/978-3-031-25726-1_6

This contribution focuses on the discursive construction of migrants at the sub-state level in general, and in minority regions in particular. The rescaling of socio-economic and cultural policies to the subnational level has, combined with decentralization reforms, turned immigrant integration into a competence of subnational authorities. While the nation-state is still an important redistributor of revenue, many local and regional governments are now the key actors responsible for the allocation of public services (such as health care or social assistance). Regional policies affecting, or directly addressing, migrants also shape (through a spill-over effect) their political participation, support for the government and their probability of voting, as well as their likelihood of seeking naturalization (Bennour, 2019; Filandra & Manatschal, 2019).

Substate actors, especially governments, therefore rely on immigrant integration policies in the socioeconomic, cultural and increasingly also the political realm, to turn 'immigrants into regional citizens' (Manatschal et al., 2020). They rely on concrete policies, such as access to the labour market, social benefits, political rights and even enfranchisement to strengthen non-citizens' identification and political engagement with the respective regions. Underlying frames of belonging or not belonging influence those policy choices and motivate regional governments either to turn migrants into regional citizens, or to design policies that do not support the long-term settlement of migrants in that territory. Hence, underlying frames also tell us whether immigration is perceived as supporting or hindering the development of the territory, its society and its identity.

Collective identity is a particularly sensitive issue in regions with a distinct history of statehood and/or a distinct cultural and linguistic identity (known as Rokkan regions, following Hooghe et al., 2016), embedded within multinational states (Gagnon & Tully, 2001). In those territories there is a strong connection between immigration and collective identity (Barker & Zapata-Barrero, 2014), leading to a prevailing engagement of Rokkan regions with sociocultural immigrant integration policymaking, either to protect their distinctive collective identity within the state vis-à-vis migrants, or to further carve out those distinctions through pronounced and divergent regional models of integration, often characterized by assimilationist approaches (Manatschal et al., 2020).

Regional immigrant integration policies are inspired by discursive frames regarding who should become a new citizen of a region, which translates into the question of 'who belongs to us', and under which conditions. Who belongs to the minority region and who is part of the subnational 'we' is thus an important question. By focusing on the underlying frames of constructed regional citizenship, this contribution complements an emerging line of scholarship engaging with the territorial rescaling of citizenship to the 'meso' level, namely to regions, provinces and cantons (Arrighi & Stjepanović, 2019; Hepburn, 2011; Manatschal et al., 2020; Xhardez, 2017). Showing how processes of 'othering' turn immigrants either into 'unwanted others', 'wanted migrants' providing services to the regional community (without becoming an accepted part of it) or into 'integrated citizens' ultimately advances our understanding of immigrant integration policymaking at the substate level.

Finally, processes of 'othering' migrants redefine the boundaries of the sub-state nation.

Relying on a structured comparison of the various Stateless Nationalist and Regionalist Parties (SNRPs) in the Basque Country (Spain), Corsica (France), South Tyrol (Italy), and Scotland and Wales (UK) I show that these parties engage, through processes of 'othering', in the creation of a hierarchy of diversities, differentiating between markers of diversity based on the perceived proximity of immigrants to the collective identity of the in-group, as well as their constructed distance to the identity of the state in which the minority region is situated. Hence, the construction of 'wanted' and 'unwanted' migrants and, in the long run, 'wanted' and 'unwanted' citizens, reflects the perceived potential of newcomers to strengthen the SNRPs' vision of the territory, their nationalist mobilization and their nation-building project, which then becomes the salient criterion for the inclusion or exclusion of migrants into the construction of regional citizenship.

6.2 Actors and Processes of Constructing Regional Citizens through 'Othering'

There is a continuous process of constructing, negotiating and reconstructing the collective identity that defines a territorially bound society at all levels, be it the state, the region or the city. This even occurs at the supranational level, as in the case of the European Union and its struggle for a European identity. These processes involve, first, a 'significant other' from which to differentiate (Triandafyllidou, 1998; Weber, 1976).

While it is widely acknowledged that immigration has an impact on collective identities, there is no evidence on how immigration changes them and in which particular direction (Esses et al., 2006; Hjerm, 1998; Wodak et al., 2009; Wright, 2011). But immigration 'challenges, and in some cases reaffirms, notions of national identity, sovereignty, and state control' (Bloemraad et al., 2008, 154). Minority regions are, independent of immigration, characterized by strong collective identities and nationalist mobilizations leading to conflicts between their substate identity, often referred to as 'national identity', and the state's national identity, resulting in conflicts over sovereignty and state control (Edwards & Wisthaler, 2023). Immigration into those territories is thus an additional challenge because the 'old' diversity of these territories encounters 'new' diversity, and immigrant integration is evaluated against substate nationalism (Banting & Soroka, 2012, 158; Jeram et al., 2015). A set of challenges arises: on the one hand, the territories may aim to maintain and further protect their cultural, linguistic or religious distinctiveness within a larger geographical space, and hence try to forestall further diversity. On the other hand, incorporating newcomers into the substate national community may strengthen the territory's demography by numerically boosting the population, which is coherent with the native 'mentality of "*la survivance*"' (Kymlicka, 2001, 278) .

In those territories there is therefore a strong connection between immigration and collective identity (Barker & Zapata-Barrero, 2014), which is mobilized by political parties in different ways: emphasizing the multicultural identity of the Scottish nation (Hepburn, 2011), constructing diversity as a marker of difference in the Basque Country (Jeram, 2014), aiming for the empowerment of Wales or excluding migration-related diversity from the notion of being South Tyrolean (Wisthaler, 2016). Thus, political actors construct regional identities in such a way to strike a balance between the exclusion and inclusion of others). Building on Weber (1976), and as Zolberg and Long put it, group formation therefore entails confrontation with others, and 'collective identity formation […] usually also involve[s] self-conscious efforts by members of a group to distinguish themselves from whom they are not, and hence it is better understood as a dialectical process whose key feature is the delineation of boundaries between "us" and "not us"' (Zolberg & Long, 1999, 8).

Triandafyllidou picks up this theme and argues that the 'the identity of a nation is defined and/or re-defined through the influence of 'significant others', namely other nations or ethnic groups that are perceived to threaten the nation, its distinctiveness, authenticity and/or independence' (Triandafyllidou, 1998, 594). While for minority regions the 'significant other' has traditionally been the state in which they are embedded, there might also be occasions when there is more than one 'significant other'. Laxer, Carson and Korteweg suggest that minority nations, when confronted with immigration, 'face the challenge of forging an identity defined simultaneously in opposition to two groups: the national majority, in relation to whom they form a minority, and migrants, for whom they constitute the majority receiving society' (Laxer et al., 2014, 133).

This contribution elaborates on the minority regions' relations with their 'significant others', specifically the others stemming from international migration. The boundaries of regional citizenship, or the questions of 'who are we?', becomes a question of 'who are the others?'. This contribution shows that the boundaries of regional citizenship are defined through a process of 'othering' the newcomers. While immigrants are always framed as 'others' political actors create a hierarchy of others: those 'like us' which strengthen the regional citizenry and contribute to the nation-building project, and those 'others' who undermine and eventually dilute the minority regions' collective identity.

This contribution takes an actor-centred approach to constructing regional citizens, since the role of elites in identity construction is particularly relevant (Brady & Cynthia Kaplan, 2009; Wimmer, 2008). It is the political elites 'who draw upon, distort, and sometimes fabricate materials from the cultures of the groups they wish to represent in order to protect their well-being or existence or to gain political and economic advantage for their groups as well as for themselves' (Brass, 1991, 8). There is a particularly strong relationship between SNRPs and identity politics (Massetti, 2009, 26), which is salient for immigration (Barker & Zapata-Barrero, 2014). Immigration brings additional diversity which SNRPs need to reflect and include or exclude from the construction of the national identity; it also challenges the demographic equilibrium between the national majority and the national minority (Conversi, 1997). Regionalist parties do not automatically develop a restrictive and exclusionary position towards immigration, but rather use the issue to strengthen their core interests that focus on the centre–periphery dimension (Jeram, van der Zwet and Wisthaler, 2015). Hence, regionalist parties appropriate the issue and connect their positions on immigration with their identity politics and nation-building aims. As such, political parties inclusive positions towards immigrants are a form of instrumental nationalism (Wisthaler, 2016). Jeram (2012) argues that the Basque Nationalist Party (PNV) presents migration-related diversity as a new marker of the Basque identity as open and tolerant, in contrast with the exclusionary Spanish identity. Similarly, Franco (2015) argues that the Scottish National Party (SNP) and the *Esquerra Republicana de Catalunya* (ERC) develop positions towards immigration that serve to highlight the difference between Scotland and the UK, and between Catalonia and Spain, respectively.

This article contributes to this line of scholarship by showing that migrants are not automatically excluded from SNRPs' constructions of collective identity. Rather, migrants may be used to strengthen the in-group in some cases, becoming 'new citizens', 'co-citizens', or 'citizens by adoption' and thereby furthering the nation-building project.

6.3 SNRPs in the Basque Country, Corsica, South Tyrol, Scotland and Wales

The empirical analysis draws on material from SNRPs in the Basque Country, Corsica, South Tyrol, Scotland and Wales. They were selected to represent a variety of contextual settings, ideological foci, governmental positions of the parties, and different nation-building projects.[1] A most different case study design allows for the exploration of different hypotheses on how regional citizens are constructed, as well as additional explanatory and contextual variables regarding SNRPs' reliance on one or other of the framings (Collier, 2011).

However, the cases also share important characteristics: these regions all accommodate a significant share of international migrants, but also have historical experiences with internal migration. Hence, in all cases, migrants contribute to the 'dilemma' over immigration and identity (Xhardez, 2017). Moreover, all selected SNRPs are engaged in nationalist mobilizations based on the quest for linguistic or cultural recognition of their collective identity, and the search for greater sovereignty in many policy areas including immigration and immigrant integration.

---

[1]Annex 1 provides additional information on the selected cases. It includes an overview of the SNRPs included in this article, their electoral strength over the last 20 years, and their position on the left–right as well as centre–periphery axis. Annex 2 provides an overview of the minority regions themselves, with information about their population size, share of the foreign-born population and its main countries of origin, as well as the main marker of difference between national and subnational collective identities.

Table 6.1 Data

	Nr. of party programmes	Nr. of parliamentary debates analysed	Nr. of other party documents (homepages, press releases etc.)	Total nr. of documents
Basque Country	21	74	0	95
Corsica	12	7	13	34
South Tyrol	19	76	11	106
Scotland	11	21	7	39
Wales	11	115	17	143
TOTAL	74	293	48	415

Focusing on party positions from 1992 to 2016, I rely on official party platforms, statutes and manifestos, as well as thematic documents on migration, immigration and integration together with official party press releases on these issues. These documents represent the finalized outcome of the consensus reached by the SNRPs in the particular policy areas. Additionally, parliamentary debates focusing on the introduction or reform of various immigrant integration policies have been analysed. One of the key functions of regional assemblies is that of 'attributing meaning to the region as a democratic polity' (Piccoli, 2014), and the analysis of parliamentary debates therefore reveals the reasoning behind a certain position, the underlying conflicts or justifications. Data have been retrieved either via the internet or from party and governmental archives, or collected during fieldwork in the minority regions indicated (Table 6.1).

Given the considerable scope of the research in terms of time span, number of minority regions and number of SNRPs (and thus primary documents), qualitative content analysis proves to be the most suitable method (Mayring, 2000). The structured and comparative analysis is facilitated by the computer-aided qualitative data analysis software, Atlas.ti. Relying on this software guarantees consistency in the elaboration of large amounts of text and facilitates a systematic classification process of coding and identifying themes or patterns (Hsieh & Shannon, 2005). The inclusion of a large number of quotes compensates for the subjectivity inherent in qualitative content analysis (Gerring, 2017, 20).

6.4 Regionalist Parties' Framing of Immigrants: From 'Unwanted' Migrants to 'New Citizens', 'Co-Citizens' and 'Citizens by Adoption'

The framing of migrants indicates which features or perceived characteristics are appreciated by SNRPs, and why. SNRPs might attribute certain characteristics to immigrants, portraying them as undermining the development of the territory,

Table 6.2 Frames and themes referring to 'migrants'

		Basque Country	Corsica	South Tyrol	Scotland	Wales
Not belonging	*Unwanted migrants*		Difficult ethnic background; internal migrants	Criminals; welfare tourists; social parasites; difficult ethnic background		
Belonging	*Wanted migrants*	Close to our culture		Close to our culture	High-skilled workers; students; Muslims; refugees	High-skilled workers; students; Muslims; refugees
	Citizens	New neighbours	Corsicans by adoption	Co-citizens; migrants like us	New Scots	New citizens

particularly the SNRPs' territorial projects. In these cases, immigrants are constructed as not belonging to the in-group, or as 'unwanted' migrants. Alternatively, migrants might be constructed as 'temporarily wanted', because they performe certain services and fill vacant positions in the labour market, or as generally 'wanted' because of their contributions to cultural development and their potential to strengthening the regionalist mobilization. These migrants are portrayed as belonging to the in-group. Those migrants portrayed as already belonging to the territory and society are referred to as 'citizens', with additional descriptors emphasizing the temporal aspects ('new citizens'; 'citizens by adoption') or spatial aspects ('new neighbours'; 'co-citizens') of their inclusion. Table 6.2 provides an overview of the frames used in the five minority regions.

SNRPs in South Tyrol, the Basque Country and Corsica use the terms 'migrant' or 'immigrant' (*Einwanderer/inmigrante-migrante/émigrant*) and 'foreigner' (*Ausl änder/extranjero/étrangère*) when discussing immigration flows. SNRPs in those three minority regions do not differentiate between first-generation immigrants and their descendants who were born in those regions. This differentiation is not yet salient in South Tyrol and the Basque Country where international immigration is still a fairly recent phenomenon, with a relative absence of second-generation migrants. However, in Corsica there is a substantial second and third generation. Corsican SNRPs therefore neglect the long history of immigration, as well as French nationality law, by failing to differentiate between persons who physically moved to the island and their locally born descendants. Continuing to use the term 'foreigner' for persons with a migration background underlines the distance between them and the in-group, and highlights their 'not belonging' to the territory.

The parties in South Tyrol predominantly frame immigration negatively, as a threat to the welfare system and the collective identity (Wisthaler, 2015), while SNRPs in the Basque Country, Scotland, and recently also in Wales, frame immigration as an added value to their own nation-building projects (Arrighi, 2019; Jeram, 2012). SNRPs in Corsica, on the other hand, frame internal migration from France and international migration from former French colonies as a threat to the economic and cultural development, or 'survival of the island' (Wisthaler, 2016), while international migration from other destinations is positively framed.

The framing of immigration spills over into to the framing of migrants themselves. A positive framing of immigration translates into the framing of migrants as becoming part of the in-group, and hence part of the regional citizenship. A negative framing of immigration predominantly translates into framing migrants as not belonging to the territory, as 'unwanted' migrants hindering socioeconomic development and diluting the SNRPs' territorial claims, and who are therefore excluded from the in-group.

6.4.1 Migrants – Those Who Do Not Belong to 'Us'

In South Tyrol, SNRPs construct the category of 'unwanted' migrants based on the perceived threats to security and the welfare system, and most importantly, the potential threat to the minority region's identity.

Migrants are referred to as 'social parasites' or 'welfare tourists' by opposition parties *die Freiheitlichen* (dF), *Union für Südtirol* (UfS) and *Bürgerunion* (BU), who predominantly frame immigration a threat to the welfare system (Wisthaler, 2015). dF has been proclaiming a connection between crime, security and migrants, irrespective of their legal status, since the beginning of the 1990s. They introduced this framing into the debates of the regional parliament in 1994 and have continued to do so until today. The framing of migrants as exploiters of the welfare system very much resembles the populist right-wing tradition of the Austrian Freedom party, which has always had a strong connection to the South Tyrolean dF. In contrast, the framing of migrants as criminals resembles the discourse of Italian right-wing parties, in particular the *Lega Nord* (Colombo, 2013).

Nevertheless, the most important frame determining migrants' belonging in South Tyrol is the ascribed capacity to integrate, to 'become like us' (Wisthaler, 2015). Migrants who are 'wanted' by South Tyrolean SNRPs are those who are perceived as more capable of assimilating into the German culture and language due to their linguistic, religious or cultural proximity, thereby strengthening (numerically) the German community within the minority region vis-à-vis the Italian-speaking population, but most importantly, vis-à-vis the Italian state.

While migrants with a European background are more 'wanted' than those from Third Countries, there are also differences within the European group. German-speaking neighbouring countries and those of the former Habsburg Empire are preferred.

> Experience has shown that there are differences between migrants from different countries in their ability and willingness to integrate. With European migrants there are less problems than with Arabic, African, or Asian migrants. This is due to the fact that persons with a

European cultural background are closer to our culture than others [*Südtiroler Volkspartei* (SVP) Grundsatzpapier , 2003]

We need to make sure that predominantly persons from other EU countries come, who are closer to our culture, language, and lifestyle [SVP Election Manifesto, 2008]

Preference [is] for workers from North and East Tyrol, and the rest of Austria, Germany, and other countries, whose populations we do not have integration problems with [*Südtiroler Freiheit* (SF) Election Manifesto, 2013]

Migrants from cultures considered to be closer to the Latin language and culture and thus to Italians, such as Romanians, Bulgarians and Albanians, as well as Roma and Sinti, are constructed as 'unwanted' migrants.

I talk about Romanians and Bulgarians. Although they are from EU countries, it is as if they were from non-EU countries and thus more difficult to integrate than those that are closer to us [Debate in the South Tyrolean Parliament, 06.12.2011, Pius Leitner, dF]

Muslims are considered to be distant from the Catholic culture and are therefore seen as 'difficult to integrate'.

We have a limited capacity for integration. This also requires the willingness to integrate from those that come to us. And this willingness is not there among many Muslims [Debate in the South Tyrolean Parliament, 01.12.1999, Pius Leitner, dF]

The construction of migrants' 'otherness' within South Tyrolean society resembles the discourse at the national level. As Clough Marinaro and Walston point out, the 'othering' of migrants 'serves to perpetuate the myth of a clear split between a unified national culture and identity, and 'them', the foreigners' (Clough & Walston, 2010, 6). In South Tyrol, this split is between the German minority population and the Italian state population. Migrants closer to the Italian language and culture hence further underline that division, and undermine the nationalist mobilization of German SNRPs.

In Corsica, cultural proximity to the French language and culture, and relationship to the nationalist mobilization, are decisive factors for the framing of migrants. However, in Corsica, internal migrants from mainland France are the 'unwanted' ones. Since the early 1990s, Corsican SNRPs have directly engaged with anti-internal-immigrant discourse. The nationalist camp, consisting of SNRPs and the militant *Front de libération nationale corse* (National Liberation Front of Corsica, FLNC), coined the term *I Francesi Fora*, demanding the exit of those French citizens who had migrated to Corsica from mainland France, and whose citizenship gave them political rights and the right to access jobs in public administration. Internal migrants are accused of depriving 'real Corsicans' of their island.

Each year, 4,000 newcomers come [from France] and flood the property market and labour market. They register in large numbers in the electoral lists and thus gradually deprive the Corsicans of the ability to control their own future [*Corsica Naziune Indipendente* (CNI) Party Conference, 2008]

For a short while, the slogan was adapted to migrants from the Maghreb (*Arabi Fora*), emphasizing their proximity to the French state and to the history of colonialism (Terrazzoni, 2010, 155).

Internal migrants have also been an issue in the Basque Country (Conversi, 1997, 187–221), in South Tyrol (Lantschner, 2008) in the 1950s and 1960s, and in both Scotland and Wales, where previous internal immigration from England and Ireland significantly changed the population and caused substantial internal tensions (Hussain & Miller, 2006). But in contrast to Corsican SNRPs, internal migrants are no longer constructed as the 'significant other' by Basque, Scottish, Welsh or South Tyrolean SNRPs. Instead, the construction of the 'significant other' has shifted from the population to the state and national government. Thus, the 'significant other' is the government and its alleged failure to respond to the minority regions' particularities (Wisthaler, 2016).

6.4.2 Citizens: Migrants Who Belong to 'Us'

In contrast to SNRPs in South Tyrol and Corsica, regionalist parties in the Basque Country, Wales and Scotland do not particularly engage with specific national, ethnic or religious groups, nor do they refer to a 'cultural proximity' between the newcomers and the receiving society. Hence, migrants are overarchingly framed as 'wanted' due to their contributions to the economy. They are seen as an added value to the development of the society and territory in general, and a support for the regionalist quest for territorial empowerment in particular. References to regional citizenship are salient in this regard, and become a powerful tool to promote nation building and separation from the central state (Xhardez, 2017).

In South Tyrol, seasonal workers in the tourism and agricultural sectors, and women who take care of the elderly, are perceived as a particular asset to the local labour market and were the first to be called 'co-citizens'.

> The idea that in our country there are more than 2,000 foreign co-citizens that take care of our elderly, and that we need them, should be recognized more in any heated debate and should remind us of human basic values [SVP, Election Manifesto, 2008]

The term 'co-citizens' was introduced in South Tyrol by the SVP in their 2008 election manifesto and gained prominence in the official discourse after 2013, when the new president, Arno Kompatscher, used it in a programmatic way while opening the legislative term.

> Now it's time to create the basis for the best possible integration of the new co-citizens [Debate at the South Tyrolean Parliament, 09.01.2014, Opening speech of the legislative term, Arno Kompatscher, SVP, President]

Although referring to migrants as 'co-citizens' shows a willingness to accept them as part of the 'collective we', the parties continue to highlight the necessity of integration policies, giving migrants a 'duty to integrate', focusing on language learning and access to the labour market. Failure to learn one of the official languages (German or Italian) results in limited access to welfare services (Alber & Wisthaler, 2020, 241). In other words, SNRPs in South Tyrol do not frame migrants a priori as 'co-citizens' but establish economic and linguistic conditions for becoming part of the regional citizenry (Medda-Windischer & Kössler, 2016). So rather than engaging in nation building through the construction of a regional citizenship that is open to migrants, they strengthen the collective identity of the territory by excluding 'unwanted' migrants or by pushing them to assimilate into the prevailing identity of the German minority.

In contrast, SNRPs in Corsica, the Basque Country, Scotland and Wales rely on framings of citizenship that include migrants in order to emphasize their forward-looking and modern conceptions of the minority nation. Corsican SNRPs introduced the possibility of migrants becoming 'citizens by adoption' (*Femu a Corsica* (FeC) Election Manifesto, 2010) through birth, ancestry or residence.

> The existence of the Corsican people as a historical and cultural community includes the Corsicans by origin and Corsicans by adoption [FeC Election Manifesto, 2010]

The discursive construction of 'Corsicans by adoption' opened a pathway for inclusion into the 'collective we', conditional on migrants' willingness to learn the Corsican language and support regionalist parties' claims, as well as long-term residence on the island.

At the beginning of the 1990s, Corsican SNRPs developed the concept of a 'community of destiny' with the aim of integrating those who live on the island and who share the wish to 'maintain the cultural and linguistic heritage of the historical Corsican people' (U Ribombu, 1998–2004). This construction of a larger community of Corsicans serves to strengthen the position of Corsica vis-à-vis the French state, and hence the quest for independence. An important element of the community of destiny is the Corsican language, which is declared to be the most visible element of Corsica's cultural identity. SNRPs portray the Corsican language as accessible to everyone who wants to learn it, and as a tool for strengthening social cohesion and integration. Hence, through language learning and support for the 'Corsican issue', migrants can gain access to the community of destiny:

> The Corsican language, as one of the most visible elements of the Corsican cultural identity, is a medium of communication and existence and also a factor strengthening social cohesion. Knowledge of the Corsican language is necessary for the integration of everybody who lives on the island (...) independent of his/her origins [Report to the Corsican Parliament, 10.05.2013, Proposal for a co-official status of the Corsican Language]

Since the beginning of the 2000s, the community of destiny has been complemented by proposals for a conceptual Corsican citizenship. In contrast with the community of destiny, where ancestry and birth are emphasized, the most important element of the Corsican citizenship is permanent residence on the island for a certain period of time.

> A Corsican citizenship, based on 10 years of residence, as a prerequisite to be able to purchase property [*U Ribombu*, 2010–2014]

While the community of destiny was constructed as a symbolic membership, Corsican citizenship is connected to voting rights (FeC Election Manifesto, 2010), the right to employment in public administration (U Ribombu, 1998–2004) and the right to acquire land and real estate (U Ribombu, 2010–2014). The development from the community of destiny to Corsican citizenship shows the shift from an exclusive framing of immigration towards accepting migrants as part of the in-group:

> This community of destiny, a central concept of Corsican nationalism, is composed of Corsicans by origin and Corsicans by adoption, who have intermingled with our people for centuries [Conf CNI 2008; U Ribombu, 1998–2004]

FeC has been the main driver behind the Corsican citizenship, going beyond the community of destiny by making it available to both internal and international migrants.

> To everyone, French, foreign, from the EU or not, who permanently resides on our island for a significant amount of time (as is already applied in many European regions) [FeC Election Manifesto, 2010]

Basque SNRPs also propose the establishment of a 'Basque citizenship', focusing on the local level. Framing migrants as 'new neighbours' underlines the Basque approach to immigrant integration at the local city level. Consequently, proposals for Basque citizenship rely solely on residence as the criterion for inclusion; residence is currently open to both legal and undocumented migrants who register in a municipality, and allows them access to welfare services (Ruiz-Vieytez & J., 2016).

> The requirement for access to the new citizenship is residence. The new concept of citizenship must be separated from nationality in the classical sense as well as from any other element related to identity. It must be based solely on residence [Plan Vasco de Inmigración, 2003-2005; II Plan Vasco de Inmigración , 2007-2009]

In contrast with Corsican citizenship and the South Tyrolean 'duty to integrate', the concept of Basque citizenship as promoted by all SNRPs does not focus on language as a marker of the in-group's identity. Rather, it constructs Basqueness as an open, tolerant and fluid concept, based on diverse cultures and identities. As Jeram shows, 'diversity' is constructed as a new marker of the Basque collective identity (Jeram, 2012).

> An inclusive concept of citizenship which allows the full participation of immigrants in the political community but which simultaneously allows them to maintain their identities [*Eusko Alkartasuna* (EA) Election Manifesto, 2009]

> PNV has always been conscious of the plural character of the Basque society. [...] The open, tolerant, and integrative nationalism which characterizes PNV aims for the future to support an economic, social, and cultural project for all citizens, whether they have nationalist sentiments or not, because this project does not have the slightest exclusive dimension [PNV Election Manifesto, 1998]

We find a similarly inclusive framing of the in-group in Scotland. The Labour/ Liberal Democrat coalition government officially introduced the term 'New Scots' in 2003 in the title of their strategy to attract highly skilled workers (New Scots: Attracting Fresh Talent to Meet the Challenge of Growth, 2003). The notion of 'New Scots' was also adopted by the SNP in its 2005 general election manifesto, announcing that the party aimed to 'pursue an immigration policy that welcomes new Scots' (SNP Election Manifesto, 2005a, b).

In the Scottish discourse, which is characterized by the wish to expand immigration flows and attract more newcomers, the most 'wanted' and appreciated migrants are overseas students who have studied in Scotland and are willing to remain in the minority nation after the completion of their degrees. They are the main target group of the 'New Scots: Attracting Fresh Talent to Meet the Challenge of Growth' (2003) campaign, which later expanded to workers (especially highly skilled workers) who were needed in certain sectors of the labour market. The term 'New Scots' is applied to students and highly skilled workers even before they enter Scotland, and thus does not refer to integration requirements but rather proposes a very immediate and inclusive notion of Scottishness.[2]

> We will introduce measures to encourage doctors who come from other countries to study here, to stay on and work in the Scottish NHS [National Health Service] when they graduate [SNP Election Manifesto, 2005a, b]

Since 2014, the notion of 'New Scots' has been expanded to refugees and asylum seekers through the 'New Scots: Integrating Refugees into Scotland's Community Strategy' (2014).[3]

> But in reaching out to new migrants, we should not forget those who are already here. There are many asylum seekers in Scotland who could make an enormous and long term contribution to Scottish society if only they were given the chance. The way in which some asylum seekers are treated by the UK immigration authorities is not only, on occasion, morally wrong. It also deprives Scotland of much needed talent and risks sending the wrong message about our country to the very people we are encouraging to come here to live and work [SNP Press Release, 26.11.2005a, b]

> Who shall be citizens? – All people resident in Scotland and all those who were born in Scotland [MacCormick, SNP, 1999]

A similar discourse emerged in Wales, where Plaid Cymru (PC) started framing migrants as 'new citizens' in 2007, highlighting their added value and potential for strengthening the party's quest for nationalist mobilization.

> Plaid Cymru believes we should celebrate and support the cultural riches of the diverse and vibrant communities that make up modern Wales, and welcome the input of new citizens, without in any way forgetting what makes us a unique nation [PC Election Manifesto, 2007]

Since 2016, the Welsh Government, supported by PC, has focused on a strategy to expand this approach to include asylum seekers. This resulted in Wales labelling itself 'the first nation of sanctuary' in 2019, with an action plan to support refugees and asylum seekers in their long-term settlement in Wales, including access to health care, education, employment, and English and Welsh language learning (Welsh Government, Nation of Sanctuary – Refugee and Asylum Seeker Plan, January 2019). As Edwards and Wisthaler (2023) argue, the Welsh Government attempts first to 'develop a specific Welsh approach to sanctuary that sets it apart

---

[2] Catalan SNRP *Convergència i Unió* employs a similar discourse, calling migrants 'new Catalans' (*Nous Catalans*), and has established the 'Foundation of New Catalans' (*Fundació Nous Catalans*) to support integration (Franco, 2015, 85).

[3] It has since been updated to 'New Scots: refugee integration strategy 2018 to 2022'.

from the UK Government', and second, to foster its construction of a regional citizenry through immigrant integration policies.

While Muslims are classed as 'unwanted' migrants in South Tyrol, they are 'wanted' in Scotland and Wales. The Welsh and Scottish governments, and in particular the SNP, present Muslims as a vital part of the Welsh/Scottish community whose particularities need to be protected and promoted:

> Rhodri, and other Ministers, have done their best to ensure that we consider the Muslim communities as a part of the Welsh community [Debate in the Welsh National Assembly, 06.11.2001, Paul Murphy, *Labour Party*, Secretary of the State]

> There is no doubt the Scottish Muslim community sits at the heart and in the mainstream of modern Scotland (…) Next year I hope to be Scotland's First Minister and I want to make clear that I will work to ensure that nothing threatens the place of Scottish Muslims, or any ethnic community, at the heart of our society [SNP Press Release, 20.08.2006, Alex Salmond;]

The added value of Muslims is not only celebrated in discourse, but is also embraced in practice. Candidates with a Muslim background regularly appear on the SNP's election lists, and there have been two SNP members with a Muslim background sitting in the Scottish Parliament: Bashir Ahmad (2007–2009) and Humza Yousaf (2011–ongoing), and one in the House of Commons: Tasmina Ahmed-Sheikh (2015–2017). Furthermore, the pro-independence 'Scots Asians for Independence' group, launched by Ahmad at the party's general conference in 1995, became an important part of the SNP. In Wales, PC includes black and ethnic minority candidates in its election lists and has supporter groups called 'Muslims for Plaid' and 'English for Plaid', the latter counterbalancing, to some extent, the accusations of Plaid having anti-English sentiments.

In both Wales and Scotland, residence or birth are the only criteria for being a regional citizen:

> Who shall be citizens? – All people resident in Scotland and all those who were born in Scotland [MacCormick, SNP, 1999]

In addition, PC regards the Welsh language as inherent to the Welsh nation and their uniqueness, and calls upon migrants to learn the minority language to further strengthen their ties with the territory.

> Wales has a language of its own, that we are rightly proud of. The Welsh Language is spoken throughout Wales, and you will find television and radio programmes, publications and signs in both Welsh and English. We would certainly encourage you to learn Welsh, as well as English [Government of Wales – Understanding Wales 2012]

6.5   Conclusion

The empirical analysis shows that migration contributes to and challenges collective identity-building in minority regions, but does not supersede or replace the traditional 'significant other' against whom the collective identity is constructed. Instead, migration complements and strengthens pre-existing cleavages and boundaries between groups (Wisthaler, 2015). In the case of South Tyrol, the Italian state together with its language and culture is still perceived as the main threat to the German and Ladin minorities, while migration is considered to be an additional 'other' threat (Carlà, 2018). In Corsica, the Basque Country, Wales and Scotland the collective identity is constructed as inclusive and open to new forms of belonging, whereas the French, Spanish and British states are still constructed as the main pole against which to differentiate. 'Othering' becomes a strategy of SNRPs to strengthen their quests for territorial empowerment.

This strategy of 'othering' extends to SNRPs' construction of migrants as either strengthening or weakening the in-group, with several important implications. First, these discursive constructions impact immigration and integration policymaking, influencing the material rights and benefits available to migrants and persons with a migration background. Second, the framing of immigration, and thus immigrants, also contributes to SNRPs' nation-building projects by (1) reinforcing the sociocultural uniqueness of the minority community, (2) asserting their autonomy through divergent policymaking and (3) establishing a national identity and notion of citizenship in contradistinction to the state majority.

For example, regionalist political parties in South Tyrol employ negative discursive frames, referring to migrants as 'parasites' and 'welfare tourists', contributing to the notion of the minority nation as exclusive, with strict limits on membership. This results in a hierarchy of migrants largely based on their country of origin and perceived linguistic, cultural and religious proximity to the South Tyrolean German minority, or distance from the majority Italian culture. It is also paired with expectations of assimilation into the host community, reaffirming their cultural distinctiveness.

Some SNRPs take a more civic approach to inclusion, with residence serving as the main criterion for membership of the in-group, without reference to any social or cultural markers. This positive framing contributes to the nation-building project by (numerically) boosting the minority population and its relative political and economic power, or by attracting specific 'wanted' migrants based on what they can contribute to society in terms of filling gaps in the labour market and bringing skills into the region. In addition to the intrinsic value of this approach, it also raises the region's influence vis-à-vis the state. It can also have a more symbolic value: Developing immigration and integration policies that contrast with those at the national level assert the region's right to self-determination.

Scholars show that inclusive regional integration policies, especially language policies and access to social benefits, have a positive impact on immigrant's intentions to naturalize in Switzerland (Bennour, 2019), and positively affect their political engagement and sense of belonging in the US (Filandra & Manatschal, 2019). We can therefore expect that a sense of belonging to the minority regions will increase migrants' support for SNRPs and their quests for territorial empowerment. Consequently, some SNRPs are actively engaged in supporting citizens-to-be in their long-term settlement by facilitating their access to the welfare system and the labour market. This positive discursive construction of immigration and immigrants therefore, once again, supports SNRPs by fostering a sense of belonging among New Scots, new citizens of Wales, adopted Corsicans and new Basque neighbours, whereas migrants constructed as 'unwanted', 'difficult to integrate' and 'distant to our culture' are unlikely to contribute to the nation-building project, as in South Tyrol.

Characteristics of SNRPs, such as party politics and party ideology, can account for their behaviour, but there is also evidence supporting a cleavage hypothesis, where it is the distance (spatial or ideological) between the state and the sub-nation that carries explanatory power. In this hypothesis, conflicting and fragile societal relations exert an influence on SNRPs' positions on immigration and integration, as well as on their framing of the minority nation's identity. This may account for SNRPs assimilating migration-generated diversity into their own particular framing of the collective identity, and instrumentalizing their framing of migration to support their claims for autonomy and distinctiveness within the state.

References

Primary Documents

Debate in the South Tyrolean Parliament, 06.12.2011,
Debate in the South Tyrolean Parliament, 01.12.1999,
Debate in the Welsh National Assembly, 06.11.2001,
Euska Alkarasuna. (2009). Por Euskal Herria y el estate de bienestar. *Programa Electoral, 2009.*
Femu a Corsica FeC, Un souffle démocratique, 2010.
New Scots: Attracting fresh talent to meet the challenge of growth, 2003.
PC. (2007). *Make a difference.* National Assembly Election Manifesto.
PNV, Programa Electora de EAJ-PNV, Elecciones al Parlamento Vasco, 25.10.1998.
Plan Vasco de Inmigratción, 2007–2009.
Plan Vasco de Inmigración 2003–2005.
Report to the Corsican Parliament, 10.05.2013, Proposal for a co-official status of the Corsican Language.
SNP, Our Independence Manifesto, 2005a.
SNP Press Release, 26.11.2005b.
SNP Press Release, 20.08.2006, Alex Salmond.
SNP, Election Manifesto, 1999.
Südtiroler Freiheit, Wahlprogramm 2013.
SVP, Mit Euch für Südtirol, Wahlprogramm 2008–2012.
SVP, Grundsatzpapier 2003. (Statute 2003).
U ribombo 2010–2014.pdf.
U ribombo_1998–2004.pdf.
Welsh Government, Nation of sanctuary – Refugee and asylum seeker plan, 2019.
Alber, E., & Wisthaler, V. (2020). Immigrations- und Integrationspolitik in Südtirol: Eine kontextualisierte Analyse rechtlicher Handlungsspielräume, politischer Diskurse und kommunaler Praktiken. In P. Bußjäger & C. Gsodam (Eds.), *Migration und Europäische Union: Multi-Level-Governance als Lösungsansatz* (Vol. 2020, pp. 225–258). Institut für Föderalismus, Wien, New Academic Press.
Arrighi, J. T. (2019). 'The people, year zero': Secessionism and citizenship in Scotland and Catalonia. *Ethnopolitics, 18*(3), 278–297. https://doi.org/10.1080/17449057.2019.1585091

Arrighi, J. T., & Stjepanović, D. (2019). Introduction: The rescaling of territory and citizenship in Europe. *Ethnopolitics, 18*(3), 219–226. https://doi.org/10.1080/17449057.2019.1585087

Banting, K., & Soroka, S. (2012). Minority nationalism and immigrant integration in Canada. *Nations and Nationalism, 18*(1), 156–176. https://doi.org/10.1111/j.1469-8129.2011.00535.x

Barker, F., & Zapata-Barrero, R. (2014). Multilevel governance of immigration in multinational states: 'Who governs?' Reconsidered. In E. Hepburn & R. Zapata-Barrero (Eds.), *The politics of immigration in multi-level states* (pp. 19–40).

Bennour, S. (2019). Intention to become a citizen: Do subnational integration policies have an influence? Empirical evidence from Swiss cantons. *Regional Studies, 54*(11), 1535–1545. https://doi.org/10.1080/00343404.2019.1699237

Bloemraad, I., Korteweg, A., & Yurdakul, G. (2008). Citizenship and immigration: Multiculturalism, assimilation, and challenges to the nation-state. *Annual Review of Sociology, 34*(1), 153–179. https://doi.org/10.1146/annurev.soc.34.040507.134608

Brady, E. H., & Cynthia Kaplan, S. (2009). Measuring identity. A guide for social scientists. In R. Abdelal (Ed.), *33–71*. Cambridge University Press.

Brass, P. R. (1991). *Ethnicity and nationalism: Theory and comparison*. Sage.

Carlà, A. (2018). Land of welcome, land of fear: Explaining approaches to 'new' diversity in Catalonia and South Tyrol. *Journal of Ethnic and Migration Studies, 44*(7), 1098–1116. https://doi.org/10.1080/1369183X.2017.1352465

Clough, M. I., & Walston, J. (2010). Italy's 'second generations': The sons and daughters of migrants. *Bulletin of Italian Politics, 2*(1), 5–19.

Collier, D. (2011). Understanding process tracing. *Political Science & Politics, 44*(04), 823–830. https://doi.org/10.1017/S1049096511001429

Colombo, M. (2013). Discourse and politics of migration in Italy: The production and reproduction of ethnic dominance and exclusion. *Journal of Language and Politics, 12*(2), 157–179. https://doi.org/10.1075/jlp.12.2.01col

Conversi, D. (1997). *The Basques, the Catalans, and Spain: Alternative routes to nationalist mobilisation*. Hurst.

Edwards, C. W., & Wisthaler, V. (2023). The power of symbolic sanctuary: Insights from Wales on the limitations and the potential of a regional approach to sanctuary. *Journal of Ethnic and Migration Studies*.

Esses, V. M., Wagner, U., Wolf, C., Preiser, M., & Wilbur, C. J. (2006). Perceptions of national identity and attitudes toward immigrants and immigration in Canada and Germany. *International Journal of Intercultural Relations, 30*(6), 653–669. https://doi.org/10.1016/j.ijintrel.2006.07.002

Filandra, A., & Manatschal, A. (2019). Coping with a changing integration policy context: American state policies and their effects on immigrant political engagement. *Regional Studies, 54*(11), 1546–1557. https://doi.org/10.1080/00343404.2019.1610167

Franco, G. N. (2015). Quin poble? Immigració i procés sobiranista a Catalunya. *Eines per a l'esquerra nacional*, 80–89.

Gerring, J. (2017). Qualitative methods. *Annual Review of Political Science, 20*(1), 15–36.

Hepburn, E. (2011). 'Citizens of the region': Party conceptions of regional citizenship and immigrant integration. *European Journal of Political Research, 50*, 504–529.

Hooghe, L., Marks, G., Schakel, A. H., Osterkatz, C., Sandra, N. S., & Shair-Rosenfield, S. (2016). Measuring regional authority. *A Postfunctionalist Theory of Governance, I*.

Hjerm, M. (1998). National identities, national pride and xenophobia: A comparision of four western countries. *Acta Sociologica*, 335–347.

Hussain, A. M., & Miller, W. L. (2006). *Multicultural nationalism: Islamophobia, Anglophobia, and devolution*. Oxford Universtiy Press.

Hsieh, H.-F., & Shannon, S. E. (2005). Three approaches to qualitative content analysis. *Qualitative Health Research, 15*(9), 1277–1288. https://doi.org/10.1177/1049732305276687

Jeram, S. (2014). Sub-state nationalism and immigration in Spain: Diversity and identity in Catalonia and the Basque Country. *Ethnopolitics, 13*(3), 225–244. https://doi.org/10.108 0/17449057.2013.853998

Jeram, S. (2012). Immigrants and the Basque nation: Diversity as a new marker of identity. *Ethnic and Racial Studies*, 1–19. https://doi.org/10.1080/01419870.2012.664281

Jeram, S., van de Zwet, A., & Wisthaler, V. (2015). Friends or foes? Migrants and sub-state nationalists. *Europe Journal of Ethnic and Migration Studies, 42*(8), 1229–1241. https://doi.org/1 0.1080/1369183X.2015.1082286

Korkut, U., Bucken-Knapp, G., & McGarry, A. (2013). Immigration and integration policies: Assumptions and explanations. In U. Korkut, G. Bucken-Knapp, A. McGarry, J. Hinnfors, & H. Drake (Eds.), *The discourse and politics of migration in Europe* (pp. 1–16). New York Palgrave MacMillan.

Kymlicka, W. (2001). *Politics in the vernacular: Nationalism, multiculturalism and citizenship.* Oxford University Press.

Lantschner, E. (2008). History of the South Tyrol conflict and its settlement. In J. Woelk, F. Palermo, & J. Marko (Eds.), *Tolerance through law. Self governance and group rights in South Tyrol* (pp. 3–15). Martinus Nijhoff.

Laxer, E., Carson, R. D., & Korteweg, A. C. (2014). Articulating minority nationhood: Cultural and political dimensions in Québec's reasonable accommodation debate. *Nations and Nationalism, 20*(1), 133–153. https://doi.org/10.1111/nana.12046

Manatschal, A., Wisthaler, V., & Zuber, C. I. (2020). Making regional citizens? Divers and effects of subnational immigrant integration policies. *Regional Studies, 54*(11), 1475–1485.

Massetti, E. (2009). Explaining regionalist party positioning in a multi-dimensional ideological space: A framework for analysis. *Regional & Federal Studies, 19*(4), 501–531.

Mayring, P. (2000). Qualitative Inhaltsanalyse. Forum Qualitative Sozialforschung. *Social Research, 1*(2).

Medda-Windischer, R., & Kössler, K. (2016). Introduction. Regional citizenship: A tool for inclusion of new minorities in subnational entities? *European Yearbook of Minority Issues, 13*(1), 61–78.

Piccoli, L. (2014). Regional Spheres of Citizenship. The Role of Sub-State Regional Polities in a Multi-Level Citizenship Theory. Vilnius. https://ecpr.eu/Filestore/ PaperProposal/516c9c71-2029-47b6-ac7d-00ac65cea83f.pdf

Ruiz-Vieytez, E., & J. (2016). Regional citizenship and the evolution of Basque immigration and integration policies. *European Yearbook of Minority Issues, 13*(1), 79–100. https://doi. org/10.1163/22116117_01301005

Schneider, A., & Ingram, H. (1993). The social construction of target populations. *American Political Science Review, 87.* https://doi.org/10.2307/2939044

Terrazzoni, L. (2010). *Étrangers, Maghrébins et Corses : Vers Une ethnicisation des rapports sociaux ? La construction sociale, historique et politique des relations interethniques en Corse.* PhD. Université Paris Ouest Nanterre La Défense.

Triandafyllidou, A. (1998). National identity and the 'other'. *Ethnic and Racial Studies, 21*(4), 593–612. https://doi.org/10.1080/014198798329784

Verkuyten, M. (1997). Discourses of ethnic minority identity. *British Journal of Social Psychology, 36*(4), 565–586. https://doi.org/10.1111/j.2044-8309.1997.tb01150.x

Weber, M. (1976). *Wirtschaft und Gesellschaft.* Mohr.

Wimmer, A. (2008). The making and unmaking of ethnic boundaries. A multi-level process theory. *American Journal of Sociology, 113*(4), 970–1022.

Wisthaler, V. (2015). 'Thinking in groups' as a frame for immigrant integration? *Journal of Ethnic and Migration Studies Forthcoming.*

Wisthaler, V. (2016). Immigration and collective identity in minority nations: A longitudinal comparison of stateless nationalist and regionalist parties in the Basque Country. Corsica, South Tyrol. Scotland and Wales.

Wodak, R., de Cillia, R., Reisigl, M., & Liebhart, K. (Eds.). (2009). *The discursive construction of National Identity* (2nd ed.). Edinburgh University Press.

Wright, M. (2011). Diversity and the imagined community: Immigrant diversity and conceptions of National Identity. *Political Psychology, 32*(5), 837–862. https://doi.org/10.1111/j.1467-9221.2011.00843.x

Xhardez, C. (2017). *Why integrate? Sub-state nationalism and immigrant integration in Flanders and Quebec*. PhD Doctoral, Sciences Po Paris and Université Saint-Louis.

Zolberg, A. R., & Long, L. W. (1999). Why Islam is like Spanish: Cultural incorporation in Europe and the United States. *Politics and Society, 27*(1), 5–38.

Chapter 7
Intercultural Citizenship in the Making: Public Space and Belonging in Discriminatory Environments

Ricard Zapata-Barrero and Zenia Hellgren

7.1 Introduction: The Debate on the Conditions of Interculturalism

Public space is essential to foster a sense of belonging among immigrants and racialized groups. This is especially true for groups who are still framed as different in relation to an abstract but taken-for-granted notion of we-ness that remains strongly connected to colonial thinking (Mayblin & Turner, 2021), according to which people perceived as white and western represent the norm in European societies. In this chapter we assume that there is an interrelation between the concepts of discrimination and interculturalism that is essential for the life conditions of immigrants and racialized groups. On the one hand, ethnic discrimination constitutes an impediment for the fulfilment of interculturalist policy goals, while on the other hand, interculturalism, understood as a strategy promoting contact among people from different backgrounds, including nationals, may potentially constitute a fruitful political and discursive tool to combat discrimination (Hellgren & Zapata-Barrero, 2022). In this chapter we defend that intercultural citizenship is a useful conceptual framework to analytically examine how such belonging could be constructed in multiethnic urban neighbourhoods, understanding multiplicity of linkages across ethnic divides as a key element. For such multiple ways of understanding contact (including formal/informal, conventional/unconventional, and also nonverbal communication, body language, eye contact, gestures and even silence (Samovar et al., 2015)[1] to fulfil the conditions of citizenship-making and developing a sense

---

[1] See diversity-linkage theory formulated by R. Zapata-Barrero (2019a, Chap. 5).

R. Zapata-Barrero · Z. Hellgren (✉)
Department of Political and Social Sciences, Universitat Pompeu Fabra, Barcelona, Spain
e-mail: zenia.hellgren@upf.edu

© The Author(s) 2023
R. Barbulescu et al. (eds.), *Revising the Integration-Citizenship Nexus in Europe*, IMISCOE Research Series, https://doi.org/10.1007/978-3-031-25726-1_7

of belonging need to take place under conditions of equality and power-sharing or be discrimination-free. We contend therefore that these people-to-place linkages in diversity settings are even more important than the probably more traditional people-to-people linkages that usually define interculturalism (Zapata-Barrero, 2017). For instance, migrants tend to use open public spaces, community gardens, and parks to gather and congregate in ways that are reminiscent of their home country, transforming the parks of their adoptive community into familiar spaces, creating an "autotopography" that links their daily practices and life experiences to a deep sense of place (Agyeman, 2017).

Entering in the interface between discrimination and interculturalism is not self-evident. It invites us to enter a debate on the conditions of interculturalism, namely going through the key- question on the necessary favourable conditions to ensure that the promotion of contact between diverse people is positive. The literature in general highlights two necessary conditions: equality and power sharing (Zapata-Barrero, 2019a). This essentially means that in conditions of inequality and even competitiveness, the relations between people could have the perverse effect of increasing prejudices and negative attitudes, and hence discrimination.

In the current debate, interculturalism is used in multi-scale contexts, from global politics to local setting, and there is a need to clarify the scale before properly entering in empirical insights (Zapata-Barrero & Mansouri, 2021). What is emerging anew is its application to contemporary migration-related challenges within local societies that are increasingly transnational and super- diverse. A number of other European policy documents stress the importance of cities as key actors for diversity management and cohesion promotion (e.g. European Commission, 2008a, b; 2015). One of the first EU political documents making this "city turn" explicit was the European Ministerial Conference on Integration (Zaragoza, 15–16 April 2010),[2] held under the Spanish Presidency, which underlined once again the central role of local authorities in implementing intercultural and integration programmes. Specifically, the final declaration of the conference concluded: "Considering that cities and their districts are privileged areas for fostering intercultural dialogue and for promoting cultural diversity and social cohesion, it is important for local governments to develop and obtain capacities to better manage diversity and to combat racism, xenophobia and all forms of discrimination." (European Commission, 2010; 7).

In this local scale the conditions of interculturalism requires diversity-awareness and diversity-recognition. Namely, if a person has the opportunity to communicate with others, he or she will also be able to understand and appreciate different points of views involving his or her way of life, and may also be open to change his or her views as a direct outcome of contact (Zapata-Barrero, 2017). This transformative dimension of interculturalism could take place if the public space where contact happens is free from discrimination. If this public space is instead full of

---

[2] Established by the European Foundation for the Improvement of Living and Working Conditions, the Council of Europe and the City of Stuttgart (www.eurofound.europa.eu/areas/populationand-society/clip.htm).

stereotypes, prejudices, ignorance, misconceptions, then the result of contact between people will most likely be social conflict instead of conviviality. Under favourable circumstances, feelings of belonging may instead thrive in relation to concrete everyday spaces and places. The centrality of equal forms of contact is why discrimination needs to be understood not only in racial and identity terms, but also in social-class ones. Pettigrew and Tropp (2011) highlight this social class component when dealing with diversity-related prejudices. Fainstein (2005: 13), for instance, affirms that – in opposition with the assumptions of contact theory -- the relationship between diversity and tolerance is not clear. Sometimes exposure to "the other" evokes greater understanding, but if lifestyles are seen as being too incompatible, it only heightens prejudice. Wessendorf (2013), in turn, analyses the super-diverse[3] London neighbourhood of Hackney and reveals complex codes of ethics in what she defines as "commonplace diversity": a situation in which ethnic mixing is so normalized that it is hardly reflected upon, but still continues to produce distance and differentiation between people and rarely translates into private relations. She found that the generally established "live and let live" ethos that appeared as a necessary condition for conviviality in such a heterogeneous environment was challenged "when this disengagement is coupled with contestations over space", for instance, competition over housing (ibid: 419). Just as competition, discrimination separates people, and a discriminatory context is by definition a non-shared public space. It is clearly a restrictive factor since it breaks any bridging condition and often increases social conflicts. In fact, "conflict zones" are those where racism, xenophobia, and lack of respect or tolerance prevail, together with unequal and unbalanced power relations (Zapata-Barrero, 2019a; 69).

What is particularly poignant in this context is when people restrain themselves from taking part of public spaces because of perceived (or expected) discrimination. They may for instance choose not to go to certain streets, neighbourhoods, pubs or public parks because they feel that they are not welcome (Hellgren, 2019); thereby, an interculturalist transformation of public spaces is impeded. These subtle modalities of inequalities and power shape the ways in which diversity is organized in particular places, spatializing the politics of diversification and consolidating taken for granted institutional cultural hierarchies (Ye, 2017). Public spaces constitute a resource that should be accessible to all, including old and new migrants (Peters et al., 2010). Public spaces need to be discrimination-free zones, free from diversity-related hostilities and conflicts. Studies show how discrimination may discourage the use of public parks, civic centres and other places (Wood, 2015). Moreover, this dimension needs to be brought into the intercultural debate. For instance, issues such as self-restraints and self-prevention to go to certain public spaces by racialized people because they feel unwelcome must also become an intercultural policy target for local authorities. Physical proximity of diverse populations in spaces such

---

[3] The concept of super-diversity, originally applied by Vertovec (2007), is used to define the demographic changes brought about by an increasingly diversified immigration, leading to situations in several western cities in which an increasing amount of nationalities are present in neighbourhoods, school classes, etc. (Crul, 2016).

as buses, parks, and public squares has the potential to generate hostility as much as conviviality (Ye, 2017). The existence of deeply rooted, ethno-racial hierarchies that continue to stratify people in European societies (Lentin, 2011) needs to be recognized and addressed by interculturalist theories and policies (Zapata-Barrero, 2017).

The 2013 Black Lives Matter movement belonged to this strand of the debate by claiming that such subtle forms of self-censorship need to be directly targeted by public authorities and political narratives. So, before returning to the core question linking discrimination with interculturalism, which we argue illuminates the citizenship-integration nexus by defining discrimination as a central impediment for egalitarian citizenship practices that are essential for integration to work, we need to ask: how can we promote positive contact if people live in unequal conditions in terms of legal, economic and education status, different power situations and different social statuses, and constantly are subject to racialized categorizations in everyday life (Lentin, 2011)? It is this focus that informs most understandings of intercultural policies. For instance, Barcelona and others cities within the intercultural cities programme often formulate their policies to fight against the adverse conditions for contact. A clear example is the last formulation of the Barcelona Interculturality Plan (2010), seen as an anti-racist tool and informing an anti-rumour strategy that has influenced the European Council's intercultural cities programme (https://www.coe.int/en/web/interculturalcities/anti-rumours). As is made clear from the very beginning, "The anti-rumour strategy aims to raise awareness about the importance of countering diversity-related prejudices and rumours that hamper positive interaction and social cohesion and that lay the foundations of discriminatory and racist attitudes" (Barcelona Interculturality Plan, 2010). Within this policy field there is an array of actions that go from anti-rumours, antiracism and campaigns for equality of rights and respect for human rights. The promotion of anti-discrimination (agendas and discourses) is a fundamental element of intercultural policies, since it potentially focuses on the factors that hinder the emergence of positive contact zones.

It should however be noted that an explicitly equality-oriented perspective is largely absent from anti-discrimination policies, which tend to limit themselves to promoting non-discrimination as ideal and rarely address the underlying structures and mechanisms that produce discrimination (Joppke, 2007). It has been argued that this is related to the fact that the implementation of anti-discrimination directives at the European level in the early 2000s had a significant impact since they did not challenge the foundations of the policy framework based on (neo) liberal principles: discrimination was framed as an obstacle for merit-based competition rather than linked to structural inequalities (Bell, 2002). Consequently, the Anti-discrimination directives' focus on race/ethnicity rather than on equality was widely criticized for not having sufficiently acknowledged the socio-economic vulnerability of many immigrants and ethnic minority people. This may reflect how states prefer less costly, symbolic solutions that do not challenge the overall political economy (Geddes, 2004; Bell, 2002), while it appears that anti-discrimination needs to incorporate both "race" and "class" in order to better address the disadvantages that many immigrants and racialized people face. Moreover, there are contextual, legal, institutional and structural factors that reduce people's motivation to interact and even build walls of separation between them based on misinterpretations of differences. This implies that diversity can no longer be used as a euphemism to perpetuate the us/others separation of societies, which instead of fighting against it, maintains the inequalities and unbalanced power relations in diverse public spaces.

As has already been noted (R. Zapata-Barrero, 2019a; 34) there is always a subtle semantic process (reflecting colonial thinking) when those who define diversity never include themselves within this category. Diversity is always considered by European standards to refer to non-Europeans. Europe has constructed diversity categories related to dimensions of race, ethnicity, religion, language, as being at the origin of social polarization and political conflicts (R. Zapata-Barrero, 2019b). In this sense, interculturalism charts the course, the focus, the horizon, and the direction of small-scale programs, and is becoming a strategic local project. One example is the intercultural cities program that the Council of Europe promoted as part of the European Year of Intercultural Dialogue in 2008, which today has a worldwide scope with more than 140 cities from all the continents.[4] Implementation areas can have a variable focal length within the territorial limits of the city: as an overall local project, and on a smaller scale, at the level of districts, and even streets and concrete public settings (market, playground, etc.), particular projects, either thematic and topic-oriented or targeting particular profiles of people (young people, women, artists, intergenerational projects, etc.), or seeking to foster determinate values, beliefs and life prospects.

This chapter has two central parts; one theoretical and one that is empirically oriented. In the first part, we frame the conceptual system within which we may develop a more focused empirical analysis of intercultural citizenship-making through anti-discrimination policies. In this context we are interested in how people subjectify discrimination, and even how discrimination may be a matter of subtle normalization for certain groups of people, who are aware of their difference from the mainstream society and take for granted, thereby in practice accepting, a certain degree of inequality and subordinate positions in the general power structures. These cognitive situations of self-censorship in acceding to certain public spaces and even of self-limiting their behaviour into a non-shared public space may erode the very concept of citizenship by seriously damaging the sense of belonging. Second, we integrate empirical data on immigrants' perceptions on discrimination and belonging from multiple studies on this topic conducted between 2004 and 2020. Based on these narratives, it clearly shows that self-perceived discrimination is a shared experience by people of diverse, non-Western backgrounds, and represents an impediment for their identification with society. Simultaneously, we find that experiences of inclusion in the local neighbourhood can counteract such negative experiences in the broader society and constitute a fertile construction ground for intercultural citizenship.

---

[4] see https://www.coe.int/en/web/interculturalcities

7.2 Framing the Interculturalism, Public Space and Citizenship-Making Debate

Among the multi-layered debate on interculturalism, and its epistemological endeavours Zapata-Barrero, 2019c), there is confusion sometimes between the ends of interculturalism and the means or conditions. For instance, the intercultural approach places equality not at a normative end, as multiculturalism does, but as a condition for intercultural relations. This means that its mantra is that it is very difficult to promote contact in unequal conditions, say regarding social class and education for instance, but also under different legal statuses. The foundation of interculturalism lies in the theory that states that under conditions of equality and power-sharing, inter-personal contact is one of the most effective ways to reduce discrimination. This application of the contact hypothesis (Allport, 1954) assumes that issues of stereotyping, prejudice and discrimination commonly occur between people who are in a competitive logic. Therefore, prejudices not only have an identity component, but also a social-class one (Pettigrew & Tropp, 2006). Fainstein (2005: 13), for instance, affirms that the relationship between diversity and tolerance is not clear. Sometimes exposure to 'the other' evokes greater understanding, but if lifestyles are too incompatible, it only heightens prejudice. Allport's proposal was that properly managed contact should reduce these problems and lead to better interactions. These conditions for interculturalism include equal status within difference, common goals, interdependence, cooperation and support of authorities, shared law or customs. This follows that diversity- awareness, diversity-recognition and shared public spaces becomes one of the most important conditions for positive contact-promotion. On this avenue of debate, and together with equality, we also need to place power relations, Interculturalism highlights how important it is to reach power sharing conditions for promoting contact. And when we link inequality and power relations, we conceptually enter the realm of discrimination.

Discrimination is understood as a conjugation of inequality and power relations. In this sense discrimination is seen as a factor preventing contact and an intercultural policy must place increased focus on discrimination prevention rather than equality alone. But in order to better conceptually box discrimination under an intercultural lens, we also need to include its geographical dimension. By this we mean that discrimination does not occur in abstract settings but in actual, physical or virtual places, and it is often public space-related. Interculturalism has first of all an urban view of public space. Carr et al. (1993) distinguish between 11 types of public spaces: public parks, squares and plazas, memorials, markets, streets, playgrounds, community open spaces, greenways and parkways, atrium/indoor market places, found spaces/everyday spaces and waterfronts. But, it can also be neighbourhood spaces like the residential streets and forecourts (Dines et al., 2006). We can also add community gardens, libraries, public amenities, festivals and neighbourhood spaces, as reported by Bagwell et al. (2012). We cannot overlook inside buildingseither such as supermarkets, restaurants, bars, closed leisure activities, theatres, music halls, and sport centres, even if these last may have rights of admission. Connecting spaces, such as sidewalks and streets, are also public spaces. In the twenty-first century, some even consider virtual spaces available through the internet as a new type of public space that develops interaction and social mixing. It is in fact this non-excludable nature of public space that makes the development of intercultural citizenship possible. In fact, the fact that interculturalism can mainly be applied at shared public spaces delineate the bottom-up approach for understanding its application, as a micro-politics and neighbourhood policies, as proximity policy (Zapata-Barrero, 2019a).

The argument is that public space needs to be shared and should always be open as a condition of interculturalism. When the public space is scattered and the activities of people find unjustified limits, then it is very difficult to promote intercultural relations. The importance of mobilising public spaces at the level of neighbourhoods can become imperative under circumstances in which areas that are left alone may be at risk of being managed by the market, following its consumption's logic of action, rather than that of social aims and public goods (Wood, 2015), and it can even become the concrete space of diversity-related discriminations. Following Habermas' concern, one additional problem today is that public spaces are sometimes represented as spaces of insecurity, isolation, threat, danger, conflicts, of consumption and competition, and other features that prevent diversity-contacts (Calhoun, 1992). There is also a criticism on the privatization of public spaces that may be relevant for us. The disappearance of open public spaces can generate negative social consequences and launch a spiral of decline. As the vibrancy of public spaces diminishes we lose the habit of participating in street life. The natural policing of streets that comes from the presence of people needs to be replaced by 'security' and the city itself becomes less free and more alienating. These public domain retreats are also a structural cause of lack of contact-zones for diversity-contacts promotion that we must take into account (Rogers, 2008). One condition for making public spaces work for intercultural citizenship is then to make sure they are safe spaces where people can celebrate their cultural peers with autonomy (Knapp, 2007). Here public space and discrimination represent a prominent factor for intercultural relations, since we can place discrimination issues within the framework of public space and then see how there are discriminatory public spaces. The relation between discrimination and exclusion of public space is important here and so are interrelated terms. Discrimination provokes exclusion from shared public spaces. That there are spaces that may not be fully shared by all challenges the citizenship-making process behind the intercultural strategy. This citizenship focus is also important.

Interculturalism shows its pro-active dimension in terms of fostering new forms of citizenship identity and belonging separated from birth and origin. The seminal work of Castells (1999) showed us that the question of personal identity is much more connected to how people relate to each other, rather than the traditional 'Who am I?' based on 'where I was born' (territory) or 'who my parents are' (descent). When we look at citizenship traditions, interculturalism is close to the republican tradition as a strategy connecting place-making and identity-making to frame public spaces (Zapata-Barrero, 2020).

Here the debate can spread on how far interculturalism is a strategy for community cohesion, for fostering communitarian values of respect and recognition of the other, and for creating diversity awareness. The debate, then, is not about conditions, but about outcomes of intercultural policies. The fact of citizenship-making behind intercultural strategies could be misleading if we do not consider a necessary condition for cohesion-making, namely the sense of belonging. Without a minimum feeling of belonging into a societal structure it is difficult to create cohesion and citizenship. Here citizenship-making become a channel for cohesion-making and the sense of belonging a factor for bridging citizenship and cohesion. If we go into this sense of belonging as a necessary condition of citizenship and cohesion, our society has been shaped to only give a political meaning to the sense of belonging when it is nationhood-based. This means that often the sense of belonging has been conducted around a symbolic flag. This traditional cognitive condition for citizenship and cohesion-making is today challenged by interculturalism, since the premise of making contact is a much more a cosmopolitan devise of detaching relations from racial and national dependencies (hence interculturalism adhere to post-ethnic, post-national and post- racial view of society). For interculturalism, place-making and public space become the main frameworks for developing the necessary feeling of belonging for citizenship-making.

In this conceptual system, non-discrimination plays a very important role, both for the conditions and the ends of interculturalism. From an intercultural lens, it is understood in spatial terms, at the micro level. For an intercultural mind, discrimination may prevent people from developing the sense of belonging that is necessary for citizenship and cohesion making. This hypothesis is what we would like to empirically test through different fieldworks that have been developed in recent years.

In fact, when we shift our focus from the interculturalism rhetoric towards evidences, we are still in much need of rigorous empirical studies in order to learn about the assets and shortcomings of intercultural policy, since its outcomes need to be tested, measured, compared and contrasted. It is within this line of research that we place our objectives.

7.3   Self-Perceptions on Discrimination and the Mitigating Effects of Place-Based Belonging

There is a vast body of research on the detrimental effects of the discrimination that frequently affects immigrants and racialized minorities in European societies (e.g. Crul et al., 2012; Safi, 2010; Lentin, 2011, 2014; Seng, 2012; Bobowik et al., 2014; ENAR report, 2014). There are also several works that look into the ways in which groups who often perceive exclusion and non- acceptance from the majority society construct alternative forms of belonging; for instance, in countercultures and movements (McDowell, 2016; Pilati, 2016), or in the construction of a collective identity that is closely linked to the physical space, generally the city or the neighbourhood where everyday life is played out (Oosterlynck et al., 2017; Hellgren, 2019). This identity-construction is often problematic. For people who live in marginalized housing areas, for instance, feelings of shame or anger over the stigmatization of their neighbourhood become mixed with feelings of solidarity and belonging. People who frequently experience that they are looked down upon; that their right to be in a certain place is questioned; that they are suspected of stealing or other infractions; or even are insulted, in other parts of the city, may feel more relaxed and at ease in the own neighbourhood, where they are known. The solidarity towards the neighbourhood may however also be put to a test for residents who manage to climb upwards on the social ladder, and lead to personal conflicts in taking the decision to move out or stay (Barwick & Beaman, 2019). The destructive effects of the "downward spiral" in areas marked by unemployment and social exclusion, resulting from the tendency that only those who have no other option end up staying, is well-known and documented, and needs to be taken into account in order to avoid a romanticizing and naïve view on the often harsh realities of many multiethnic neighbourhoods in European cities.

Nevertheless, what is particularly relevant in the context of this chapter is to understand the physical space – and hence to place the focus on people-to-place linkages rather than only applying a people-to-people focus, as is usually taken for granted in debates on interculturalism – as a "construction site for intercultural citizenship": how is this happening (or not), and under what circumstances? As discussed above, we consider the perceptions of discrimination – both in terms of actual experiences and of an internalized "normalization" and expectation to repeatedly be discriminated against based on one's ethnicity and previous experiences – among racialized people as an important impediment for the bottom-up construction of an intercultural citizenship based on egalitarian relations between people from the ethnic majority society as well as immigrants and ethnic minority groups.

In this section, we will provide empirical data that ground these theoretical endeavours.

First, we will briefly present the empirical studies that the data used are extracted from. Then, we will use extensive, qualitative interview data providing narratives on the character of the discrimination that the respondents perceive, and the consequences it has for them at a personal and social level. This approach is intended to provide a deeper insight into the severe consequences that also "invisible" forms of discrimination may have in terms of sense of belonging to society, illustrating empirically in what ways discrimination constitutes an impediment for the kind of intercultural citizenship that we outlined above. Finally, we shift our perspective on the empirical data and focus on the narratives on belonging and the respondents' relationship to the place where they live their lives.

7.3.1 The Empirical Material: Analysing Data from Different Research Projects

The data used for our analysis was collected for several different research projects addressing inclusion/exclusion among immigrants and racialized people.[5] This involves important advantages. First, it allows us to use extensive qualitative interview material: the literal transcripts from altogether 185 interviews conducted between 2004 and 2020 with immigrants from North and Sub-Saharan Africa, Latin America, Asia, the Middle East, and Eastern Europe, children of immigrants, and racialized citizens as the Spanish Roma population, were used. Second, the great variety of the material is enhanced by the fact that it is multi-sited: the data were collected at different sites in Spain and Sweden. For the purpose of this chapter, we were interested in explicitly contrasting the different narratives on discrimination and belonging that were included in the transcripts from these projects, regardless of the differences in framing between them. The rich data allowed for comparisons between the experiences of racialized people with different educational and income levels, between different forms of racialization (based on skin colour or prejudices about cultural or religious differences, for instance (Silverstein, 2005)), and in relation to different societal contexts. This multi-comparative approach was considered of central importance for the reliability of the findings. All of these 185 respondents declared that they experienced discrimination regularly, most typically in public spaces, in shops and supermarkets, in access to housing and employment, or as disrespect at work.

In coding the interview transcripts and conducting a thematic analysis, a distinction was first made between the respondents' narratives on how they experienced and perceived different types of discrimination, and the consequences these experienced had for them in terms of sense of belonging and identification with society. Different experiences of discrimination were categorized as "direct" or "indirect" discrimination, where the first refers to overt discriminatory experiences as racist insults or explicit forms of rejection (for example the case of a black flight attendant who was denied employment as the HR representative claimed that "this airline is not used to working with coloured people"), while the second category covers a wide spectrum of more subtle forms of exclusion or rejection. For instance, the experience of repeatedly not being selected for employment despite being a qualified candidate, or simply perceiving that one is looked down upon and avoided in a wide range of situations, based on physical features. Skin colour was common for

[5]The core results of this research is published in several journals and edited volumes (see, e.g., Hellgren, 2008, 2014, 2015, 2019; Hellgren & Gabrielli, 2021a and b). Zenia Hellgren was the PI and/or researcher and in charge of the empirical studies conducted in all of them. For a full list of these research projects, see her personal website: https://www.upf.edu/web/zenia-hellgren/research-lines. One of these projects, REPCAT (The Role of the Ethnic Majority in Integration Processes: Attitudes and Practices towards Immigrants in Catalan Institutions), received funding from the European Union's Horizon 2020 research and innovation programme under the Marie Sklodowska-Curie grant agreement No. 747075.

many of the respondents, and severely harmed their self-esteem and sense of belonging to society at a general level. In this context, specific attention was paid to the dimension of self-restraint that we discussed in the theoretical section above, as this was considered an essential factor for the willingness to interact with others in public spaces and thereby participate actively in the "making of intercultural citizenship". Finally, the respondents' narratives on their relationship with the place where they live were coded, including both positive and negative aspects of such identification.

7.3.2 Self-Perceptions on Discrimination

The analysis of the 185 interviews about self-perceived discrimination clearly show that visible difference such as skin/hair colour, "indigenous features" (salient among Latin American migrants in Spain, particularly for those of Bolivian origin), or religious clothing in the case of Muslim women, were overall perceived as the principal cause for both overt forms of racism and more subtle forms of rejection. Overt discrimination was most common in the narratives of people of African descent, (visible) Muslims, and Roma. Particularly among the Roma respondents, it was common to express how the perception is passed from generation to generation that one will (in these respondents' view, inevitably) be exposed to racism and rejection because of their belonging to the Roma ethnicity.

> I was in a playground with my daughter and another mother yelled at her little son, loud and just in front of me 'look how dirty you have gotten, you look like a gypsy'. This kind of things happens all the time and it is hard to explain to my children, I try to protect them but they begin to understand now, how people look at them. –*Roma woman, 2020*

This kind of experiences contributed to the widely shared sentiment that one is safer in their own neighbourhood, and that it is not worth the exposure to humiliation that is often involved in trying to access places that are perceived as "not for us."

> Always, always, when I go to *Zara* downtown for instance, a security guard shows up and walks closely behind me all the time. So, I prefer to buy my clothes at the market in *La Mina*, because there they treat me well, even if I like the clothes at *Zara* better. –*Roma woman, 2018*

There are also many narratives that illustrate how the subtler forms of rejection, most typically that of never being selected for employment, influence on the affected persons' self- esteem and sense of identification with the broader, mainstream society, even if many of the respondents also express how they actively struggle against the negative effects of discrimination at the individual level.

> I know when I don't get a job because of my skin colour. After so many years of being exposed to it [discrimination], one knows just by the way people look at you, or talk you to. But once when I applied for a job as shop assistant, the lady actually told me that she could not hire me because the clients cannot identify with a black person. –*Woman of Burundian origin, 2014*

I try not to think that it is because I am black if I don't get a job or a rental contract, and I am still applying for these things. I have to be aware of the problem [with racism] without becoming paranoid. I cannot assume that it is because of my origin every time I am rejected, and I am not going to stop wanting things just because I may have fewer chances. –*Man of Guinean origin, 2013*

Many of the respondents felt significantly limited by the fact that they had experienced discrimination in the past, and therefore expected to experience it again, which made them avoid situations where this was considered likely to occur. Overall, the analysis of the interviews lends empirical support to assert that the damage caused by discrimination is severe in terms of self- limitations and nonbelonging – even if it, as Crul et al. (2012: 28) points out actually "only happened once or twice in a lifetime". This is also where the link between (both actual and expected) discrimination and the relationship to place becomes particularly evident: while discrimination thus hampers the feeling of identification with and sense of entitlement to the place (for instance, youngsters who perceive that they are unwelcome outside their own neighbourhood may claim that the city is "not theirs"), a positive relation to the physical space that is significant for the individual, most importantly their own neighbourhood, may counteract negative experiences of discrimination in society as a whole and create a sense of belonging that is essential for the person's wellbeing, even if it is a form of "underdog belonging" (Hellgren, 2019; Barwick & Beaman, 2019).

7.3.3   The Relation to Place and the Construction of Belonging

The importance for developing a sense of belonging of immigrants' and racialized people's identification with the physical space where everyday life is played out, most typically the neighbourhood, has been stressed by numerous authors (e.g., Oosterlynck et al., 2017; Crul, 2016; Wessendorf, 2013). It has also been argued that for people who are exposed to discrimination based on their origin, the local level is more central for processes of identification and belonging than the national level (Barwick & Beaman, 2019). The relationship with place can apparently, at least to some extent, compensate for the discrimination and marginalization that racialized people often experience in their contacts with the mainstream society. It may, for instance, be far easier for an immigrant to identify as "Barcelonian" than "Catalan" or "Spanish." In one of the research projects used for this article, the main conclusion was that experiences of racism and discrimination were similar among racialized immigrants and minorities in Stockholm and Barcelona, but the sense of wellbeing and identification with the city was overall far greater among the respondents in Barcelona. The city's more "cosmopolitan" character and ethnically mixed public spaces were given as the main reasons for this, while on the reverse, the high degree of spatial segregation in Stockholm, where most non-white people live in high-rise buildings in the outer suburbs, was considered a central reason for discontent and detachment, and directly counterproductive for integration processes (Hellgren, 2019).

In understanding multi-ethnic environments as potential construction sites for an intercultural citizenship from below, the liberating effect that such spaces have for many of the respondents provides important insights. Overall, the respondents express that they feel more comfortable and experience a greater sense of belonging in ethnically mixed surroundings, and some of them who had positive experiences abroad consider melting pots such as London, New York, or Brussels, as the ideal places to live.

> When I was a teenager, we went to visit family in Brussels in the summer holidays. There is a much larger African diaspora there, many black people, mainly from Congo. That feeling, of not being a minority, not looking different... I did not realize until I came back home how relaxed I had felt [in Brussels], without really knowing why. Also in the US, people ask me where I'm from, but they mean from which American state! I did not feel so exotified there. There is much racism but people don't find it strange to see black people everywhere, even as bosses. –*Woman of Congolese origin, 2014*

In most of the narratives used for this chapter, the yearning to feel that one is treated "like anyone else" is central. This is, for many of the racialized respondents, only possible, to some extent, in their own neighbourhood, or in other multi-ethnic neighbourhoods. However, this does not mean that multi-ethnic places are safe-guarded from racism and discrimination. As Barwick and Beaman (2019: 2) point out, "even in super-diverse cities and neighbourhoods, ethnic and religious minorities often experience stigmatization and discrimination".

Furthermore, there are important complexities involved in the different forms of identification with the physical space that racialized people construct. Indeed, many of the super-diverse neighbourhoods in European cities with high proportions of residents who have their roots in other countries are also marked by severe socio-economic difficulties (Crul, 2016). As Crul (ibid) points out, this "super-diversity" does often not involve the native population, who lives and works in other, mainly white neighbourhoods and hardly sees how "the other half" lives. This consequence of urban segregation may be the focal point that needs to be addressed in order for the ideal construction of an egalitarian intercultural citizenship that we defined in the theoretical section above to become more of a reality: such a project can hardly work if it does not involve a majority of natives as well.

As for now, the forms of belonging and intercultural identification that emerges in super- diverse neighbourhoods is often what best may be described as an "under-dog identity," which is often based on shared experiences of exclusion and discrimination (Hellgren, 2019; Barwick & Beaman, 2019). This sentiment is reflected in many of the respondents' accounts on how they perceive that others see them as inhabitants of a stigmatized housing area.

> Have you seen the streets? There is garbage everywhere, they don't even care about cleaning here. But we are actually a part of Badalona though it doesn't feel like it, we even speak about it like that, 'are you going to Badalona?' And if we go to the centre, people look at us like... it bothers them. This [the own neighbourhood] is the only place where I feel comfortable. –*Roma man, 2020*

> I went to high school in a fancy neighbourhood, with lots of ethnic Swedes, quite upper class…and when everyone talks of integration, they usually mean that I should integrate into their society, but not so much that these rich ethnic Swedes should integrate into our society, into my neighbourhood where lots of people have an immigrant background. So, I feel that there are two sides of the coin, so to speak, but only one part is expected to integrate and adapt to the other. –*Man of Eritrean origin, 2014*

There are also narratives of the kind of stigmatization that may affect racialized people who move upwards on the social ladder. This highlights the challenges involved in breaking destructive mental schemes that prevail among the mainstream society, according to which racialized people are automatically assigned pejorative labels as "underclass," or, if wealthy, "probably a gangster." This respondents' experiences are similar to Barwick and Beaman's (Barwick & Beaman, 2019: 10) finding that second-generation Turks in middle-class German neighbourhoods feel that they must be cautious to avoid negative attention, for instance to not buy a fancy car:

> The neighbours were suspicious, my name being the only foreign one. 'How can he afford to live here, is he a criminal?' And I had to work very hard, to not end up in [marginalized suburb], but I did not want that for my children. –*Man of Chilean origin, 2015*

Similarly, Schuster (in Barwick & Beaman, 2019: 10) found that the fear of suffering mistreatment in predominantly "white areas" may lead ethnic minorities to avoid such places, and that for this reason they may prefer to continue living in marginalized housing areas even if they can afford to move out – thus preventing the middle- and upper-class areas where mainly white people live from becoming more ethnically diversified. Indeed, such examples illustrate how deeply incompatible prejudice and discrimination are with the construction of an intercultural society, and also, how essential it is to combat urban segregation in order for the sense of belonging that emerges in relation to public space to be inclusive also of the native population.

7.4   Concluding Remarks: Interculturalism from below

The debate on interculturalism needs to be more practice-oriented and its main argument better evidence-based. This chapter tries to contribute to this research avenue within interculturalism by linking several theoretical and empirical arguments. The premise is that interculturalism is a policy strategy that is basically intended for citizenship-making in diverse societies. As a strategy it needs to focus its conceptual and policy efforts to better connect the ends and means it seeks to put forward to reach these policy ends. Interculturalism has no strong normative dimensions in its core concept, as was the case with multiculturalism, often driven by a sense of justice and equality (Fossum et al., 2020). But this normative-free dimension of interculturalism does not imply that it does not need to deepen its engagement with the conditions that make positive contact possible in ethnically diverse societies. At this juncture, the debate on the conditions of interculturalism is straightforward, since we cannot take for granted that the environment where contact takes place does not affect the citizenship-making process of interculturalism.

We have considered equality, power sharing and belonging as the main components of successful citizenship-making, and we have focused our argument on the basic structural restrictions that people may encounter in their everyday practice, which affects to what degree they are open to relate to other people. The main argument put forward here is that people-to-place linkages may be determinant for people-to-people linkages, which is as we understand interculturalism. This people-to-place linkage needs to be discrimination-free, and empirical findings from diverse settings and contexts show us that there is a self-censorship pattern that may prevent people to be motivated to relate with other people, across ethnic, racial, and other barriers. These subtle and often very difficult-to-prove self-behaviours, together with other more explicit forms of discrimination, often further contaminate public space, which is already contaminated by market inequalities and physical insecurity. Hence, the conditions of interculturalism are key to better shape the intercultural debate when the focus is on public space, belonging and discriminatory practices.

The empirical data from several research projects has helped us to better ground these conceptual endeavours. These multi-sited data lend support to the argument that people who are visibly different from the white, western norm feel more at ease in public spaces with high degrees of ethnic mixing. Several scholars have engaged with identity-formation in multiethnic or "super-diverse" neighbourhoods, where many different nationalities, colours, cultures and religions meet, and young people grow up with hybrid identities and form solidarity and a sense of belonging across ethnic boundaries (e.g., Barwick & Beaman, 2019; McDowell, 2016; Hellgren, 2008; Stevenson, 2003). If we dare to be optimistic, perhaps this ongoing process of emerging identities could be described in terms of "interculturalism from below," grounded in attitudes and practices at the micro level. This ought to be fundamental for an actual interculturalist transformation of society to take place, beyond the political and academic debates and agendas.

There is however still a gap regarding the involvement of the native-origin population in these processes. Ethnically mixed or super-diverse neighbourhoods generally count on low levels of native inhabitants, and those who do live in such areas and share public spaces with newcomers and racialized minorities are often natives in vulnerable positions and with low socio-economic status, who share many of the disadvantages that affect racialized people to a high extent. As discussed above, thus, the type of intercultural identity-formation that takes shape in these areas is often what we denominated as underdog belonging, based on a shared situation of disadvantage, and sometimes, distancing from the mainstream (McDowell, 2016; Pilati, 2016; Hellgren, 2019). In that sense, such identities would rather be in opposition with the construction of an intercultural citizenship, based on egalitarian relations between minorities and natives.

What kind of ideal scenario would we then imagine, if intercultural ideals were successfully translated into the construction of more egalitarian, discrimination-free (super)diverse public spaces? Several of the respondents mentioned multiethnic cities such as New York, London, or Brussels as closer to their ideal cosmopolitan urban space than their own residential areas in Spain or Sweden. As discussed above, there were also salient differences between the relationship to space between the interviewed residents of Barcelona and Stockholm. People of diverse origins expressed more satisfaction in relation to the public spaces of Barcelona than Stockholm, because they perceived Barcelona as less segregated, more open-minded and more visibly ethnically mixed (Hellgren, 2019). Naturally, we need to be cautious in order not to romanticize the ideal of harmonic coexistence in "cosmopolitan" spaces. All the aforementioned cities are for instance strongly segmented across socio-economic divisions. Also, as Wessendorf (2013) argued, diversity per se does not imply that solidarity or identification between people is automatically fostered.

Rather, in the best of cases, the kind of conviviality that emerges in superdiverse urban settings seems to be that of "respectful indifference". Yet, in line with the recent handbook of the governance of migration and diversity in cities (Caponio et al., 2019), we may conclude that apparently, immigrants and racialized people experience a greater sense of belonging in more diverse public spaces, and that part of the intercultural project inevitably needs to consist of a struggle against discrimination and spatial segregation, involving both ethnic majorities and minorities.

References

Agyeman, J. (2017) Interculturally inclusive spaces as just environments, *Items*. Social Science Research Council (items.ssrc.org/interculturallyinclusive-spaces-as-just-environments/).

Allport, G. W. (1954). *The nature of prejudice*. Addison Wesley.

Bagwell, S., et al. (2012). *Public space management: Report to the Intercultural Cities Research Programme*. Cities Institute, London Metropolitan University. (rm.coe. Int/CoERMPublicCommonSearchServices/DisplayDCTMContent?documentI d=09000016803009c0).

Barcelona Interculturality Plan. (2010). Barcelona City Council. https://ajuntament.barcelona.cat/bcnacciointercultural/sites/default/files/documentos/web_bcn_angles.pdf

Barwick, C., & Beaman, J. (2019). Living for the neighbourhood: Marginalization and belonging for the second-generation in Berlin and Paris. *Comparative Migration Studies, 7*(3), 1–17.

Bell, M. (2002). *Anti-discrimination law and the European Union*. Oxford Studies in European Law.

Bobowik, M., Basabe, N., & Páez, D. (2014). 'Heroes of adjustment': Immigrants' stigma and identity management. *International Journal of Intercultural Relations, 41*, 112–124.

Calhoun, C. J. (Ed.). (1992). *Habermas and the public sphere*. MIT Press.

Caponio, T., Scholten, P., & Zapata-Barrero, R. (Eds.). (2019). *The Routledge handbook of the governance of migration and diversity in cities*. Routledge.

Carr, S. F. M., Rivlin, L. G., & Stone, A. M. (1993). *Public space*. Cambridge University Press.

Castells, M. (1999). *The rise of the network society: The information age: Economy, society, and culture*. Wiley-Blackwell.

Crul, M. (2016). Super-diversity vs. assimilation: How complex diversity in majority–minority cities challenges the assumptions of assimilation. *Journal of Ethnic and Migration Studies, 42*(1), 54–68.

Crul, M., Schneider, J., & Lelie, F. (2012). *The European second generation compared: Does the integration context matter?* Amsterdam University Press.

Dines, N., et al. (2006). *Public space and wellbeing: Public spaces and social relations in East London*. The Policy Press.

ENAR (European Network Against Racism) report/book. (2014). Invisible visible minority. Confronting Afrophobia and Advancing Equality for People of African Descent and Black Europeans in Europe. https://www.enar-eu.org/Invisible-visible-minority-ENAR-book-on- people-of-African-descent-in-Europe

European Commission. (2008a). Intercultural dialogue in Europe. Available at: https://ec.europa.eu/culture/policy/strategic-framework/intercultural-dialogue_EN.htm

European Commission. (2008b). Highlights of the European year of intercultural dialogue. Available at: https://eur-lex.europa.eu/legal-content/EN/TXT/?uri=URISERV%3A129017.

European Commission. (2010). European ministerial conference on integration, Zaragoza, 15–16 April. Available at: https://ec.europa.eu/migrant-integration/librarydoc/declaration-of-the-european-ministerial-conference-on-integration-zaragoza-15–16-april-2010.

European Commission. (2015). Recommendation CM/Rec(2015)1 of the Committee of Ministers to member states on intercultural integration. Available at: https://search.coe.int/cm/Pages/result_details.Aspx?ObjectID=09000016805c471f

Fainstein, S. (2005). Cities and Diversity: Should we want it? Can we plan for it? *Urban Affairs Review, 41*(1), 3–19.

Fossum, J., Kastoryano, R., Modood, T., & Zapata-Barrero, R. (2020) Governing diversity in Europe's plural spaces: A path to new normativities. GRITIM-UPF working paper series, no. 46 (winter) http://hdl.handle.net/10230/45565

Geddes, A. (2004). Britain, France, and EU anti-discrimination policy: The emergence of an EU policy paradigm. *West European Politics, 27*(2), 334–353.

Hellgren, Z. (2008). (De)constructing European citizenship. Political mobilization and collective identity formation among immigrants in Sweden and Spain. In I. Bondebjerg & P. Madsen (Eds.), *Media, democracy and European culture*. Intellect. ISBN 9781841502472.

Hellgren, Z. (2014). Negotiating the boundaries of social membership. Undocumented migrant claims-making in Sweden and Spain. *Journal of Ethnic and Migration Studies, 40 (7-8)*, 1175–1191.

Hellgren, Z. (2015). Markets, regimes, and the role of stakeholders: Explaining precariousness of migrant domestic/care workers in different institutional frameworks. *Social Politics, 22*(2), 220–241.

Hellgren, Z. (2019). Class, race - and place: Immigrants' self-perceptions on inclusion, belonging and opportunities in Stockholm and Barcelona. *Ethnic and Racial Studies, 42*(12), 2084–2102.

Hellgren, Z., & Gabrielli, L. (2021a). Racialization and Aporophobia: Intersecting Discriminations in the Experiences of Non-Western Migrants and Spanish Roma. *Social Sciences, 10*(5). https://doi.org/10.3390/socsci10050163

Hellgren, Z., & Gabrielli, L. (2021b). The Dual Expectations Gap. Divergent Perspectives on the Educational Aspirations of Spanish Roma Families. *Journal of Intercultural Studies*, https://doi.org/10.1080/07256868.2021.1883569

Hellgren, Z., & Zapata-Barrero, R. (2022). Discrimination meets interculturalism in theory, policy and practice. *International Migration, 00*, 1– 13. https://doi.org/10.1111/imig.13048

Knapp, C. (2007). 8 lessons to promote diversity in public places. *Project for Public Spaces*. www.pps.org/article/diversityinpublicspaces

Lentin, A. (2011). *Racism and ethnic discrimination*. Rosen Publishing Group.

Lentin, A. (2014). Post-race, post politics: The paradoxical rise of culture after multiculturalism. *Ethnic and Racial Studies, 37*(8), 1268–1285.

Mayblin, L., & Turner, J. (2021). *Migration studies and colonialism*. Polity Press.

McDowell, A. (2016). "This is for the Brown kids!": Racialization and the formation of "Muslim" punk rock. *Sociology of Race and Ethnicity, 3*(2), 159–171.

Oosterlynck, S., Schuermans, N., & Loopmans, M. (2017). *Place, diversity and solidarity*. Routledge.

Peters, K., Elands, B., & Buijs, A. (2010). Social interaction in urban parks: Stimulating social cohesion? *Urban Forestry and Urban Greening, 9*(2), 93–100.

Pettigrew, T. F., & Tropp, L. R. (2006). A meta-analytic test of intergroup contact theory. *Journal of personality and social psychology, 90*(5), 751.

Pettigrew, T. F., & Tropp, L. R. (2011). *When groups meet: The dynamics of intergroup contact* (1st edn). Psychology Press.

Pilati, K. (2016). *Migrants' participation in exclusionary contexts: From subcultures to radicalization*. Palgrave Macmillan.

Rogers, R. (2008). *Cities for a small planet*. Basic Books.

Safi, M. (2010). Immigrants' life satisfaction in Europe: Between assimilation and discrimination. *European Sociological Review, 26*(2), 159–176.

Samovar, L. A., et al. (2015). *Intercultural communication: A reader*. Cengage Learning.

Seng. (2012). Marginalized identities, discrimination burden, and mental health: Empirical exploration of an interpersonal-level approach to modelling intersectionality. *Social Science & Medicine, 75*(12), 2437–2445.

Silverstein, P. A. (2005). Immigrant racialization and the new savage slot: Race, migration, and immigration in the new Europe. *Annual Review of Anthropology, 34*, 363–384.

Stevenson, N. (2003). *Cultural citizenship: Cosmopolitan questions*. Open University Press.

Vertovec, S. (2007). Super-diversity and its implications. *Ethnic and Racial Studies, 30*(6), 1024–1054.

Wessendorf, S. (2013). Commonplace diversity and the 'ethos of mixing': Perceptions of difference in a London neighbourhood. *Identities, 20*(4), 407–422.

Wood, P. (2015). Meet me on the corner? Shaping the conditions for cross-cultural interaction in urban public space. In R. Zapata-Barrero (Ed.), *Interculturalism in cities: Concept, policy and implementation* (pp. 53–75). Edward-Elgar Publishing.

Ye, J. (2017). 'Contours of urban diversity and coexistence. *Geography Compass, 11*(9), 1–8.

Zapata-Barrero, R. (2017). Interculturalism in the Post-Multicultural Debate: A defence. *Comparative Migration Studies, 5*, 14.

Zapata-Barrero, R. (2019a). *Intercultural citizenship in the post-multicutural era*. Sage Swifts Publishing.

Zapata-Barrero, R. (2019b). Rebooting European identity: Intercultural citizenship for building the future of a diverse Europe. *Journal of Contemporary European Studies, 28*(2), 153–166.

Zapata-Barrero, R. (2019c). Guest editorial: Methodological Interculturalism: Breaking down epistemological barriers around Diversity management. *Ethnic and Racial Studies, 42*(3), 346–356. https://doi.org/10.1080/01419870.2019.1538527

Zapata-Barrero, R. (2020). Republicanism, diversity and public space in contemporary political theory: The normative basis of intercultural citizenship. *Citizenship Studies, 24*(8), 1066–1183. https://doi.org/10.1080/13621025.2020.1769028

Zapata-Barrero, R., & Mansouri, F. (2021). A multi-scale approach to Interculturalism: From globalised politics to localised policy and practice. *Journal of International Migration and Integration, 23*, 775.

Chapter 8
"In London, I Am a European Citizen": Brexit, Emotions, and the Politics of Belonging

Nando Sigona (iD) **and Marie Godin** (iD)

8.1 Introduction

London hosts by far the largest population of non-national EU citizens in Europe. It is also home to roughly one-third of the entire EU citizen population living in the UK. London's population changed rapidly following EU enlargement in the 2000s in terms of its size, the variety and number of nationalities it hosts, and its socio-demographic profile (Lessard-Phillips & Sigona, 2018). These changes have intensified and shaped the process of 'diversification of diversity' captured in the late 2000s by anthropologist Steve Vertovec in his seminal work on superdiversity (Vertovec, 2007). Despite Britain's exit from the EU, its new geopolitical orientation (towards a more 'Global Britain') and the new immigration regime that has come to replace the EU's freedom of movement, this diversification process has continued. For example, between 2016 and 2020, live births among EU mothers in London have roughly stayed the same - only marginally declined from 17.52 to 17.18 per cent of the total number of live births in London, with Poland, Romania, Germany and Lithuania among the top 10 countries of birth for non-UK mothers in the city (ONS, 2021; see also Lessard-Phillips & Sigona, 2019).

Despite vague reassurances from politicians during the referendum campaign, the outcome of the 2016 EU referendum – which saw the 'Leave' campaign winning popular support across every region in England and Wales with the exception

N. Sigona
Chair of International Migration and Forced Displacement, Department of Social Policy, Sociology, and Criminology at the University of Birmingham, Birmingham, UK
e-mail: N.Sigona@bham.ac.uk

M. Godin (✉)
Refugee Studies Centre, Oxford Department of International Development,
University of Oxford, Oxford, UK
e-mail: marie.godin@qeh.ox.ac.uk

© The Author(s) 2023
R. Barbulescu et al. (eds.), *Revising the Integration-Citizenship Nexus in Europe*, IMISCOE Research Series, https://doi.org/10.1007/978-3-031-25726-1_8

of Greater London – led to an extended period of uncertainty for over three million EU citizens living in the UK concerning their legal status and rights after Brexit. Over several months of bilateral negotiations that followed the vote, EU citizens made their concerns, anxieties and frustrations heard through social media and political activism, lobbying their MPs, joining existing civil society organisations, and creating new ones. In the months leading to the referendum and during the negotiations that followed, anti-EU and anti-immigration sentiments were evident across the British mainstream media. This along with an increase in hate crime, and the fear of becoming a target of the UK's hostile environment policy contributed to heightened concerns among EU citizens. The reassurance that came with the introduction of the EU Settled Status (EUSS) programme for EU citizens in June 2018 was short-lived; the prospect of a 'no deal' Brexit seemed highly probable until the end of negotiations in early 2020. Uncertainty continues to the present day around the Northern Ireland protocol and its implications for the implementation of the Trade Agreement.

Examining the geographical distribution of the Brexit vote, Johnston et al. (2018: 162) showed that, 'of the fifty local jurisdictions where the vote to remain in the EU was strongest, only eleven were not in London or Scotland, and most of these were areas with large universities', with London standing out 'from the rest of England, even when its population composition had been taken into account' (p.180).

Acknowledging London's substantial support for remaining in the EU, one month after the referendum the Mayor of London, Sadiq Khan, launched the campaign #LondonisOpen[1] to reassure all EU citizens in London and EU institutions and businesses abroad that 'London is united and open for business, and to the world, following the EU referendum.' In the months that followed, Sadiq Khan embarked on a tour of European capitals to strengthen the economic and social ties between London and EU cities. He then intensively lobbied for continued visa-free travel to the UK for European citizens trying to ensure that London remains 'a leading global business capital'. The EU Londoners Hub was created to provide EU citizens and their families with information about life in London and advice on how to apply for the EU Settlement Scheme (EUSS).

The EU-UK Withdrawal Agreement was signed on 17 October 2019 and entered into force on 1 February 2020. It set the terms for the UK's departure from the EU, including the rights for EU citizens living in the UK and British citizens living in the EU. Between March 2019 and 30 June 2021, EU, EEA and Swiss citizens and their families who had resided in the UK as of 31 December 2020 – the date which marks the end of freedom of movement – could secure their residency rights through the EUSS. Soon after the implementation of the EUSS, concerns were raised about the vulnerability of groups who were at greater risk of being excluded from the scheme and the risk of inequality in the future (see Godin & Bica, 2019; Sumption & Fernández-Reino, 2020; Jablonowski & Pinkowska, 2021). While not an exhaustive list, among those who were deemed more vulnerable to fall through the cracks of

---

[1] https://www.london.gov.uk/what-we-do/arts-and-culture/london-open

EUSS were victims of exploitation or trafficking, people with mental health problems, children in care and care leavers, victims of domestic violence, homeless people, older people, people with significant language barriers, people who are digitally excluded, unpaid carers and people working cash in hand. Romani communities were also singled out as particularly vulnerable. The transition from pre-settled to settled status presents additional challenges for these communities, with IT digital literacy constituting an important divide up to now (Doležalová et al., 2021).

This chapter portrays the emergence of a new politics of belonging following the 2016 EU Referendum that reconfigures discursively and legally who belongs to, and who is excluded from the post-EU 'Global Britain' from the unique standpoint of London, the city with the largest and most diverse population of EU citizens in Europe. Firstly, through an intersectional lens, we examine how EU families living in London experienced the prolonged Brexit negotiations and what mitigation strategies they were able to put in place to cope with it, according to their resources, circumstances and social status. EU nationals have not only been impacted differently by the uncertainties surrounding the Brexit referendum; but their perceptions and responses to Brexit are very much shaped by their social locations both in the UK and at home as well as sense of entitlement and self-worth. Secondly, the analysis of the responses of EU citizens to Brexit provides the conceptual underpinning to investigate the nexus between integration, citizenship and belonging in a highly diverse and stratified migrant population. We will highlight the significance of positionality, scale and place-based attachments in people's perception and understanding of belonging, and the uniqueness of London's superdiversity in enabling a multi-scalar articulation of citizenship decoupled from nationality.

8.1.1 Belonging and the New Politics of Belonging as EU Citizens in Post-Brexit Britain

As far as EU citizens are concerned, Brexit involved a legal transition from being *EU mobile citizens living* in another EU member state with rights and protections enshrined in the EU law, to being EU *immigrants* living in the UK under the UK's immigration regime (D'Angelo & Kofman, 2018). This legal transition was managed through the EUSS for those already living in the UK or via the mainstream immigration system for newcomers. This change of legal status, which applies also to British citizens living in the EU (Benson, 2020), also change people's claims to belonging and access to rights (Erel & Ryan, 2019; Yuval-Davis et al., 2018). To mitigate the consequences of Brexit, some have chosen to apply for naturalisation (see for example Sigona & Godin, 2019a; Godin & Sigona, 2022).

Nira Yuval Davis' three-pronged analytical framework for the study of belonging (Yuval-Davis, 2011) – in terms of social locations, people's identifications and emotional attachments to various collectivities and groupings, and the ethical and political value systems with which people judge their own and others' belonging – offers a useful conceptual framework for the analysis of the impact of Brexit on EU mobile citizens in London. Yuval-Davis points out, that while belonging as emotional attachment tends to be naturalised, 'particular political projects of belonging select specific signifiers of belonging from different analytical levels in order to construct their projects' (2006: 199). The analytical distinction between belonging and the politics of belonging is particularly relevant we argue, in the context of Brexit which marked a major geopolitical shift for the UK that carried with it a new political project of belonging. This project has reshaped the boundaries of belonging for UK residents, British citizens and non-citizens alike. In that sense, the politics of belonging is not only about 'the dirty work of boundary maintenance' (Favell, 1999), creating both a symbolic and physical separation between 'us' and 'them', but also about the reshaping of these boundaries, and new contestations, challenges as well as resistance by those who are 'newly' excluded. In the chapter we will show how the outcome of the EU referendum generated a range of emotional responses among EU citizens, emotions which reflect situated and intersectional politics of belonging (see Anthias, 2002; Mc Ghee et al., 2017; Botterill et al., 2019; Lulle et al., 2019; Guma & Dafydd Jones, 2019; Sotkasiira & Gawlewicz, 2021).

After the Brexit vote, our research (Sigona & Godin, 2019b) shows that while in England many EU families felt rejected and unwelcome, in Scotland they were more willing to say that they felt at home. A number of people pointed to the exclusion from the EU referendum franchise and inclusion in the Scottish independence referendum as further evidence of how much more valued they feel themselves to be in Scotland. To explain the different treatment EU citizens were experiencing in England, EU citizens in Scotland often referred to the political trope of Scotland as a 'nation of immigrants'. This echoes a narrative which has been pushed strongly by the Scottish Government in the last decade aimed at 'ensuring that appeals to nationhood in Scotland can be meaningfully calibrated to include minorities too' (Meer, 2015: 2). While public opinion surveys have consistently shown that this more positive narrative on immigration does not necessarily translate into a more positive public attitude towards migrants, they also show that EU migrants are perceived more positively overall in Scotland as they also benefit from the pro-EU message coming from the political leadership. In this political context, EU citizens consider Scottish identity as being more inclusive than English identity, allowing EU citizens to feel both Scottish and European, while simultaneously embracing their own national identity (Sigona & Godin, 2019b). Building on Berg and Sigona's work on the 'diversity turn' in migration studies (Berg & Sigona, 2013), we argue that public narratives about Scotland being a 'multicultural nation' (El Fekih Said, 2018) have been re-appropriated by EU citizens to re-legitimize their presence in the UK. As we will discuss shortly, the possibility of feeling comfortable carrying multiple identities, without being forced into binary dilemmas also surfaces frequently among our London-based participants. In London, however, diversity is not only celebrated as a narrative or as a policy but is also a 'fact of life', as one of our interviewees stated. The global city, a node in the neoliberal global economic system produces unprecedented degrees of socio-demographic and cultural diversification; it is a 'living multi-culture (Neal, 2015; Back & Sinha, 2018) in which diversity is 'commonplace' (Wessendorf, 2013) shaping, we argue, the unique ways in which EU families are able to articulate their situated sense of belonging to the city, as well as embodying possibilities for articulating more open, supra- and post-national politics of belonging, such as EU citizenship.

Drawing on the interviews with London-based EU citizens, we will examine the Brexit politics of belonging in London, emplacing Brexit in the London milieu. By doing so, this chapter aims to provide a better understanding of the significance of London as a place of urban *citizenship* as well as a place where different notions of 'European citizenship' are produced. It shows how different projects of belonging as 'Europeans' as well as 'Londoners' not only can coexist confirming the importance of adopting a multi-scalar approach to belonging (Erdal, 2020), but are also enabled by the local condition of superdiversity (Vertovec, 2007). To achieve this, we take into consideration what happened before reaching the city of London, adopting a transnational lens (looking at the experiences prior to migration to the UK) in combination with an intersectional lens (capturing the influence of power, privilege, and social status).

8.1.2 Methodology

This chapter draws on sixty in-depth semi-structured interviews that were collected after the EU referendum from families living in London with members from over fourteen EU member states.[2] It includes families of mixed nationality and mixed ethnicity, those long-established and those more recently settled in the UK, and a variety of family configurations. Our typology of EU families includes five types (see Table 8.1). In order to be included in the study, a family had to include at least one child and one EU-born parent. To capture variations in family responses to the opportunities and challenges presented by Brexit, both from a legal and a personal perspective, we have included a range of family configurations. Parents' country of

Table 8.1 Five types of EU families

	Type of family	Count
Type 1	EU same	24
Type 2	EU-UK	20
Type 3	EU different	8
Type 4	EU single	2
Type 5	EU-TCN	6
	Total	60

[2] Born in France (8); Italy (9); UK (7); Romania (5); Germany (4), Slovakia (2), Greece (1), Ghana (1), Bulgaria (1); Hungary (1); Denmark (1); Belgium (1); Sweden (1), Slovenia (1), US (1) and Poland (1) (N = 45) (Eurochildren database).

origin is relevant in this regard since it affects the capacity of members to secure their legal status, and in terms of remigration and settlement options available.

The typology of family configurations aims to capture diversity in the nationality and country of birth of each parent in the families selected for interview. Type 1 refers to families in which both parents were born in the same EU country (EU-same), Type 2 refers to families where one parent is EU-born and the other is UK-born (EU-UK). These are the most prevalent groups in our sample. We then have 'EU families' composed of two parents born in different EU countries (EU-different, type 3). Type 4 refers to EU-born single parent families (EU-single, type 4). Type 5 consists of families with one EU-born parent and one third-country-national parent (EU-TCN) (see Table 8.1).

Among the families that participated in our study, there were families with children only born in the UK, only born elsewhere in the EU, and families with children born in both. Paying attention to the country of birth of children is relevant, not only because it has implications on their legal status and access to citizenship (Yeo, 2018a, b) but also because it affects family strategies for Brexit mitigation (Sigona & Godin, 2019a). Many of the children from the EU families we interviewed have dual citizenship (a British and an EU passport) which they either acquired through their parents' residency rights in the UK as EU citizens or because one parent is British by birth or was naturalised at the time of birth. To capture children's voices, we also interviewed EU citizens who were over 18 years old and living with their parents. This included those that were born in the UK or who had been born outside the UK but brought over by their parents as younger children. Lastly, to capture the voices of younger children, we put in place a participatory photo and audio project entitled "In the Shadow of Brexit"[3] offering a space for participants to articulate their voice and agency on this subject. The participatory photo project aimed to capture the diversity of the EU population in the city and to explore whether the way these people feel about the protracted uncertainty of the Brexit process depends upon where they live. Overall, 15 family-portraits were taken and audio-recordings were made at the beginning of the photo-shoot as well as during the session and were used as tools to elicit meanings and understandings of belonging. These short narratives mixing both children's and parents' voices explore the family's everyday life and plans for the future.

All interviews were conducted in English by researchers involved in the 'EU families and Eurochildren in Brexiting Britain' project. The recruitment process took place with the assistance of three grassroots organisations (i.e. The 3Millions,[4] Migrant Voice[5] and the Roma Support Group[6]). All the interviews were transcribed,

---

[3] The team for this participatory photo research project includes Crispin Hughes and Francesca Moore (photographers), Marie Godin (researcher) and Nando Sigona (PI Eurochildren project). More information can be found at: https://eurochildren.info/2019/11/05/in-the-shadow-of-brexit-launch-and-debate/

[4] https://www.the3million.org.uk/

[5] https://www.migrantvoice.org/

[6] https://www.romasupportgroup.org.uk/

and analysed using NVivo software with thematic coding applied across the entire dataset.

In the following section, we will discuss the empirical data, focusing on three articulations of the new politics of belonging stemming from the Brexit referendum. Firstly, we will examine the range of emotional responses to Brexit among EU citizens in London highlighting the role of social hierarchies and positionality in defining our participants' emotions, feelings and affects about Brexit. We then move the focus to the role of London as a city in our participants' narrative of Brexit and how the city offers opportunities and spaces for articulating ideas of new forms of belonging and citizenship. Finally, our attention moves to focus on the meaning of EU citizenship and its availability for EU citizens to make sense of their emotions.

8.1.3   Brexit, Emotions and the Intersectional Politics of Belonging

A sense of betrayal was one of the primary feelings expressed by EU mobile citizens living in London at the time of Brexit. Albert is in his fifties and identifies with three nationalities – French by his mother, Italian by his father and British because he was raised in the country. To him, London is the 'offshore capital of Europe, really multinational, really cosmopolitan, multicultural, multi- whatever you want', which has suddenly fallen apart. He feels very much like a Londoner and does not necessarily 'feel typically English, whatever that might mean'. He also acknowledges that, to his surprise, these nationalistic ways of identifying oneself are relevant to a lot of people, including those living in London, 'now even more than in the past', he adds. Apart from the practical effect that Brexit will have on his life and his children, the main change for him is the feeling he carries with him that the country and city he lives in are regressing. Since the referendum, his daily social interactions are defined by the Remain/Leave divide. However, while being critical about London, he also acknowledges that London as a city has not fallen enough in his esteem and other cities and countries in Europe have not risen enough for him to decide, 'Right, time to go'. Brexit has shaken but not destroyed Albert's attachment to the city.

For other EU families, the feeling of being betrayed led them to consider leaving the city. As this extract from an Italian-Venezuelan couple with one EU-born child indicates, Brexit produces inter- and intra- generational tensions that reverberate within the family.

> We woke up in a different country and it was a different situation. Even though London is different from the rest of the UK, but still. Within the couple, I'm the one for whom is easier to leave … Brexit only accelerated the desire to go and live somewhere else, but the rest are happy where they are.

While he had a strong desire to leave, he made it clear during the interview that the family will probably stay because of the strong sense of belonging to London that his child has and also for his wife, who is not from Italy and could not consider Naples as a city to return to; it is too 'provincial', he says reporting his wife words. Aspirations to return and leave the city of London, as a result of the Brexit referendum, are not necessarily shared by every member of a family, particularly in the case of mixed-status EU families.

This Finnish mother, married to an Italian, explained to us how her UK-born daughter changed from identifying as a Londoner to reclaiming her Italianness:

> Her identity changed very dramatically after Brexit. She is 14 now and since she was born she has been a London girl really through and through. I mean to the point that she misses London physically, she becomes physically sick for how much she misses London. After Brexit she has become Italian [...] She has changed her whole identity. She has felt so deeply rejected. Yes, she started to watch various BBC programmes about Italian food, Italian history, Italian art [...] she started to identify nationally as Italian for the first time ever [...] you know like previously she would be really insisting that she is not a foreigner and now she will say she is Italian.

In other EU families, men such as Thomas, who is a French Cameroonian father of two, are less enthusiastic about London and the UK more specifically. He says, 'if you are Black and immigrant, Brexit hasn't changed much [how you are treated'. His wife, Sonia, echoed his point, explaining, 'Because he is Black, and I'm white, Brexit doesn't feel the same'. However, they both agree that, for their children, Zoe and Leo, London is a better place to grow up than most cities in France. Similarly, a mother of two who is French-Hungarian and married to a dual citizen with French and Vietnamese citizenship also believes London is the best place for their children: 'Yes, I have to say that my husband is half Vietnamese, half French. And he also has this mixed identity which my children also have. At the moment, I still feel that London is one of the most tolerant cities in Europe.'[7] For all the mixed-race couples we interviewed, London is still a better and safer place for their children to grow up in. Its superdiversity offers a safer and more welcoming space than elsewhere in Europe for EU citizens from various social, cultural and ethnic backgrounds to meet, mobilise, and build relationships, including intimate ones.

8.1.4   Emplacing Brexit and Urban Citizenship

For many EU Londoners, the idea that everything has changed but at the same time nothing had changed was often mentioned:

> I don't think much will change for us. We've been here for 15 years, always living here, paying the taxes. We've got all the evidence, all the proof, and I have nothing to fear, to be honest. I'm relaxed but still, I mean, the feeling of living here changed. I mean, the perception of the country, the perception of the people in this country, how you fit within the society. As I said, London is one thing, the rest of England is quite another [Louise, from France, 39 years old, in London since 2001, UK-EU].

---

[7] Ana, French-Hungarian, 43 years old, in London since 2010.

Many described London as a world apart from the rest of the country. Some, half-jokingly, even advocated for an independent London that leaves the UK and remains in the EU. Looking at the percentages of votes for remain/leave, they identified even more with London as a place for Remainers, with a general feeling that people living in London – with the right to vote – had predominantly voted to remain. Jeremy, 24 years old, born in London to French parents, explains:

> we grew up with a lot of people that were European families – because we have the Eurostar and flying anywhere in Europe is so easy, we're in constant contact with Europeans. So, the general opinion for everyone was remain.

London is often framed as a bubble, a place of refuge, a place outside England. Marie is French Beninese, but also identifies as French, Beninese, British, European; most of all, she feels like a Londoner, she says. Married to British-born Paddy, she says: 'In London, diversity is a fact of life, and everyone can thrive to live comfortably in their own skin.' In France, she felt that there was still a stigma attached to being different, and more specifically to being Black. After she felt discriminated against when looking for jobs as a young professional, she decided to go to the UK. She felt that London was a place where she could be herself, where she did not have to be 'so self-conscious about being Black and where everyone seemed to be accepted for the way they were'. Friends at home kept asking her when she would return but, so far, she sees no reason for doing so, 'I love the open-mindedness that England had and I still feel like we are a long way from that in France, especially open-mindedness in terms of origin'. Regarding Brexit, she admits that it felt like 'a slap in the face'. She also realised that the open-mindedness that she loved so much about England was actually more of 'a London way of looking at things'. However, both she and her husband are still very confident that London is the best place to continue raising their mixed-race children. They agree that, in the city, 'the population is what it is, unless all the multicultural people disappear … London is such a mixed place'. As Marie says of her children's classes, 'everyone is so different, they don't know any other way', while her husband adds, 'it is amazing to see so much diversity in the next generation'.

Despite shared concerns surrounding the disruptive impact of Brexit and the uncertainty surrounding the future, for mixed-race families there is also an awareness that life may not be easy for them elsewhere in Europe, where immigrants, and ethnic and religious minorities, experience frequent discrimination and are the target of xenophobic and racist political movements. This shows the importance of considering the social location of EU families and the ways in which they have experienced Brexit as an 'unsettling event' (Kilkey & Ryan, 2021) but also in terms of the impact it has had on their lives and the ways in which they had to re-articulate their sense of belonging (or non-belonging) to the city, to the UK and in regard to the European project (as described hereafter).

For Mihai, a Roma activist from Romania, this is clear: 'Despite things getting worse in the UK as a result of Brexit, London is still one of the best places in Europe for a Roma to live.' Considering the wave of anti-immigration politics spreading across Europe (Godin & Sigona, 2022) and the discrimination that Roma people still suffer in Romania, raising his children in the city of London is still the most secure place for them to grow up. All these narratives about London reveal how EU citizens have developed a strong sense of "city-senship" to the city of London. Describing her idea of what a *true* Londoner is, Martine – who has lived in London for over twenty years – explains:

> I think it is someone who is quite open, someone mobile, someone happy to meet people from any kind of other horizons, any religions, any backgrounds. And I think London has shown that it is like the mayor would say it is an open place [...] the diversity makes it so interesting. It is very cosmopolitan and the arts, I mean there are so many things [...] So for me London is everything. But I don't feel English, I don't feel British. I feel like a Londoner. [Martine, from France, 42 years old, in London since 2000].

The sense of disconnect from the rest of the country is produced also from the realisation that most neighbours are likely to be originally from somewhere else in the world and therefore not responsible for the Brexit vote.

> Where I live in London and especially in our block of flats it is like 70 different flats and most of us are foreigners to be honest, both from EU countries and from outside of Europe so I don't feel the immediate impact on my life. Which would certainly be different if I moved somewhere to a British community.' [Yvonne, from Germany, 39 years old, in London since 2007].

London is often not only constructed in juxtaposition to the rest of England, but also to some extent to Europe. It is its unique position as global, open and superdiverse city that makes it a point of reference for European youth.

> I've never been anywhere else outside of London, I always live in London. You will feel a massive difference between London and the rest of the UK. Philip and I always say, if we come out of London, we wouldn't be able to live on the other side [...] London is not England'. (Isabel, born in the UK, French citizen, 40 years old).

Comparing her sense of belonging to London to how it feels to go back to France, she continues, saying:

> There is a sense of in common there, I don't know what it is, it's a shared history or.... feel like a younger generation in Europe is quite similar in the way that they think, they come to London because London is so different, they come to London because London is original. London is...the island here in the UK.

8.1.5 *'In London, I am a European Citizen': EU Citizenship and the Nested Politics of Belonging*

Among the EU citizens that we interviewed, many from 'old' member states described themselves as Europeans first and foremost, before defining themselves as a national of an EU member state. The following extract from a French woman in her fifties living in London is particularly evocative of this approach:

> Yeah, in London I'm a European citizen. Yes, I am French, but I'm here, and I've been allowed to live in this country because of the European Union. So, I feel like, yeah, we are

European, it's what we've got in common, all of us in London – most of us I mean. Got a large number of Italian, Spanish, German, Dutch, Belgian – we know people of every single nationality. [Anne-Laure, from France, 50 years old, in London since 2004, Type 2, EU-UK, one child born in the EU, one in the UK].

London's diversity and its connections with the rest of Europe are often referred to as what makes the city unique. This quote and the next show that being European is not just about making use of the right to freedom of movement; it is also about how this right translates pragmatically in real life, creating a strong sense of European belongingness through the city of London especially after the referendum:

So far I kept a very good balance because I was able to spend part of the time in France, part of the time in Italy and part of the time in England so I never really felt I missed anything. And I do feel very good in London because it is very multicultural so probably out of everything, London I feel like is more like home. [Susanna, Italian, single mum, mother of two London-born children and one born in Italy).

Local urban embeddedness can be combined with a solid sense of transnational belonging, making the city of London a 'European anchor' that has allowed EU citizens to conduct a transnational life and maintain over time a sense of multi-embeddedness in different places and across generations. London, as a city, took an active role in welcoming European citizens from diverse transnational contexts. Transnational practices across the continent and the UK have, in many ways, contributed to a growing sense of what it is to be European and transnational, while at the same developing a strong attachment to the city where you live. As an example, a Polish family with both parents born in Poland and with their two UK-born children explained to us what it means to be European in a city like London:

If you meet other parents, there are French parents, Bulgarian parents, Romanian parents or German or Spanish parents, it brings us closer together because when you do talk about Britain *versus* the rest of the Europe, we are all in the pot of sort of [we are all unwanted here]...in a sense it creates a bond, a stronger bond with them, because we have this subject to talk about... they are like us, they want to stop Brexit, they want to remain as well and it would be sort of hypocrite if I thought otherwise. So that is what is happening so in a sense, it is bringing us together, yes, and this why we believe we made a home here in London in Great Britain because of those friendships, the bonds that we have with all the Europeans with European nationalities basically including Great Britain. It is only when Brexit come on the table, then when the referendum started and after, that I think we felt a little bit sad and less welcome. [Polish dad, from Poland, in London since 2004, type 1, EU-same, two UK-born children].

Sharing with us how they are raising their kids, they explain how they are preparing them for the eventuality that they will one day move out of the UK. To be 'European' is to be mobile and to achieve this; to master more than one European language is an asset. Teaching French as well as Polish to their children, this is what they tell us about the future of their kids:

It will give them more opportunities for their future wherever they decide to be. They are citizens of Europe so to speak. I think it is great that we can move without frontiers and limits, it is a great thing, we feel like European... free movement we really embraced it.

This extract reveals the importance of 'mobility capital' to EU parents. Mobility capital as put forward by Moret (2020) is a factor for social differentiation. Acquired via socialisation and experiences, it 'can be transmitted from generation to generation and necessitates investment in terms of time and economic capital'.

The outcome of the Brexit referendum in some cases has made attachment to the European identity stronger, sometimes alongside a rejection of Britishness including London as a city. The story of this Italian mother recalling how it felt after the referendum exemplifies this point:

> …that morning I was taking the kids to school and being consoled by all the well-meaning British middle class parents and I remember thinking, do you realise what it means for you? You are no longer Europeans? but yes actually that reaction and that dilemma, this gut feeling that although the fact that I was getting a lot of sympathy was not making it any better because the same people that were giving me sympathy were the same people that had not been able to not let this happen. Including Londoners and London as a whole. I don't take much solace in the fact that London is different.[…] because London first of all is where Britishness is born and is bred in some ways' [Clara, from Italy, 47 years old, in London since 1997, EU same].

For others, their country of origin was not even part of the EU when they migrated to the UK. Having lived in London led to progressively developing a sense of European identity, which was not necessarily present before leaving their country of origin. This shows how Europeanness as an identity can also emerge over time. This is the case of many interviews we conducted with Roma people in London. This Roma father arrived with his parents in 1994 at the age of three from Romania. When asked whether he feels European, he replied, 'Sometimes when I go to work and people think, oh, you are South American most likely or Mexican or whatever, and I say, no, I'm European. When I say that, I say it like I'm proud of it for some reason, I'm not saying South American – it's not a bad place, but I'm happier about it saying that I'm European for some reason.'

He recalls saying it before the referendum, and this was mainly due to the fact that England was part of the EU. However, if the question comes up again, he does not know yet what he will say:

> I wouldn't know what it's going to be like saying it, you know. Depends on the circumstances I suppose, if England has a thing against it or not, because they were part of it (Mirku, from Romania, 27 years old, lived in London since 1994).

This quote indicates a shift in the politics of belonging in the context of the Brexit referendum and post-Brexit Britain and how some of the discourses about who belongs and who does not belong to the nation have situated people differently. It also shows, as argued by Tuuli Lähdesmäki et al. (2021), how the 'notions of "Europe" and what it is to be and feel "European" is fluid, changing and contextual.

The change in the politics of belonging in the UK and in the city of London, of who belongs and who does not, and the dialectics of "us" versus "them" have created different kinds of uncertainties for EU citizens as well as different ways to reposition oneself and the "EU family" in terms of their sense of belonging to the city and/or a nation. It also reveals something about the borders of Europe and its polity as, for a long time, citizens of old member states were offered as an example of the

Europeanness of the city. As a result, for some EU citizens from Central and Eastern Europe, the label "European" was not available to them for a long time and did not resonate entirely with their own experience, leading to a volatile sense of belonging to a European imagined community. Therefore, the experience of Brexit for EU families has not been a homogeneous one, with some having been more affected than others by the uncertainties that surrounded the protracted negotiations. Their sense of belonging and their responses have been substantially shaped by social status, sense of entitlement and self-worth, as well as for many their long-lasting experiences of EU citizens that were already 'migrantized' before the event of Brexit (see Anderson, 2019). In other cases, as the story of Marie illustrates, living in the UK – in particular, London – has been the only way for her to become truly 'European' leading to a more grounded sense of belonging to an imagined EU community.

At the end of our interview, Marie, a black EU citizen, reflects on the reactions of 'Europeans' – referring to white EU citizens from Western EU countries – to being rejected, as it is something that "they" have been doing to so many countries that are not part of Europe, and African countries in particular. Selective immigration is not something that has ever been imposed upon these Europeans. For the first time in their lives, "they" (as she recalls) are being rejected, being told that they are not so welcome anymore and experiencing what migrants from poorer countries have been experiencing for so long. As Marie says, 'they are now living what it feels – a little bit though – to being rejected just because you are now someone else's "other"'. This also indicates that Marie has experienced racism in her life, especially as living in France as a Black woman has forced her to move to the UK, and London in particular, to finally be herself: a French Beninese, a Londoner and a European. It is through her experience of moving from London to France that she could finally experience her 'Europeanness' in addition, and not in opposition, to her African/Beninese identity. As she says,

> I feel like a citizen of the world and this all idea is to me thanks to the EU having taken off barriers, making it possible to decide wherever I want to live in Europe, and this is almost magical, this is amazing [...] what we eat, the all diversity is very much influenced by that, we don't realise it because it has become an everyday thing.

8.1.6 Conclusion: London's Unique Position as the Hub of the Largest EU 'Diaspora' Outside the EU

Through an intersectional and situated perspective, this chapter captures the emergence of a new politics of belonging, which reconfigures discursively and legally who belongs to a post-EU Britain from the perspective of EU families living in the city of London. The geopolitical earthquake produced by Brexit and its aftershocks shook the foundations on which generations of EU citizens have built their lives and their sense of belonging in the UK and London, forcing them to reconsider their migration projects and how they present themselves to others. London's unique position as a global hub of neoliberal globalisation and a former Empire capital produced the conditions for unparalleled socio-demographic diversification that enabled the formation of a more open, progressive and liberal idea of "Europe", yet we have revealed how this very identity has been denied to some, particularly racialised communities and Central and Eastern Europeans (Zorko & Debnár, 2021). London is a unique, yet fragile, laboratory of a possible "Europolitanism", a pan-European and post-national sense of belonging including different diaspora points nested in the formation of an 'imagined EU diaspora' (Vathi & Trandafoiu, 2022). Our analysis casts light on the significance of positionality, scale and place-based attachments in people's perceptions and understanding of the new politics of belonging at a time of rapid and turbulent political transformation. It shows how London in acting as an enabler of a multi-scalar and more open articulation of both a different sense of belonging (and non-belonging) to the city and to Europe.

Acknowledgments Authors would like to thank the anonymous reviewers for their valuable comments on the manuscript and Dr Laurence Lessard-Phillips, and Dr RachelHumphris, Migrant Voice and The 3 Million for their contribution to data collection.

References

Anderson, B. (2019). New directions in migration studies: Towards methodological de-nationalism. *Comparative Migration Studies, 7*(36). https://comparativemigrationstudies.springeropen.com/articles/10.1186/s40878-019-0140-8.

Anthias, F. (2002). Where do I belong?: Narrating collective identity and translocational positionality. *Ethnicities, 2*(4), 491–514.

Back, L., & Sinha, S. (2018). *Migrant City*. Routledge.

Benson, M. (2020). Brexit and the classed politics of bordering: The British in France and European belongings. *Sociology, 54*(3), 501–517.

Berg, M. L., & Sigona, N. (2013). Introduction: Ethnography, diversity and urban space. *Identities: Global Studies in Culture and Power, 20*(4), 347–360.

Botterill, K., McCollum, D., & Tyrrell, N. (2019). Negotiating Brexit: Migrant spatialities and identities in a changing Europe. *Population, Place and Space, Special Issue: Negotiating Brexit: Migrant spatialities and identities in a changing Europe 25:*e2216

D'Angelo, A., & Kofman, E. (2018). From Mobile workers to fellow citizens and Back again? The Future Status of EU Citizens in the UK. *Social Policy & Society, 17*(2), 331–343.

Doležalová, M., Barbulescu, R., Mirza, N., & Bica, M. (2021). *Closure of EU settlement scheme risks leaving migrant Roma behind'. Report. Policy Leeds*. University of Leeds.

El Fekih Said, W. (2018). Reconstruction and multiculturalism in the Scottish nation-building project. *Études écossaises, 20*. https://journals.openedition.org/etudesecossaises/1418.

Erdal, M. B. (2020). Theorizing interactions of migrant transnationalism and integration through a multiscalar approach. *Comparative Migration Studies, 8*, 31.

Erel, U., & Ryan, L. (2019). Migrant capitals: Proposing a multi-level Spatio-temporal analytical framework. *Sociology, 53*(2), 246–263.

Favell, A. (1999). To belong or not to belong: The post-national question. In A. Geddes & A. Favell (Eds.), *The politics of belonging: Migrants and minorities in contemporary Europe* (pp. 209–227). Taylor and Franci.

Godin, M., & Bica. M. C. (2019). It took 2 hours and one third Didn't get through": Piloting the settled status application with Roma migrants. Eurochildren website. https://eurochildren. info/2019/01/21/it-took-2-hours-and-one-third-didnt-get-through-piloting-the-settled-status-application-with-roma-migrants/

Godin, M., & Sigona, N. (2022). Intergenerational narratives of citizenship among EU citizens in the UK after the Brexit referendum. *Ethnic and Racial Studies*. Special Issue: Good Citizens, Permitted Outsiders - Conditional Inclusion and Citizenship in Comparison, *45*(2), 1–21.

Guma, T., & Dafydd Jones, R. (2019). Where are we going to go now? European Union migrants' experiences of hostility, anxiety, and (non-)belonging during Brexit. *Population, Space and Place*, Special Issue: Negotiating Brexit: Migrant spatialities and identities in a changing Europe, *25*:e2198

Jablonowski, K., & Pinkowska, P. (2021). Vulnerability in the EU Settlement Scheme: looking back, going forward. A review of evidence from Law Centres' casework. Available at https://www.lawcentres.org.uk/policy/news/news/better-support-for-vulnerable-people-needed-in-eu-settlement-scheme-new-report

Johnston, R., Manley, D., Pattie, C., & Jonesa, K. (2018). Geographies of Brexit and its aftermath: Voting in England at the 2016 referendum and the 2017 general election. *Space and Polity, 22*(2), 162–187.

Kilkey, M., & Ryan, L. (2021). Unsettling Events: Understanding migrants' responses to geopolitical transformative episodes through a life-course lens. *International Migration Review, 55*(1), 227–253.

Lähdesmäki, T., Mäkinen, K., Čeginskas, V. L. A., & Kaasik-Krogerus, S. (2021). *Europe from below: Notions of Europe and the European among participants in EU cultural initiatives* (European studies, Vol. 38). Brill.

Lessard-Phillips, L., & Sigona, N. (2018). *Mapping EU citizens in the UK: A changing profile? From 1980s to the EU referendum.* Eurochildren Research Brief Series, no.3.

Lessard-Phillips, L., & Sigona, N. (2019). *UK-born Children of EU Nationals in the UK.* Eurochildren Research Brief Series, no. 5.

Lulle, A., King, R., Dvorakova, V., & Szkudlarek, A. (2019). Between disruptions and connections: "New" European Union migrants in the United Kingdom before and after the Brexit *Population Space and Place*, Special Issue: Negotiating Brexit: Migrant spatialities and identities in a changing Europe, *25*:e2200

Mc Ghee, D., Moreh, C., & Vlachantoni, A. (2017). An 'undeliberate determinacy'? The changing migration strategies of Polish migrants in the UK in times of Brexit. *Journal of Ethnic and Migration Studies, 43*(13), 2109–2130.

Meer, N. (2015). Looking up in Scotland? Multinationalism, multiculturalism and political elites. *Ethnic and Racial Studies, 38*(9), 1477–1496.

Moret, J. (2020). Mobility capital: Somali migrants' trajectories of (im)mobilities and the negotiation of social inequalities across borders. *Geoforum, 116*, 235–242. https://doi.org/10.1016/j.geoforum.2017.12.002

Neal, S. (2015). *Living multiculture: The new geographies of ethnic diversity and the changing formations of multiculture in England. [data collection].* UK Data Archive. https://doi.org/10.5255/UKDA-SN-851852

ONS. (2021). Births by parents' country of birth, England and Wales: 2020. Annual statistics on live births including countries of birth for non-UK-born mothers and fathers. https://www.ons.gov.uk/peoplepopulationandcommunity/birthsdeathsandmarriages/livebirths/bulletins/parentscountryofbirthenglandandwales/2020

Sigona, N., & Godin, M. (2019a). Naturalisation and (dis)integration Eurochildren Brief Series, no. 6.

Sigona, N., & Godin, M. (2019b). EU families feel more welcome in Scotland than they do in the rest of the UK, LSE blog, https://blogs.lse.ac.uk/europpblog/2019/10/10/eu-families-feel-more-welcome-in-scotland-than-they-do-in-the-rest-of-the-uk/

Sotkasiira, T., & Gawlewicz, A. (2021). The politics of embedding and the right to remain in post-Brexit Britain. *Ethnicities, 21*(1), 23–41.

Sumption, M., & Fernández-Reino, M. (2020). Unsettled status – 2020: Which EU citizens are at risk of failing to secure their rights after Brexit?, *The Migration Observatory*, https://migrationobservatory.ox.ac.uk/resources/reports/unsettled-status-2020/

Vathi, Z., & Trandafoiu, R. (2022). A post-national EU diaspora? Political mobilization of EU citizens in the UK post-Brexit. *Global Networks*. https://doi.org/10.1111/glob.12373

Vertovec, S. (2007). Super-diversity and its implications. New Directions in the Anthropology of Migration and Multiculturalism. *Ethnic and Racial Studies, 30*(6), 1024–1054.

Wessendorf, S. (2013). Commonplace diversity and the 'ethos of mixing': Perceptions of difference in a London neighbourhood. *Identities: Global Studies in Culture and Power, 20*(4), 407–422.

Yeo, C. (2018a). The impact of the UK-EU agreement on citizenship rights for EU families., Eurochildren Research Brief Series, no. 2. https://eurochildren.info/publications/

Yeo, C. (2018b). The impact of the UK-EU agreement on residence rights for EU families., Eurochildren Research Brief Series, no. 1. https://eurochildren.info/publications/

Yuval-Davis, N. (2006). Belonging and the politics of belonging. *Patterns of Prejudice, 40*(3), 197–214.

Yuval-Davis, N. (2011). *The politics of belonging*. Sage Publications Ltd.

Yuval-Davis, N., Wemyss, G., & Cassidy, K. (2018). Everyday bordering, Belonging and the Reorientation of British Immigration Legislation. *Sociology, 52*(2), 228–224.

Zorko, Š. D., & Debnár, M. (2021). Comparing the racialization of central-east European migrants in Japan and the UK. *Comparative Migration Studies, 9*, 30.

Part III
Integration from Above

Chapter 9
"It Just Feels Weird" – Irish External Voting and the 'Brexit Irish'

Vikki Barry Brown

9.1 Introduction

Ireland is a country with a generous citizenship offering but restricted external voting rights. The first (or emigrant) generation lose the right to vote eighteen months
after departure; other non-resident citizens, including those in Northern Ireland (NI)
are currently ineligible to vote. In November 2020 the Irish Government committed
to holding a referendum which if passed, would give all Irish citizens, resident and
non-resident the right to vote in Presidential elections.

Irish citizens living in Britain and NI have come under the spotlight since 2016
following the United Kingdom's (UK) decision to leave the European Union (EU).
Colonialism, historical migratory patterns and the Good Friday Agreement have
meant a great number of UK-born people have eligibility for Irish citizenship which
many enacted in what has been perceived to be a post-Brexit rush to retain European
citizenship. Whilst assertions have been made as to the motivations of this population, who I term the 'Brexit Irish', my research and that of others has demonstrated
a myriad of reasons as to why people have felt compelled to obtain Irish citizenship
post-Brexit. Given the forthcoming referendum in Ireland, the 'Brexit Irish' may
soon be able to vote in Irish Presidential elections – but do they want or feel entitled
to this right?

I will begin this chapter with an overview of external voting, briefly engaging
with arguments for and against the practice which I will then explore further in the
context of Ireland, recounting political and campaigning milestones. Following this,
I introduce the 'Brexit Irish' through engagement with relevant literature and an
overview of the wider research project from which my data arises. I will then
consider responses from participants on the subject of Irish external voting.

V. Barry Brown (✉)
Leverhulme Trust Doctoral Scholar, School of Geography, Queen Mary,
University of London, London, UK

© The Author(s) 2023
R. Barbulescu et al. (eds.), *Revising the Integration-Citizenship Nexus
in Europe*, IMISCOE Research Series, https://doi.org/10.1007/978-3-031-25726-1_9

The respondents almost overwhelmingly communicated an unwillingness to participate in Irish elections, which I conclude may demonstrate a lack of connection between Ireland and non-resident Irish citizens, in particular those in NI and beyond the emigrant generation.

9.2 External Voting

The right to vote is generally accepted as one of the key aspects of democratic citizenship, however this right has often had conditions attached on the basis of residency (Honohan, 2011). Since the late nineteenth century, countries across the world have permitted external voting for citizens outside of their usual national territory, albeit for small and specific subsets of the population (Lafleur, 2015). Those awarded such rights tended to be military or diplomatic workers stationed outside of the national territory and in some cases, votes were granted to seafarers (Lafleur, 2015). This practice has changed over time, as countries have – particularly since the 1990s – increasingly removed voting restrictions on external citizens (Spiro, 2006; Lafleur, 2015). By 2013 it was estimated that 129 countries allowed external voting of some iteration; in the same year just three of the 47 Council of European states did not permit external votes (or restricted it only to those abroad on an official capacity) (Lappin, 2016).

Approaches to and provision of external voting systems vary across the world (Lafleur, 2015). In Canada, Australia and the UK, prior residency is a requirement, with the right to vote permitted only for a set time after leaving (O'Neill, 2019). Amongst the EU 27, 22 countries do not have residency requirements, nor do they set time limits following departure (O'Neill, 2019). Under the EU, member states are tasked with establishing their own national voting rights, however The European Commission (EC) has issued guidance strongly suggesting that states who do not provide external voting take action 'so that citizens can get back on the electoral role of their home country' (European Commission, 2014). This is considered particularly important by the EC as whilst EU citizenship provides EU citizens residing in another EU country *'the rights to vote and stand as candidates in Local and European elections in their EU country of residence'* (European Union, 2020), they are not permitted to take part in national elections unless they acquire citizenship of that country. The process of meeting residency and other stipulations in order to achieve citizenship in some EU countries may take in excess of ten years. Therefore, an individual moving from a state which does not permit external voting could result in the individual being disenfranchised from national voting for a number of years.

There are many arguments for and against the provision of voting rights for citizens living abroad. Common factors held up as cautionary points include (but are not limited to): whether or not those who are not subject to the politics and laws of a country should have a voice after leaving (López-Guerra, 2005); if those with 'tenuous connections' to a country can make an informed vote (Green, 2007:94) if people should be entitled to representation without taxation (Hickman, 2016) and that large external voting populations may 'swamp' a 'home' electorate (Honohan, 2011). It has been suggested that ruling parties who may consider an external voting population as opponents to their electoral interests might choose to deny non-resident voting rights in order to protect their position (Spiro, 2006). Conversely, an incumbent party may perceive the introduction of extraterritorial votes as assistive to their remaining in power and proceed to extend the franchise.

Those in support of external voting may counter: that modern interconnectivity provides sufficient opportunities for external engagement with a 'home' country (European Commission, 2014) and that external enfranchisement may encourage life-long links or even the return migration to their country of origin (Honohan, 2011). Equally, counterpoints to concerns over 'swamping' of 'home' votes can include: that interest in home affairs can wane across time and generations (Fitzgerald, 2006); that emigrant voting globally tends to draw a consistently low turnout rate (Hutcheson & Arrighi, 2015); and that the creation of dedicated external vote constituencies can channel the impact of large external electorates (O'Neill, 2019).

9.3   The Irish Context

9.3.1   Emigration and Diaspora

The question of non-resident citizenship and voting is particularly pertinent to the Republic of Ireland (ROI) which has a lengthy history of emigration. Across the nineteenth and twentieth centuries thousands in each generation of Irish people emigrated, fleeing 'poverty and social repression to seek work and new lives abroad' (Crowley et al., 2006). Irish emigration has continued into the twenty-first century, particularly following the 2007 collapse of the 'Celtic Tiger' economy (Ryan & Kurdi, 2015); a quarter of a million Irish citizens departed Ireland between 2008 and 2014 with more than 70 per cent of this cohort in their twenties when they left (O'Neill, 2019). According to the Department for Foreign Affairs (DfA), it is thought that worldwide up to 70 million people claim Irish ancestry (DfA, 2015:10). Irish citizenship can be claimed down to the third generation and an estimated 3.8 million citizens live outside Ireland - up to half of this number reside in NI (Hickman, 2020). Ireland, in line with other countries has since the 1990s increasingly recognised benefits associated with diaspora engagement (Devlin Trew, 2018) however these efforts have received some criticism, accused of being overly concerned with the extraction of money or capital from the Irish abroad (Boyle & Kavanagh, 2018; Hickman, 2020). In response, the Irish Government has increasingly acknowledged the diaspora as both 'an asset and a responsibility', with a recognizable broadening of strategies including the funding of projects that support welfare, advocacy and connectivity amongst the Irish abroad (Boyle & Kavanagh, 2018:68). Nevertheless, a notable absence within these strategies is the provision of external voting for citizens abroad (Devlin Trew, 2018; Hickman, 2020).

9.3.2 Irish External Votes – Policy & Campaigning

At the time of writing (May 2022), Irish emigrants retain the right to vote in Irish elections for just 18 months after leaving, and in order to enact this entitlement they must return to vote in-person (Mackle, 2018). Returning to Ireland and voting in an election after the 18-month period is classed as a criminal offence (O'Neill, 2019). There are some exceptions to these rules. Firstly, diplomatic staff and military personnel posted abroad can vote in all elections by postal ballot (Honohan, 2011). Secondly, graduates of the National University of Ireland and Trinity College Dublin cast votes in Seanad Éireann (the Upper House) elections to elect six Senators, this is enacted by postal vote, papers are sent to the voter wherever they live, globally (National University of Ireland, 2020). As Conor O'Neill points out, this means that a proportion of Irish citizens have the ability to vote in Irish elections from outside of the ROI 'simply by registering a foreign address with the relevant university and returning their ballot by post' (O'Neill, 2019:109).

Non-resident voting for Irish citizens has arisen a number of times with increasing regularity since the early 1990s (Honohan, 2011) with lobby groups founded from the late 1980s onward – Glór an Deorai in Britain, Irish Votes Abroad in Australia and the Irish Emigrant Vote Campaign in the USA (Hickman, 2016). In 1991 Glór an Deorai published a policy document calling for an extension of voting rights to emigrants for up to twenty years after leaving Ireland, this was followed by a private member's bill instigated by the then Labour spokesman on emigration Gerry O'Sullivan TD (Glynn et al., 2013; Hickman, 2016). The bill was marginally defeated by four votes (Honohan, 2011: Hickman, 2016; O'Neill, 2019). Just before Christmas the same year, the Irish Emigrant Vote Campaign chartered a plane from New York to Dublin using the flight as 'a combination symbol of return and faith', to demonstrate their strength of feeling toward securing external voting (Mulkerns, 1991). A plan to have three dedicated seats in the Seanad to represent the emigrant population was proposed during the mid-1990s (Honohan, 2011), however as campaign groups had tended to focus on Dáil (lower house) representation and a voice in Presidential elections, this proposal was 'generally seen as a red herring' (Glynn et al., 2013).

Arguments against giving Irish emigrants the vote during the 1990s centred mainly around two points, both of which have been roundly discredited by Mary Hickman. The first – that constitutional issues prevented the extension of the franchise is, according to Hickman a misnomer, because the Irish constitution does not contain any clause that disbars Irish citizens abroad from voting in national elections, instead a legislation change would be required (Hickman, 2016). The second was the suggestion that there should be no representation without taxation, which Hickman describes as a diversionary argument of little substance, pointing to other countries who allow non-resident voting (Hickman, 2016:15). Linking financial contributions and political rights is provocative, unsettling the idea that differing social statuses should not affect the rights and obligations of citizens (Lappin, 2016). Contribution models, according to Iseult Honohan can be 'under-inclusive in defining the demos', excluding those who for reasons such as age or health are unable to contribute (Honohan, 2011: 547).

In 1997 Fianna Fáil's election manifesto pledged to introduce external voting by 2000, yet despite the party winning the election, the promise did not materialise (Hickman, 2016). 2002 saw a report of the Oireachtas All-Party Committee on the Constitution recommend that only resident citizens should have the right to vote in the Dáil elections (Honohan, 2011), advising that the Taoiseach designate a senator(s) who 'can cater for groups such as our emigrants' (Government of Ireland, 2002). Designating a dedicated constituency or representative is a way in which other countries have dealt with the possibility of large emigrant votes 'swamping' an election (Honohan, 2011). This may have been on the mind of the Irish Government when in 2009 they proposed an Electoral Commission to investigate feasibility into external voting in Presidential elections (Honohan, 2011).

2011 saw the establishment of VICA (Votes for Irish Citizens Abroad), a London-based group who campaign for Irish citizens to have the right to vote in elections and referendums in Ireland (VICA, 2020a; b). In 2013 the issue of external voting in Presidential elections was referred by the Government to the Convention on the Constitution, who balloted in favour of the move (O'Neill, 2019). The Convention voted separately on 'citizens outside the state' and 'citizens resident in NI' with the 'yes' votes coming in for both at 78 per cent and 73 per cent respectively, additionally the Convention signalled votes be open to all citizens, not just those with prior residency (Convention of the Constitution, 2013).

During 2015, the government published *Global Irish: Ireland's Diaspora Policy* in which it acknowledged campaigning groups on the issue of voting and the importance of external voting to non-resident Irish citizens (Hickman, 2016). The document took a cautious approach, stating that the introduction of external voting would be 'challenging to introduce and to manage' commenting that the Government had asked for further analysis to take place (DfA, 2015: 21). A year later, the first Irish emigrant to be appointed to the Senate took his seat, Chicago-based Billy Lawless (Kenny, 2016). A passionate advocate and campaigner for the Irish abroad, Lawless is also a co-founder of the international coalition of Irish emigrant voting rights organisations, VotingRights.ie. (Kenny, 2016).

Two oft-cited arguments against extending votes to citizens abroad are that those who are not subject to the laws and political decisions of a country should not have a say in elections and that those who have migrated are unable to maintain a significant interest, connection and understanding of the country they left. These arguments came to the fore in Ireland during 2015 and 2018 with the Marriage Equality and Repeal the 8th Referendums. Prior to the Marriage Equality Referendum, the Twitter hashtag #HomeToVote was recorded 72,000 times in 24 hours as Irish emigrants from across the world made their way to Ireland to cast their vote (Mackle, 2018). Those unable to vote joined in with social media posts, with some posting online about calling family in Ireland, encouraging them to vote 'Yes' (Fottrell, 2015; Mackle, 2018). Danielle Mackle describes this as the diaspora mobilising 'to make their voices heard in the hope of creating a more open and tolerant society at home to which they may someday return' (Mackle, 2018:119). Similar scenes could be witnessed around Repeal the 8th; post-referendum media spoke of emigrants motivated to return to vote, many of whom expressed a desire to make change in an Ireland they hoped to return to in the future (Ryan, 2018,Kenny, 2018: O'Neill, 2018). Return migration is sometimes viewed as the pinnacle of the diasporic dream (Ní Laoire, 2008) and in 2012 research into the lives of recent Irish emigrants found that 72 per cent indicated 'a high intention to return' (Devlin Trew, 2018). A year later University College Cork's Emigre project reported their respondents (recent emigrants) felt that those who intended to return should have an input in Irish elections (Glynn et al., 2013). The Emigre team recounted that only a minority of interviewees didn't view losing their right to vote on exit as a major issue (Ibid, 2013). The Irish Government has expressed great interest in encouraging the return of emigrants, stating in 2015 an intention to attract 70,000 people back to Ireland by 2020 (Devlin Trew, 2018).

Between 2017 and 2019 the Irish Government announced intentions to hold a referendum on external voting in Presidential elections, however these plans have been repeatedly postponed due to the impact of the prolonged Brexit process (Carswell, 2017; Carswell, 2020).

In November 2020, the Irish Government launched *'Global Ireland: Ireland's Diaspora Strategy 2020 – 2025'* in which they committed to holding a referendum on voting rights in Presidential elections for external citizens (DfA, 2020a; b). The document claimed that 'Greater engagement of our citizens outside of the State in our democracy will strengthen the connection between the diaspora and Ireland' and set intentions to 'sustain and renew a meaningful connection' with the Irish diaspora (DfA, 2020a, b). VICA welcomed the strategy and the planned referendum, writing in their November 2020 campaign newsletter 'The president represents the entire Irish nation, and all citizens should be invested in their election.' (VICA, 2020a; b).

In recent years, as intentions to hold a referendum on Presidential elections for non-resident citizens have been announced, Irish media outlets have provided comment and content on the subject. With an apparent lack of 'bottom up' academic research on external voting for Irish citizens in NI and Irish citizens beyond the emigrant generation, Irish media has in its stead delivered podcasts on the topic (see in particular 'The Irish Passport Podcast': Mc Inerney & O'Leary, 2019) as well as articles and reports (see for example: Carswell, 2017; Gilligan, 2019; O'Riordan, 2019; Spillane, 2020). Articles featuring 'vox pops' from resident and non-resident citizens often cite the arguments for and against external voting already discussed in this chapter, in addition to more specific concerns such as anxieties about the potential influence of "nostalgic" and "conservative" Irish Americans having a vote (O'Riordan, 2019).

9.4   Brexit; Irish Citizens in the UK and NI

There are approximately 1.9 million Irish citizens resident in NI and an estimated 412,658 ROI-born people living in the UK (Hickman, 2020). The DfA takes a maximalist approach (based upon people in NI having the right to be British, Irish or both) in estimating that there are in the region of 356,589 people in Britain who are the children of people born in the ROI or NI (DfA, 2017a; b; c).

In the aftermath of the 2016 'Brexit' referendum, many British citizens rushed to find ways to retain access to EU rights, with some newspapers publishing articles advising how UK-born people might access a passport from an EU state (Wood & Gilmartin, 2018). In response to a reported rise in British citizens seeking advice on emigration immediately following Brexit, publications also ran articles informing readers of 'politically progressive' countries that they could move to, with the New Statesman including Ireland as part of its '7 of the best' (Rampen, 2016). It wasn't long before applications for Irish citizenship and passports began to rise. Less than two months after the referendum The Telegraph reported a 70 per cent surge in Irish passport applications by British people, and a 63 per cent increase in applications from NI (Harley, 2016). Figures in the UK media varied and conflicted, but in January 2017 the DfA stated that 2016 NI applications saw a 26.5 per cent rise over the 2015 figures, whilst applications from Britain increased by 40.6 per cent in the same period (DfA, 2017a, b, c). This trend continued throughout 2017, 2018 and 2019 (DfA, 2017a, b, c, 2018, 2019). In NI (which had returned a majority 'remain' vote in the referendum) people who might not have traditionally opted to apply for Irish citizenship submitted applications (de Mars et al., 2018; Wood & Gilmartin, 2018). Indeed, this action was encouraged by British MP and Democratic Union Party member Ian Paisley Jr. who, along with his party campaigned for the Brexit leave vote (Irish Independent, 2016).

9.4.1   Irish Citizenship Eligibility for UK and NI Born Residents

Irish citizenship for UK and NI born residents can be accessed via two methods, ancestry or birthright provision:

1. *Ancestry:*

   (a) Having a parent who was born on the island of Ireland on or before 31 December 2004;

or

   (b) By being the grandchild of someone born on the island of Ireland on or before 31 December 2004 and having their own birth registered on the Foreign Birth Register or

(c) Being the great-grandchild of someone born on the on the island of Ireland on or before 31 December 2004, provided a parent is registered on the Foreign Birth Register before the birth and their own birth is subsequently also registered on the Foreign Birth Register (Department of Foreign Affairs, 2020a; b).

2. *Birthright Provision:*

The constitution of Ireland was changed following the Good Friday Agreement in 1998 stating eligibility to Irish citizenship for any person who was born on the island of Ireland (The Belfast Agreement, 1998). This eligibility changed, however, just five years later when it was removed by the 2004 Citizenship Referendum which set out a system whereby a person born on the island of Ireland could only automatically qualify for Irish citizenship if they had an Irish parent who was already a citizen or who met a three-year residency requirement prior to the child's birth (Wood & Gilmartin, 2018).

9.5 The 'Brexit Irish'

Thus far, little has been published academically on the subject of the 'Brexit Irish', however, research is taking place; Brexit is a seemingly ever-evolving situation and the machinations of publishing take time. Nevertheless, there are notable exceptions. Patricia Burke Wood and Mary Gilmartin undertook an investigation of Irish identity and citizenship following the Brexit referendum via analysis of media reports, social media and government press releases (Wood & Gilmartin, 2018). Of particular relevance are the two categories of new Irish passport holders that the authors identify (ibid). Firstly, 'Pragmatic cosmopolitans' – those who see national identity as fluid, who wish to retain the convenience of a European citizenship 'in order to facilitate other lifestyle choices' but make little to no mention of Irishness (ibid:231). The second category 'Ethnic apologists' according to the authors, justify their passport or citizenship application by claiming connectivity to Ireland, often referring to their 'sense of Irishness' (ibid). The authors continue to discuss these categories in the context of new NI applicants from Unionist backgrounds; people who may be initially perceived as 'Pragmatic cosmopolitans' yet far less likely to consider national identity as a fluid conception (Wood & Gilmartin, 2018). This study is interesting and informative, providing two useful categories with which to explain a phenomenon, however having carried out empirical research within this population, I propose that many more motivations and explanations beyond those suggested by Wood and Gilmartin are at play.

In the Irish Times article 'Are Irish passport applicants in Britain becoming 'more Irish'?' Marc Scully considers if those in Britain applying for Irish passports at this time are formalising an existing Irish identity, or undertaking an identity change (Scully, 2018). The article combines a speculative prelude to Scully's ongoing research into this area, as well as drawing on his extensive previous work on people of Irish descent in Britain (ibid). Scully highlights the complexities around the claiming of a hybrid British / Irish identity and wonders if some of those applying for Irish passports might begin to 'claim Irishness in certain strands of their lives where they hadn't before' (ibid). There are a number of reasons as to why claiming Irishness as a second or third generation person in Britain may be complicated. The behaviour of migrants in a 'host' country may be concerned with fitting in, which can lead to the suppression of certain aspects of identity in themselves and their children (Hickman, 1996). In the case of Irish families, parents and grandparents may have felt compelled to encourage their offspring to hide their Irishness in Britain, particularly during periods such as the Troubles (Walter, 2001). Authenticity and the policing of Irishness is also important: what constitutes authentic Irishness outside of Ireland is consistently contested and remade (Scully, 2012). The trope of the 'Plastic Paddy' endures, an accusation suggesting a fake or inauthentic claim upon Irishness, usually aimed at someone born outside of Ireland (Walter, 2008; Scully, 2009). Bronwen Walter has written about accents and identity amongst first- and second-generation Irish people in England, demonstrating how some of her respondents felt unwelcome in Ireland with their English-accented Irish identities (Walter, 2008). In some cases, Walter's interviewees had internalised these feelings, stating that their accents 'precluded them from claiming an Irish identity' (Walter, 2008:179). In concluding his article, Scully speaks of the fluidity of Irish identity in Britain and how it is undoubtedly shaped by 'the broader cultural and socio-political environment' (Scully, 2018). Scully has since spoken about early responses to his project and whilst cautioning against terming these as findings at that stage, he suggested that the people he had spoken to were in many ways re-evaluating their relationships to Britishness (Scully, 2019).

9.6   Project and Method

The discussion that follows draws upon a wider research project which considered the experiences and motivations of UK-born people who applied for or were considering applying for an Irish passport following the result of the UK's 2016 referendum to leave the EU. I undertook fourteen qualitative interviews with fifteen people (the sample included a couple) during June and July 2018; interviews were conducted via video call with the exception of two which took place over email. The interviews were semi-structured, beginning with set questions and ending with open discussion allowing me to go behind the statistics and gain insights into the personal experiences and behaviours of the respondents. I recruited through social media, personal contacts and snowballing via both methods. The respondents had been born in England or NI but were living at the time of the interviews in Scotland, England and the Czech Republic. Participants' backgrounds and claims to citizenship were diverse, nine had at least one ROI-born parent; one had a ROI-born grandparent. Two had at least one NI-born parent from a Catholic background; two were

NI-born from Protestant Unionist backgrounds and one would be eligible if her NI-born British Grandmother would agree to apply for Irish citizenship (she had so far refused). Respondents were aged between twenty and sixty-five, comprising of eight men and six women. Two participants had teenage children for whom they had been going through the passport application process for; they discussed their own experiences, as well as those of their respective children. Pseudonyms have been used throughout this discussion.

The data discussed here derives mostly from participants' responses to being asked if they felt that they as Irish citizens should be able to vote in Irish politics. Whilst the focus of this chapter is not the participants' motivations for pursuing an Irish passport, it would be remiss not to give a brief insight into this key information. All of the participants had voted to 'remain' and whilst Brexit acted as a catalyst in passport acquisition interviewees often cited additional motivations. Convenience for travel was a consideration, as was a desire to retain European identity; others sought to distance themselves from or rebel against Britishness. Some had held long-term aspirations to possess an Irish passport, but had faced barriers such as financial constraints or the need to engage with estranged family members – in these situations, Brexit came to symbolise a tipping point. Motivations could be complex and overlapping, demonstrating the need to explore beyond the limitations of binary categorizations.

9.7 External Voting and the 'Brexit' Irish

9.7.1 A Move to Vote?

Overwhelmingly, participants did not feel that they should have the right to vote in Irish elections, with only one respondent – Jamie – feeling that it would be appropriate. Jamie lived in London at the time of the interview, having grown up in northern England. His claim to Irish citizenship was through his Irish father who had moved to England from NI as a child, however, Jamie was yet to visit the Island of Ireland. Politically knowledgeable and a supporter of the EU, Jamie's belief that he should have the right to vote appears framed by his intention to move to the ROI in the future:

> Er yes, I believe so. I mean at some point I do intend on living there, so when I do, I will be able to, obviously after a period of time… –Jamie

Throughout our conversation, Jamie positioned Ireland as "moving forward" and the UK as "regressing", citing the recent referendums in Ireland as socially positive moves and Brexit as a backward step. His motivation to apply for an Irish passport was to retain the freedoms that EU citizenship had afforded him, and he felt that his "liberal kind of open beliefs" were more "embodied in Ireland" than they were in England.

The narrative of Ireland as progressive and 'Brexit Britain' as backward was a common thread across the participants many of whom, to varying degrees of seriousness were considering a move to Ireland. Discussion of political rights often led directly into this, with participants pointing out that whilst they didn't agree with external voting, they felt very strongly that if they moved to Ireland, they should have a right to vote. Alan, in his late thirties presented an alternative view, telling me that watching the Repeal the 8th Referendum play out a month earlier had made him want to take an active role in Irish citizenship:

> So, almost the very fact that I can't vote, that I can't engage actively as a citizen and engage in Irish politics has made me think "maybe we should move there!" so I can. –Alan

I explored earlier the suggestion that non-resident voting for the emigrant generation may be a factor in return migration, so it is intriguing therefore that for Alan, a third-generation Irish citizen *not* having a vote may motivate a move to Ireland. Alan's eligibility for Irish citizenship came via his estranged maternal grandfather and he didn't grow up with a connection to Ireland. His initial rationale for acquiring Irish citizenship was to distance himself from Britain following the 2015 Conservative-won election and Brexit in addition to the retention of European rights. As Alan and his mother navigated the "tricky" bureaucratic process of locating documents, he became aware of unknown family members and became interested in finding out more about where his grandfather was from. Alan's desire to leave the UK after Brexit was not, as noted earlier, a unique standpoint: perhaps Alan's decreasing satisfaction with Britain and increasing connection to Ireland drew him to feel he could move to a country and make a difference.

9.7.2   Connections/Disconnections

Edie, a student in her early twenties, claimed Irish citizenship through her ROI-born mother who had moved to England with her parents. She told me she had always wanted to describe herself as Irish, declaring that having the passport meant that she could do that "officially". Despite this, Edie said she would be reluctant to identify herself as Irish to an Irish-born person on the basis that they might find it "annoying" or "superficial", particularly because she has an English accent. She didn't think that she should have the right to vote in Irish elections, telling me:

> Look I know I'm not fully Irish, and I know that some people might be offended potentially or a bit iffy –Edie

Throughout the interview, Edie expressed feelings and beliefs which, as previously referenced, are commonly reported in research on second-generation Irish people in Britain – contested claims on Irishness; an English accent as a barrier to claiming Irish identity; a perception that 'real' Irish people may be irritated by identity claims from those born outside of the state. If Edie is uncomfortable claiming Irish identity, it's unsurprising that she would also feel uncomfortable claiming a political stake in Ireland.

Another participant who expressed discomfort with claiming Irish identity, albeit to a greater extent than Edie, was Stephanie. Stephanie was born and raised in London by her Irish parents. In her late twenties, she had spent the last decade living in Scotland. Stephanie had wanted to apply for an Irish passport for some time having felt that in some countries an Irish passport might be more welcome than a British one. Stephanie described herself as being "of Irish heritage", as opposed to "Irish - because it would be a bit disingenuous", explaining that this was mainly because her parents had always told her that she was English:

> Like, not in a mean way.... [laughing] but, they just they didn't want me to be like, I dunno, I think – you know when you see some people, some children of Irish immigrants and they cling onto it so much that it becomes a kind of bastardization of what it actually is, we particularly had some relatives in America who were a bit like that, and I think they just found that a bit like hard erm to see so I think they were just a bit wary of that happening to us... –Stephanie

Stephanie didn't feel that she should have an entitlement to vote in Irish elections, but observed that current rules excluded emigrants, which she disagreed with, stating that she felt her mother would probably vote if she had the opportunity.

That Stephanie and Edie feel reluctant to vote could be a demonstration of interest in the 'home' country dissipating across generations and time (Fitzgerald, 2006). However, that they have both perceived and experienced policing and suppression of Irish identity could be significant in the shaping of their external voting opinions.

Concealment of Irishness was also raised by Nathan, a second-generation Irish citizen living in the Czech Republic. Both of his parents were Irish, having met in the Birmingham dance halls during the 1970s where they initially found it easy to integrate. However, following the Birmingham IRA bombings and experiencing local hostility, his parents decided to assimilate, becoming "more English than the English". Behind closed doors, he said that his parents told stories, talked about Ireland and took him there for childhood holidays, but that:

> Like a lot of people in Britain, a lot of people in the West Midlands do, I felt disconnected – Nathan

Nathan said that he was developing more of an Irish connection and that like Alan and Jamie, was considering moving to Ireland. He stated that with regards to voting, it was easy for him to have opinions from the outside, but that he had far less of an understanding of Ireland than he would like to if he were to be casting a vote.

9.7.3 Reluctant to Influence

A reluctance to affect the lives of people living in a different country was emphasized by almost all of the respondents. Grace, who had grown up in London with her Irish mother and English father the found the idea of voting in Irish elections odd:

> I would feel strange about having an influence on the lives of people whose daily experience I do not share... I would no more think about remotely influencing the outcomes for Irish people than I would any other country –Grace

Grace's views were echoed by Linda, who additionally referenced a lack of a shared experience as a mark against external voting:

> I haven't had to grow up in that society or struggle for the right to abortion or you know, all those, even contraception, all those things that women there have had to fight for, I haven't had to fight for that yet, maybe in the future we will, but right now... –Linda

Dermot, a father of two teenagers from Yorkshire initially felt quite strongly against having an external vote in Irish elections:

> I don't think you have the right to influence where other people live if you don't have any vested interest in it and, it just feels a bit weird, I'd be perfectly happy not to vote in Ireland because I don't live there. –Dermot

However, later in the interview Dermot wondered about these feelings in the context of his personal situation:

> If I was living in Ireland and my kids were here [England] and the government were about to do something really bad here and I could come back to vote, I probably would but it wouldn't make a difference. A little bit I want my cake and eat it there. –Dermot

As indicated in the overview of the project, all of the participants had been 'remain' voters who disagreed wholeheartedly with Brexit. Two years after the referendum they were still unsettled, angry and hurt by a decision they felt had been imposed upon them. In this context, it might be a natural reaction for those respondents to view external voting as a problematic situation. Regardless of the accuracy of this assumption, it appears clear that participants often felt disconnected from 'home' citizens and didn't feel part of Irish citizenship as a whole.

9.7.4   Northern Ireland

A third of respondents were either from NI or descended from a NI person. Two participants, Peter and Geoffrey came from Protestant Unionist backgrounds and were now living in south-east Scotland and southern England respectively. Peter, in his late thirties, viewed his Irish citizenship acquisition from a purely practical standpoint, aligning with Wood and Gilmartin's description of NI Unionist applicants - 'pragmatic cosmopolitans' who did not subscribe to identity as fluid (Wood & Gilmartin, 2018). Peter described himself as British and did not feel he should vote in Irish elections.

Geoffrey, who was about thirty years older than Peter, came from a similar background but told me that having had republican and socialist sympathies, he'd felt out step with his community. Geoffrey described his motivations as "partly emotional and partly practical" – a desire to retain the ability to live in any European country and to reject what he saw as the 'parochial bigotry' of the Brexit campaign. He felt voting should be limited to people who live in Ireland; pay tax; or 'have some skin in the game'. Geoffrey differentiated between residents and taxpayers, which was an alternate view to other participants who strongly linked taxation and political representation. He also stated that he hadn't "invested" in his "new Irishness yet", suggesting that there may be a point in the future where he might feel comfortable holding an external vote.

Ryan, thirty-five, told me that he'd been brought up in a "really Irish kind of family", in an area of northwest England "where most people are of Irish descent". As a child he frequently spent holidays in Co. Derry where his father was from. When asked about voting, Ryan told me that it had only recently occurred to him that members of his family in Co. Derry didn't have the right to vote in the ROI:

> Errm, well I thought about it recently because of the abortion vote and then that's when I realised that even the Northern Irish didn't get a vote in that.
>
> I don't live there, I don't really know anything about Irish politics, 'cos even my family are from Northern Ireland so it's different. Anyway. –Ryan

Ryan's position is layered; on the one hand he identified as a second-generation Irish person living in England, yet his father, who he viewed as an Irish emigrant was at no point in his life entitled to a vote, even when he was living on the island of Ireland. The distance between Ryan and a stake in Irish politics appeared significant, as did the distance between himself and the ROI. These may be contributory factors in why Ryan felt that having a vote in Irish elections was unimportant.

9.8   Conclusion

It is apparent, with the exception of Jamie, that the cohort felt to varying degrees that they, as external citizens should not have the right to vote in Irish elections. This may be reassuring information for those reluctant to extend the franchise, and for some it might seem a logical consequence of perceived pragmatic moves to preserve European rights, as demonstrated by Peter. However, my research has demonstrated that in addition to a multitude of motives driving Irish passport and citizenship applications, the views of participants on external voting may also reflect a disconnection from Ireland, be that through estranged family, suppression of an Irish identity, the policing of Irishness and the ambiguity of Irish citizens of NI.

Undertaking the research so soon after the Brexit referendum meant that most of the respondents were only recent holders of Irish citizenship and it felt to me that each of the respondents were only just beginning to make sense of what this meant for them and their own identity. In light of this, it would be fascinating to revisit their lives now, over two years later to canvass their opinions in a post Brexit-world.

It will be interesting to see if and how the intentions set in the Irish Government's 2020 Diaspora Strategy develop, however, I believe, in the case of the 'Brexit Irish' who took part in this study, that using Presidential external voting rights to connect the state with the diaspora might be bypassing a vital step in the process – that to be interested in voting, external citizens may first need to feel connected to, and a part of, Ireland.

References

Agreement between the Government of the United Kingdom of Great Britain and Northern Ireland and the Government of Ireland (with annexes) (Belfast/Good Friday Agreement). (1998).

Boyle, M., & Kavanagh, A. (2018). The Irish Government's diaspora strategy: Towards a care agenda. In J. Devlin Trew & M. Pierse (Eds.), *Rethinking the Irish diaspora after the gathering*. Palgrave Macmillan.

Carswell, S. (2017). Voting for a vote for the Irish abroad, *The Irish Times*, 18 March. Available at: https://www.irishtimes.com/life-and-style/abroad/voting-for-a-vote-for-the-irish-abroad-1.3013105. Accessed: 28 Dec 2020.

Carswell, S. (2020). Emigrants who 'left in crisis' to be embraced in new diaspora strategy, *The Irish Times*, 18 November. Available at: https://www.irishtimes.com/life-and-style/abroad/emigrants-who-left-in-crisis-to-be-embraced-in-new-diaspora-strategy-1.4412420. Accessed: 28 December 2020.

Crowley, U., Gilmartin, M., Kitchin, R., (2006). Vote yes for common sense citizenship: Immigration and the paradoxes at the heart of Ireland's "Céad Míle Fáilte" working paper series. No 30. Working paper. NIRSA – National Institute for regional and spatial analysis. Available at: http://mural.maynoothuniversity.ie/1541/. Accessed: 28 Dec 2020.

de Mars, S., Murray, C., O'Donoghue, A., & Warwick, B. (2018). *Bordering two unions*. Policy Press.

Department of Foreign Affairs. (2015). Global Irish: Ireland's Diaspora Policy. Available at: https://www.dfa.ie/media/globalirish/global-irish-irelands-diaspora-policy.pdf. Accessed: 17 Nov 2020.

Department of Foreign Affairs. (2017a). *733,060 Irish passports issued in 2016 – Minister Flanagan* [Press Release]. 5 January. Available at: https://www.dfa.ie/news-and-media/press-releases/press-release-archive/2017/january/passport-numbers-2016/. Accessed: 26 Dec 2020.

Department of Foreign Affairs. (2017b). *Irish emigration patterns and citizens abroad*. Available at: https://www.dfa.ie/media/dfa/alldfawebsitemedia/newspress/publications/ministersbrief-june2017/1%2D%2DGlobal-Irish-in-Numbers.pdf. Accessed: 29 Dec 2020.

Department of Foreign Affairs. (2017c). *Record number of Irish passports issued in 2017* [Press Release]. 29 December. Available at: https://www.dfa.ie/news-and-media/press-releases/press-release-archive/2017/december/record-number-of-irish-passports-issued-in-2017/. Accessed: 26 Dec 2020.

Department of Foreign Affairs. (2018). *Tánaiste statement on 2018 passport figures* [press release]. 31 December. Available at: https://www.dfa.ie/news-and-media/press-releases/press-release-archive/2018/december/tanaiste-statement-on-2018-passport-figures-.php. Accessed: 26 Dec 2020.

Department of Foreign Affairs. (2019). *2019 sets new record for Irish passports* [Press Release]. 27 December. Available at: https://www.dfa.ie/news-and-media/press-releases/press-release-archive/2019/december/2019-sets-new-record-for-irish-passports.php. Accessed: 26 Dec 2020.

Department of Foreign Affairs. (2020a). Citizenship. Available at: https://www.dfa.ie/citizenship/. Accessed: 30 Dec 2020.

Department of Foreign Affairs. (2020b). *Global Ireland: Ireland's diaspora strategy 2020–2025*. Available at: https://www.dfa.ie/media/globalirish/Diaspora-Strategy-2020-English.pdf. Accessed: 26 Dec 2020.

Devlin Trew, J. (2018). Diaspora engagement in Ireland, north and south, in the Shadow of Brexit. In J. Devlin Trew & M. Pierse (Eds.), *Rethinking the Irish diaspora after the gathering*. Palgrave Macmillan.

European Commission. (2014). *Disenfranchisement: Commission acts to defend voting rights of EU citizens abroad* [press release]. 29 January. Available at: https://ec.europa.eu/commission/presscorner/detail/en/IP_14_77. Accessed: 27 Dec 2020.

European Union. (2020). *European Elections: Your Right to Vote.* Available at: https://europa.eu/youreurope/citizens/residence/elections-abroad/european-elections/index_en.htm. Accessed: 27 Dec 2020.

Fitzgerald, D. (2006). Rethinking emigrant citizenship. *New York University Law Review, 81*(1), 90–116.

Fottrell, Q. (2015). Emigrants Don't Have a Vote, But We Do Have a Voice, *The Irish Times*, May 10. http://www.irishtimes.com/life-and-style/abroad/generation-emigration/emigrants-don-t-have-avote-but-we-do-have-a-voice-1.2208051. Accessed: 29 Dec 2020.

Gilligan, A., (2019) Should Irish Citizens Abroad be able to vote in Presidential elections? *Lunchtime Live, Newstalk*, 10 July. Available at: https://www.newstalk.com//podcasts/highlights-from-lunchtime-live/irish-citizens-abroad-able-vote-presidential-elections (Accessed: 15 November 2020).

Glynn, I., Kelly, T., Mac Éinrí, P. (2013) Irish emigration in an age of austerity, Department of Geography, University College Cork., http://www.ucc.ie/en/emigre/emigrereport. Accessed: 24 Dec 2020.

Government of Ireland. (2002). *Seventh Progress Report of the All-party Committee on the Constitution*: Parliament (Dublin: Stationery Office). Available at: https://www.oireachtas.ie/en/debates/debate/seanad/2002-04-18/7/. Accessed: 30 Dec 2020.

Green, P. (2007). Entitlement to vote. In A. Ellis, C. Navarro, I. Morales, M. Gratschew, & N. Braun (Eds.), *Voting from abroad, the international IDEA handbook*. International IDEA.

Harley, N. (2016) Number of Irish passport applications rises by 70 per cent after Brexit, *The Telegraph*, 6 August. Available at: https://www.telegraph.co.uk/news/2016/08/06/number-of-irish-passport-applications-rises-by-70-per-cent-after/. Accessed: 14 June 2018.

Hickman, M. J. (1996). Incorporating and denationalizing the Irish in England: The role of the Catholic church. In P. O'Sullivan (Ed.), *The Irish worldwide, (volume 5), religion and identity* (pp. 196–216). University of Leicester Press.

Hickman, M. J. (2016). An issue that will not go away – Votes for Irish citizens abroad. *History Ireland, 24*(3), 14–15.

Hickman, M. J. (2020). Diaspora policies, consular services and social protection for Irish citizens abroad. In J. M. Lafleur & D. Vintila (Eds.), *Migration and social protection in Europe and beyond (volume 2)*. IMISCOE Research Series.

Honohan, I. (2011). Should Irish emigrants have votes? External voting in Ireland. *Irish Political Studies, 26*(4), 545–561.

Hutcheson, D. S., & Arrighi, J. (2015). "Keeping Pandora's (ballot) box half-shut": A comparative inquiry into the institutional limits of external voting in EU member states. *Democratization, 22*(5), 884–905.

Irish Independent. (2016). Rush for Irish passports as Paisley advises getting one. The Irish Independent, 27 June. Available at: https://www.independent.ie/business/brexit/rush-for-irish-passports-as-paisley-advises-getting-one-34835841.html. Accessed: 27 Dec 2020.

Kenny, C. (2016). Billy Lawless: the emigrant Senator, The Irish Times, 3 June. Available at: https://www.irishtimes.com/life-and-style/abroad/generation-emigration/billy-lawless-the-emigrant-senator-1.2671525. Accessed: 30 Dec 2020.

Kenny, C. (2018) Nine out of 10 emigrants surveyed would have voted for repeal', The Irish Times, 27 May. Available at: https://www.irishtimes.com/life-and-style/abroad/nine-out-of-10-emigrants-surveyed-would-have-voted-for-repeal-1.3510191. Accessed: 28 Dec 2020.

Lafleur, J. (2015). The enfranchisement of citizens abroad: Variations and explanations. *Democratization, 22*(5), 840–860.

Lappin, R. (2016). The right to vote for non-resident citizens in Europe. *International and Comparative Law Quarterly, 65*, 859–894.

López-Guerra, C. (2005). Should expatriates votes? *The Journal of Political Philosophy, 13*(2), 216–234.

Mackle, D. (2018). Marriage equality north and south: The journey after the gathering'. In J. Devlin Trew & M. Pierse (Eds.), *Rethinking the Irish diaspora after the gathering*. Palgrave Macmillan.

Mc Inerney, T., O'Leary, N. (2019). *Why Can't all Irish citizens vote?* [podcast]. 5 August. Available at: https://www.theirishpassport.com/podcast/s3-episode-6-irish-citizens-want-voting-rights/. Accessed: 21 Oct 2020.

Mulkerns, H. (1991). When the "New Irish" were fighting for the right to vote, 1991. Available at: http://helenamulkerns.com/when-the-new-irish-were-fighting-for-the-right-to-vote-1991/. Accessed: 29 Dec 2020.

National University of Ireland. (2020). Seanad Éireann Election 2020. Available at: http://www.nui.ie/elections/seanadelection2020/default.asp. Accessed: 27 Dec 2020.

Ní Laoire, C. (2008). Complicating host-newcomer dualisms: Irish return migrants as homecomers or newcomers? *Translocations: Migration and Social Change, 4*(1), 35–50.

O'Neill, C. (2018). #HomeToVote should inspire Ireland and embarrass politicians, *The Irish Times*, 5 June. Available at: https://www.irishtimes.com/life-and-style/abroad/hometovote-should-inspire-ireland-and-embarrass-politicians-1.3520045 (Accessed: 29 December 2020).

O'Neill, C., (2019). A stake in the outcome? External voting rights for Irish citizens. Emerging voices – A future of Europe anthology. The Institute of International & European affairs. Available at: https://www.iiea.com/wp-content/uploads/2019/06/A-Stake-in-the-Outcome.pdf. Accessed: 3 Nov 2020.

O'Riordan, E. (2019). I don't believe the 3.6 million Irish abroad should have the right to vote, The Irish Times, 8 July. Available at: https://www.irishtimes.com/life-and-style/abroad/i-don-t-believe-the-3-6-million-irish-abroad-should-have-the-right-to-vote-1.3949147. Accessed: 29 Dec 2020.

Rampen, J. (2016). Hate Brexit Britain? 7 of the best places for political progressives to emigrate to, New Statesman, 24 June. Available at: https://www.newstatesman.com/politics/uk/2016/06/hate-brexit-britain-7-best-places-political-progressives-emigrate. Accessed: 27 Dec 2020.

Ryan, O. (2018). A defining moment for our generation: Why emigrants are coming home to vote, The Journal.ie, 24 May. Available at: https://www.thejournal.ie/home-to-vote-eighth-amendment-4029675-May2018/. Accessed: 29 Dec 2020.

Ryan, L., & Kurdi, E. (2015). 'Always up for the craic': Young Irish professional migrants narrating ambiguous positioning in contemporary Britain. *Journal for the Study of Race, Nation and Culture, 21*(3), 257–272.

Scully, M. (2009). 'Plastic and proud'?: Discourses of authenticity among the second-generation Irish in England. *Psychology and Society, 2*(2), 124–135.

Scully, M. (2012). Whose day is it anyway? St. Patrick's day as a contested performance of national and diasporic Irishness. *Studies in Ethnicity and Nationalism, 12*(1), 118–135.

Scully, M. (2018). Are Irish passport applicants in Britain becoming 'more Irish'?, *The Irish Times*, 4 May. Available at: https://www.irishtimes.com/life-and-style/abroad/are-irish-passport-applicants-in-britain-becoming-more-irish-1.3484245. Accessed 7 Sept 2020.

Scully, M. (2019). Negotiating Irishness – Ray French interviews Marc Scully about his research into hybrid identities. In R. French, M. McCrory, & K. Mckay (Eds.), *I wouldn't start from here: The second-generation Irish in Britain* (pp. 99–110). The Wild Geese Press.

Spillane, R., (2020). I'm Irish and I live Abroad, *The Irish Times*, 27 January. Available at: https://www.irishtimes.com/life-and-style/abroad/i-m-irish-and-i-live-abroad-why-have-we-been-forgotten-in-election-2020-1.4152683. Accessed: 27 Dec 2020.

Spiro, P. (2006). Perfecting political diaspora. *New York University Law Review, 81*(1), 207–233.

The Convention of the Constitution. (2013). Fifth report of the convention on the constitution: Amending the constitution to give citizens resident outside the state the right to vote in presidential elections at Irish embassies, or otherwise. November 2013.

VICA. (2020a). *November 2020 Campaign Newsletter.* Available at: https://mailchi.mp/
ab47e20cc934/votes-for-irish-citizens-abroad-reminder-next-volunteer-meeting-1589701.
Accessed: 24 Dec 2020.

VICA. (2020b). *About us.* Available at: http://www.vica.ie/about-us/. Accessed: 29 Dec 2020.

Walter, B. (2001). *Outsiders inside: Whiteness, place and Irish women.* Routledge.

Walter, B. (2008). Voices in other ears: "Accents" and identities of the first- and second-generation
Irish in England. In G. Rings & A. Ife (Eds.), *Neo-colonial mentalities in contemporary Europe?
Language and discourse in the construction of identities.* Cambridge Scholars Publishing.

Wood, P. B., & Gilmartin, M. (2018). Irish enough: Changing narratives of citizenship and national
identity in the context of Brexit. *Space and Polity, 22*(2), 224–237.

Chapter 10
Between Integration and Dissociation: Intra-European Immigrants' Life Experiences in Romania

Bogdan Voicu and Alin Croitoru

10.1 Introduction

Increasingly visible migrant communities that coexist within transnational spaces (Vertovec, 2009) are part of a contemporary world marked by a changing political approach to immigration, in which integration is the key word. The vagueness of the term (Schinkel, 2017) is compensated by the potential benefits derived from its usage. Given its multidimensionality (Harder et al., 2018; Voicu & Vlase, 2014), integration allows observing a liquid migration. The term was developed in relation to intra-European migration (Engbersen, 2018), to stress the encapsulation of such spatial movement into a more complex set of social changes, and to stress the flexibility of migration itself. Such fluidity implies a series of temporary states in the personal life, that is appropriate for the case of high-skilled intra-European migrants.

When moving from an EU country to another, EU citizens form a sort of internal migration flow (Jong, & de, and Helga de Valk., 2020). Although citizenship is not challenged due to their EU nationality, and their rights are virtually the same irrespective of the country of residence within European Union, EU migrants still face difficulties. Civil servants may mistreat them, and they also may encounter ignorance and discrimination. One should add the difficulties to understand the culture

Bogdan Voicu's work on this paper was partly supported by grant GAR-UM-2019-XI-5.3-9. Alin Croitoru's work was supported by a grant of the Romanian Ministry of Education and Research, CNCS– UEFISCDI, project number PN-III-P1–1.1-TE-2019-0238, within PNCDI III.

B. Voicu
Romanian Academy, The Research Institute for Quality of Life, Bucharest, Romania

Lucian Blaga University of Sibiu (Romania), Sibiu, Romania

A. Croitoru (✉)
Lucian Blaga University of Sibiu (Romania), Sibiu, Romania

of the host country and to properly use a structure of opportunities that they do not know in intimate details and often they cannot understand.

Highly skilled migrants might show a different story (Leinonen, 2012), in particular when they migrate to less developed European countries from wealthier ones (Andrejuk, 2017). In such instances, they can convert prestige associated with their own expertise and with their country of origin to foster integration and to receive much higher gratifications and social status as compared to what most could have hoped for in the country of birth.

In this paper, we move the typical story of integration of immigrants to a different context and ask how integration occurs when a high-skilled intra-European migrant moves to a rich region located in a relatively poor country. We consider intra-European highly-skilled migrants to Bucharest, the capital city of Romania, a country with real GDP per capita of 8700 Euro in 2018, largest only to Bulgaria (6500) and almost three times lower than the EU average of 27,640, according to Eurostat.[1] Based on such conditions, one should expect integration in a select bubble of foreign citizens, and low interaction with local society. However, Bucharest is special in the sense that it is wealthier than almost any Southern and Eastern European NUTS2 regions and is hectic as cultural and social life. We argue that such context changes the type of interaction with local society and leads to blending of the high-skilled migrants rather in the upper strata of the local society than in an expat bubble.

We consider a definition of integration that takes into account the economic, social and cultural domains, particularized through four areas of life: employment, accessing health services, participation in local social life, and learning Romanian language.

For empirical documentation, we use 11 in-depth interviews carried out in July 2017–May 2018 with EU mobile citizens in Bucharest. A fast-integration process is observed. European citizenship becomes a de facto given, that on long term, we expect to lead to a category of new Romanian residents that become influent in local communities and society as part of the critical upper strata of the society.

In the following, we briefly discuss the concepts that we employ. Then we depict the context of the research, that is the Romanian society as a migration country, and we derive our hypotheses. Then we describe the methods and data employed in this paper. Findings are structured around the four themes of integration and show a genuine integration into the higher stratum of the society. A final conclusive section includes a discussion on policy and research implications.

10.2   Mobile EU Citizens and Integration

Mobile EU citizens that move from Western to Eastern European countries are often among the privileged migrants (Kunz, 2016). Being highly skilled, they might be labelled as expatriates, expats, professional migrants, etc., terms that typically share

---

[1] https://ec.europa.eu/eurostat/databrowser/view/sdg_08_10/

as common features the image of someone that migrates temporally but lives abroad for long, and is typically employed by a transnational corporation as a professional (Baubock, 2007; Fechtter, 2007; King, 2002; Meier, 2014; von Koppenfels Amanda, 2014). In this sense, that is also our definition, they are seen as "migrants of privilege" (Croucher, 2009, 2018), sometimes expressing lifestyle migrations (Benson & O'Reill, 2009; Hayes, 2014) or deriving gratifications from diving into cosmopolitanism (van Bochove & Engbersen, 2015), sometimes pursuing migration pathways as means to develop a career (Favell, 2008; Leinonen, 2012; Piekut, 2012), for family reasons (Becker & Teney, 2020), and in search for welfare arrangements dependent on life cycle (Jong, & de, and Helga de Valk., 2020). In general, EU highly-skilled migrants are invisible from ethnic-racial point of view, being similar to the local population (Leinonen, 2012), and are subject to transnational professional inclusion (Iredale, 2001), and play an important role as transmitters of cultural norms and social values (Beaverstock, 2002), even though they typically live in their own bubbles with little interaction with the local society (Favell, 2008; Fechtter, 2007). This poses a challenge in assessing integration.

On the one hand, the complexity of the process of integration is shaped by the individual's cultural, economic and social background, as well as their willingness to integrate at destination. On the other hand, the host country's institutional web can facilitate or inhibit integration through public policies targeting immigrants and by enhancing personnel' capacity to interact with immigrants. Based on these aspects, integration processes are usually understood and characterised as multidimensional processes both in academic approaches (Harder et al., 2018; Snel et al., 2006; Voicu & Vlase, 2014; Wrigley, 2012) and in public views (Sobolewska et al., 2017). Both agency and structure of opportunities play their roles in the process (Lutz, 2017).

Individuals richer in human and material capital are well equipped for human agency (Inglehart & Welzel, 2005). Consequently, through their privileged positions, highly-skilled migrants can manipulate both the environment, that they can even ignore and engage solely with their bubble, and to manifest agency by their own in shaping their lives as they wish. This applies quite well in countries where they enter directly into a dominant class.

Integration of high-skilled is considered by existing policy (Kennedy, 2019; Kolbe, 2021; Kolbe & Kayran, 2019; Triadafilopoulos & Smith, 2013). On one hand, there is a natural preoccupation for the well-being of the immigrants themselves, as human beings. On the other hands, societies are interested in having residents that are integrated and contribute to their life, both social, cultural, and economic.

The process of integration may occur in various areas of life. Given the limited space of this chapter, we opt for a narrow selection of such areas, option which is common to other works as well (Snel et al., 2006; Voicu & Vlase, 2014). We consider mastering the language, as pathway to ability for in-depth experiencing and understanding local society. We also investigate employment and entrepreneurship, therefore integration on the labour market and relation to economy. We analyse aspects linked to accessing health services as part of using the welfare state as ordinary citizens. Last but not least, we consider social participation and developing relations with citizens in the host society, in order to tap for informal engagement with the local society.

Our choice of dimensions reflects the categorization by Snel et al. (2006). Learning the language is a first step towards endorsing local norms, which are otherwise addressed as side-topic in all four domains. Integration on the labour market taps for structural integration along with education. We do not discuss education, since it was set up as selection criteria for our target population, and children education comprises complications due to temporality in the migration decisions. The second facet of integration according to Snel et al. (2006) referred to social and cultural integration. On one hand, this implied relations to natives, on the other the endorsement of norms and values of the host society. Relations to natives are reflected in our choices of dimensions through the social participation, that taps for informal relations, and through accessing the health services, which stands for a more formal relationship to the society, and as indicator for understanding local institutions as sets of formal norms and informal practices.

10.3   Immigration to Romania and Previous Evidence on Integration

Romania is a major country of emigration, with over 3,five million of its citizens officially resident in other EU countries (EUROSTAT, 2020). In this context, the stock of immigrants in Romania is expected to fill in some of the labour gaps resulted from this massive emigration even if these flows are far from being equivalent (Anghel & Coşciug, 2018). To understand the incoming flows, firstly we outline the stock of foreign citizens in Romania and its structure by paying attention to immigrants who are EU citizens. Secondly, we portray the participation of these two categories of foreign citizens on the Romanian labour market.

As compared to a population of roughly 20 million, the total of foreign citizens was around 137 thousand registered in Romania at the end of the year 2019 are like a drop of water into the sea, despite the increase in recent years [in 2018, the stock of foreign citizens was around 120 thousand; while in 2017 it was near the value of 117 thousand - (Coşciug et al., 2019)]. Most of them hold a non-EU citizenship (61,2%), while 38,8% are foreigners with EU citizenship. Italy, Germany and France are the main sources of incoming intra-European migration flows (Table 10.1).

Table 10.2 offers insights on the occupations performed by intra-European immigrants in Romania and also pays attention to specificity of the country's Bucharest capital region. In 2019, there were over 76 thousand work contracts registered for foreign citizens at national level and about half of these are concentrated in the Capital Area (otherwise, about 12% of Romania's total population is located in this region). About 25% of the EU foreign citizens who work in Romania are registered

Table 10.1   Number of foreign citizens in Romania in 2019

	Total	Citizenship	Number	Percentage	
Foreign citizens Non - EU	80,417	Moldova	12,190	8.9	58
		Turkey	10,603	7.7	
		China	8458	6.1	
		Other countries	49,166	35.7	
Foreign citizens EU	53,331	Italy	15,228	11.1	39
		Germany	6719	4.9	
		France	6712	4.9	
		Other countries	24,672	17.9	
Refugees and asylum seekers	3871	Syria	2083	1.5	3
		Iraq	880	0.6	
		Afghanistan	148	0.1	
		Other countries	760	0.6	
Total			137,619	**100**	

Source: General Inspectorate for Immigration in Romania (CRCMIS, 2021)

Table 10.2   Immigrants' work contracts registered in 2019

ISCO[a] (MG: Major Groups)[a]	Romania – National Level		Region of the Capital (Bucharest and ILFOV)	
	Foreign citizens (UE, EEA, and Switzerland)	Foreign citizens NON - (UE, EEA, and Switzerland)	Foreign citizens (UE, EEA, and Switzerland)	Foreign citizens NON - (UE, EEA, and Switzerland)
MG 1 – Managers (%)	24.8	4.7	21.9	7.0
MG 2 – Professional (%)	19.3	6.7	37.2	12.4
MG 3 - technicians and associate professionals (%)	12.3	5.4	19.6	8.0
MG 4 - clerical support workers (%)	3.7	2.8	6.6	6.3
MG 5 - service and sales workers (%)	7.1	11.0	3.7	13.9
MG 6 - skilled agricultural, forestry and fishery workers (%)	0.4	0.3	0.0	0.1
MG 7 - craft and related trades workers (%)	7.1	24.6	3.3	17.3
MG 8 - plant and machine operators, and assemblers (%)	11.2	8.8	3.4	3.2
MG 9 - elementary occupations (%)	14.2	35.7	4.4	31.9
Total (percentage and number of contracts)	100 19,816	100 56,191	100 9376	100 27,098

Source: Work Inspection, Ministry of Labour and Social Protection (CRCMIS, 2021)[a]

in the top job category (Managers and other top executives' positions), while the correspondent percent within the non-EU foreign citizens is less than 5%. The first three ISCO job categories group 57% of the EU foreign workers in Romania (within the capital region it grows to 79%), while among the non-EU workers the corresponding figure is 17% (rising to 27% for the capital region). In brief, the EU workers are concentrated at the top of the job hierarchy, while the non-EU population is rather over-represented within the last three categories of occupations (MGs 7 to 9 cumulate 70% of the non-EU workers countrywide and 52% in the capital Region). Such occupational discrepancies frame individuals and their families' life in Romania.

While labour market integration is a standard dimension of immigrant's integration into the destination context, the share of managerial and professional occupations of EU-migrants as compared to others is not only impressive, but also provide a hint on the integration within society. Immigrants entrepreneurship depend on their access to economic resources, social capital at destination and mobilization of ethnic capital (Cederberg & Villares-Varela, 2019; Waldinger & Ward, 1990), as well as the transfers of skills, abilities or knowledge gained in other national contexts (Williams, 2007). Individuals' work trajectories are influenced by their level of education (Marvel et al., 2016) and their capacity to navigate within the destination context (Harder et al., 2018). Linguistic capital (Dustmann, 1999) and previous experiences of running business (Ucbasaran et al., 2008) also matter.

The difference between the capital region and the rest of the country is easy to be explained by the migration magnet that the first became in recent decades. The number of inhabitants make Bucharest the tenth largest European city. Excluding non-EU cities, Bucharest is the sixth, after London, Berlin, Madrid, Rome, and at basically the same size as Paris (roughly 2.1 million) when not including the metropolitan area. In terms of richness, the GDP/capita in the Bucharest/Ilfov NUTS2 area was in 2018 larger than in any region South of it, including the ones in Italy, Spain, or Southern France. According to Eurostat,[2] there are only a few regions in the Northern and Western Europe to overpass existing yearly produced wealth in Bucharest and surrounding areas, while in Central and Eastern Europe (CEE), only Budapest and Warsaw experience similar levels, while Bratislava and Prague are even richer.

Eurostat data for 2018 reports very high inequality for Romania: the GINI coefficient was 35.1, surpassed only by Latvia, Lithuania and Bulgaria (39.6 – the highest in the EU), and much higher than the EU average of 30.4. All Western societies were more equal, while figures for other countries in the CEE were substantially lower: Hungary (28.7), Poland (27.8), Czechia (24.0), Slovakia (20.9).[3]

---

[2] https://ec.europa.eu/eurostat/databrowser/view/tgs00005/

[3] https://ec.europa.eu/eurostat/databrowser/view/tessi190/

10.3.1 Expectations: An Atypical Integration

Bucharest is a large and wealthy city well served by good international transport links, with a vivid night and cultural life, where high inequality directs most of the wealth to the privileged class, making the place attractive for those in search for high living standards, high incomes, or eager to experience life-style migration.

Within this set up, EU mobile citizens in Bucharest meet the needs under the particular drivers of their migrations. But they also face a local elite in full ascension, in particularly boosted by the discussed inequality. In the perspective on migration as liquid, it becomes critical to see integration as part of wider social changes that occur within the immediate context.

With the depicted interplay of differences in status between the society of origin and the host country, and in adjustments of personal status, as well as considering the inequalities to be found in Romania, *we expect that integration of highly-skilled EU mobile citizens does not occur in a bubble of foreigners, but rather in a mix of foreign citizens and tiny social class of wealthy Romanians*. Citizenship plays a secondary but important role, since the migration flow that we consider is located between international and internal migration in particular due to EU citizenship.

In the following, we inspect the four domains of integration with the aim to depict the situation of our subjects and their coping with Romanian society. We keep in mind the question whether they act as "regular" members of society, as members of a self-selected bubble of foreigners, or as part of a tiny mixed layer of wealthier people at the top of a poorer European society.

10.4 Data and Methods

To inspect the type of integration of the EU mobile citizens to Bucharest, a set of interviews with 11 such high-skilled Europeans is employed. The interviews were carried out in 2017–2018, by a team led by the first author of this chapter. Recruitment of interviewees was done using direct contact, after identifying them over social networks or through personal recommendations. Three criteria were employed for selection: (1) at least one year of living in Romania, in order to be sure that they had the opportunity to emerge into interaction with the local society; (2) having a family, in order to increase the probability of interacting with social services, including health, education, social insurance etc.; (3) being highly-educated non-Romanian EU citizens.

Out of the 11 interviewees, one had neither partner, nor kids at the time of interview, but we have considered that the interaction with the local society was assessed as deep enough on the basis of his previous experiences (he had a partner for a while living into the country, and also presented various examples during interview of interacting with service providers, including health care, public administration etc.).

The sample reflects the distribution by occupations observed at national level. Intra-EU movers in Romania are professionals in the corporate sector, or entrepreneurs. Most arrived initially for professional reasons, while two come as part of a life-style migration flow. We examine integration of high skilled, mobile EU citizens in four dimensions: linguistic, economic, access to health care, and social integration (seen through volunteering, interest in politics, and connecting with locals). The four themes were part of the interview guide, and were addressed by all the interviewees. The entire set up of the discussion was free with respect to structure, but it started in all cases with the story of coming to Romania. When the mentioned topics were not addressed spontaneously, specific questions were asked on current employment and history of employment, informal relations with Romanian society, interaction with local service providers, family life, knowledge of Romanian language, future intentions. The questions were not standardised, but the themes in the interviews were (Table 10.3).

Nevertheless, the support provided by eleven interviews can be questioned from the point of view of number of interviewees. However, various accounts from late career researchers in the field lead to a canonical view that the optimal number of interviewees in qualitative research is provided by the proverbial "it depends" and it is actually determined by the old saying that one keeps interviewing until information is saturated (Baker & Edwards, 2012). Numbers may become problematic in this respect, and one might need experimental design to test which is the optimum. In such an experiment, Guest et al. (2006) analysed 60 in-depth interviews and concluded that saturation was reached for sure after 12, and "basic elements for metathemes were present as early as six interviews." (p. 59). Hennink et al. (2017) worked with 25 interviews to determine that 9 were enough for reaching saturation with a shorter code structure, and 16–24 for more refined approaches. Hagaman and Wutich (2017) identified that one needs 4–6 interviews to correctly identify for the first time the three most common themes, and then, the sample size increases to 8, 9 and 12 for identifying again the first, second, and third most important themes. Therefore, our 11 interviews sample, also considering the noted saturation of information, can be considered as relevant for the aims of this study.

10.5   Results

We present the findings starting with linguistic integration given that this is the first and most obvious sign in any interaction, since language is key to communication. Then we discuss economic integration, which is the typical mean to access material resources in any society. Then we approach interaction with health care systems, which is also related to tangible needs. Lastly, we consider social integration, which is related to higher-level needs as compared to the others.

Table 10.3 List of interviewees

Respondent	AT1	CZ1	DE1	ES1	FR1	FR2*	FR3	IT1	PL1	PT1	UK1
Age	56	35	~40	35	30	39	45	40	~42	39	~55
Gender	m	m	m	f	m	m	f	m	f	m	m
Arrival RO	2008	2015–2017, 2017-	2017	2009–2013, 2017-	2014	2000	2013	2001 (w. breaks)	2003	2008–2013, 2014-	1998
Motives to immigrate to Romania	Professional	Professional	Professional	Professional	Life-style	Life-style	Professional	Professional	Professional	Professional	Professional
Job	Entrepreneur	Corporate // entrepreneur	Corporate	Teleworking // mother	Entrepreneur	Entrepreneur	Corporate	Corporate	Corporate	Corporate // entrepreneur	Corporate
Current partner	AT-divorced // RO	SK	US	ES	–	RO, divorced	FR	RO	BE	RO, divorced	RO
Children	2 + 1	2	2	2	–	1	2	–	2	2	2
Recruitment	Rec	D.R.	Rec	Rec	Rec	Int	D.R.	D.R.	Int	Int	D.R.
Language of the interview	EN	EN	EN	RO	FR	RO	FR	EN	RO	EN	EN

Rec by recommendation, *D.R.* desk research (Internet), *int* desk research (social media)

10.5.1 Linguistic Integration: Romanian Proficiency

Seven interviews were carried out in English, the language in which we have approached the interviewees. Two interviewees were approached directly in French, their native language, while three switched to Romanian language from the very beginning, as expression of their own preference. Out of the seven interviewees that preferred discussing in English, three have or had Romanian spouses. Another one, CZ1, which is the only one to be reticent to learning or try learning the language, has a Slovak wife that speaks Romanian. Her reasons to learn the local language relates to using it both in business, and for interacting with the school of their children.

Beyond the mere information about the language preferred in communication with the interviewer, all interviewees mentioned the use of English in work-related communication, but also some knowledge of the local language. The reference for English in work-related situation is justified by one of the interviewees through its higher precision as compared to Romanian and the interviewee's native language – Portuguese.

> I understand [Romanian]. I think it's like Portuguese or English for me in terms of listening, but because I never practice [...] I cannot speak. It's missing me the vocabulary, the training and ... All the environments I live in, everybody speaks in English, it's a business environment so you need to be sharp, clear and Romanian language is not clear. I used to say to my employees "Come on guys, you are speaking between you in Romanian, and you don't understand each other. I say to you in English and is clearer [...] It is a good way in fact to contact business in English because it's much clearer than Romanian. It is a Latin language, like the Portuguese, the same thing. [...] Latin languages have a lot of ... things that for business are not so good. English is the perfect language for these things. So, I understand really good, people can tell me whatever they say and because I understand well but I keep speaking in English because I know it better, on my day to day this is the language I use. (PT1).

Except for the three interviews carried out in Romanian, IT1 was also fluent in the language of the host country. All others reported limited knowledge that enabled them to understand enough Romanian for managing in daily interaction, but not for more.

Most of those working at the time of interviews or in the past in the local corporate sector reported taking Romanian classes as part of their first interactions with the local society.

Only three of the interviewees (CZ1, FR3, and DE1) mentioned no or very little knowledge of local language. Out of them, DE1 was taking Romanian classes from time to time, but the very busy schedule was impeding him to perseverate. CZ1 was against learning the local language, basing on the above-mention family division in language skills.

Overall, the impression is that Romanian language was not rejected, but actually used as a tool. Contrary to expectations, access and use to Romanian was not find preponderantly among those natives in Roman languages, and is moderated by having a spouse that is native in Romanian or speaks Romanian as foreign language.

Therefore, the focus remains on the apparent non-rejection of the local language, which also ease the interaction with locals. This is contrary to the studies carried out in Poland (Andrejuk, 2017; Piekut, 2012) that located high-skilled immigrants in enclaves of foreigners with no or little interaction with natives.

10.5.2 Economic Integration: Employment and Entrepreneurship

In correspondence with the EU legal framework, Romania's legislation distinguishes between intra-EU migrants and immigrants who are third-country nationals (extra-EU), as well as refugees and asylum seekers. Our study included people who took advantage of the legal status of intra-EU migrants and this offered them access to the labour market (Voicu et al., 2020). At the same time, their high level of education and training makes them suitable employees for large multinational corporations with subsidiaries in Romania or contributed to their entrepreneurial projects. The two categories of immigrants, highly-skilled employees and entrepreneurs, allow us to illustrate various aspects of their work life.

Firstly, the work in a multinational corporation frames individuals' work in a cosmopolitan social milieu in which most of the people are willing to comply to economic, cultural and social values which have a transnational/globalized nature (e.g., sustainable use of resources, accepting diversity in terms of sexual orientation, promoting gender equality). It provides knowledge about the Romanian society, but this is mostly limited to the urban and highly-educated young people who qualifies to work in these companies.

Secondly, depending on the market in which the company operates, broader access to the Romanian society can be derived from contacts with production workers or company's clientele. There are interviewees who point out that within corporations they make efforts to solve local issues through mechanisms based on a deeper understanding of the social problems. However, some of the practices encountered within host country challenge individuals' migrants economic and work values.

> We had a project in Ferentari [a poor neighbourhood in Bucharest], dedicated to energy theft, to address the problem, but without punishing those who do it. At some point those who steal have high costs, it's a social explanation. You, as a corporation, have to be an actor in the company, which proves that you understand how the company works. (...) Romania was always very conservative; it did not have a disruptive element to change. (IT1).

All our interviewees but one had experiences of living and working in other countries before Romania. For half of them, previous migrations included non-EU countries, but all have at least one experience in another EU country apart for the country of birth.

Their decisions to move in Romania were influenced by work motivations linked to the development of their professional career or to other opportunities from this area. Due to this fact, they have certain expectations from the host country, and they evaluate their work experiences in Romania in contrast to their former (or potential) experiences from other countries.

The organization is much smaller. Very dynamic. The market is kind of growing but not as developed and not as mature (...) You need to have a significantly higher level of flexibility because you are facing things that you wouldn't expect. Wouldn't happen in other places. So, I think that is also something that you see in the country where this type of organization there is a lot of growth here which is very good. There's a lot of flexibility here when it comes to processes being established and kind of how you run the company. (DE1).

[In Romania] (...) I'm going as an expat for a management position and not really going... to... and Romania... has a lot of opportunities and that is a lot of growth. In Portugal is quite stable... so for a young manager, Romania is much more increasing ...intergrowth... giving opportunities and you come with a new vision and this is appreciated in here. In Portugal you wait for the elders to retire so that you can grow. (...).

Otherwise, Romania is full of opportunities because there are a lot of things to do. (PT1)

I came to open the XXX Hotel, that's... that's what I came for... I've been abroad in my career once before, I've been to Kiev, Ukraine (...) I was back in London and I was looking for another job. (...) At that time, it was one of the main hotels, if not the main hotel in Romania, in Bucharest. So, it was certainly a step up and it was certainly I looked upon it as a challenge and something good for my... for my career. (...) Generally it's an expatriate you pay very well. (UK1).

Those who hold managing positions undertake active roles in changing mentalities within their social circle and companies. Some put emphasis on Romanians lack of self-confidence or on their feelings of inferiority when compared to foreigners. At the same time, some interviewees criticize certain aspects of the Romanian society and emphasize differences between foreigners and Romanians.

Interviewee: I think you are still a bit like this... and you still have a sentiment of ...
Interviewer: inferiority?
Interviewee: ... inferiority. There is no reason anymore, maybe there was in the past, I don't know I'm not sure, but as today there is no reason for this feeling in Romania anymore and I am spending my time to say it to my friends and my team there is no reason. Is not because we are foreigner that we are better by default and there is nothing to be ashamed for. (...) you always have this feeling that people have this this sentiment of inferiority. (FR3).

Working as an entrepreneur offers a broader image on the host society due to the various interactions with business partners, employees, clients, public institutions, etc. Romania was perceived at the time of migration as an attractive market for developing a business and several participants in our study were motivated to move in Romania by business reasons. They used economic resources and human capital transferred from abroad, but the experience is embedded in the social and institutional milieu of the host society.

Basically, this challenge gave me the possibility to learn out how to be an entrepreneur somehow, because I remain alone, let say, in the business, trying to do something (...) it was a great opportunity to learn, to develop. At a certain moment I had this invitation from a friend that I met here to start a new business, a platform for health business, and I said OK, fine, I like the ideas, let's do it (...). I like Romania because the location of Romania is perfect. I adapt really good to the country. (PT1).

I have a business and I still have a business in Czech Republic and I tried to expand (…)
It's time for expansion, where the market is bigger (…) So, Bucharest was like I wouldn't
say perfect but it was good (…) that's why we choose Romania due to being the biggest
capital…. Eastern … Southern Europe… (CZ1).

In some cases, the road to entrepreneurship is paved with obstacles that need to be overcome. However, among our interviewee, for some entrepreneurship was the main option from the very beginning of settling in Bucharest, while others followed this path on the way. Among the main challenges for entrepreneurship can be noted language barriers in relation to public authorities and difficulties derived from social interactions and business partnerships. Respondents included in this study managed to overcome these aspects either by constant readjustments of their practices (including or excluding Romanians in their businesses).

(…) language barrier is there, and there I learned if I need something from authorities, I
need to have a Romanian beside me. (CZ1).
   I met some people here and I started a business that lasted a year and a half. Then, I
didn't want to have an associate anymore, I thought it was better alone because that's how
I see the situation much more clearly and then I kind of changed the approach in terms of
trust [in business partners at the destination]. (PL1).
   [in Bucharest] people are nice, people here are very entrepreneurial and this is a thing
I like very much and when I speak about opportunities there are always opportunities (…).
Business life promote that people are very open but it's quite unstable. This is a character-
istic of a country that is still growing, so it's lacking the maturity of .. you start a project and
you know it takes time to succeed, [in Bucharest] people are still looking for the fast prod-
uct… This is general, the Romanian culture is still lot based on short-cuts, this is something
that I conflict more with the culture. (…)
   This is the biggest challenge for me let's say, it is … to conciliate my vision that is always
medium-long term with the vision that the most people have which is very, very short, this
is the thing that has been hard for me to conciliate all the time. (PT1)

Within our sample, an interesting case is the one of FR2. He doesn't believe in the state, and for him it was hard at first, and everything seemed to be going very slowly. He had a negative experience when he opened his first company, he was perceived as a stranger because he moved to a country where people wanted to leave. He also worked for others, as employee, but preferred to be on his own. At the moment of interviewing, he had no employees, he only worked with an accountant. FR2 had at that time no days off, but he has learned not to stress. The program was flexible and decided by FR2 himself, which gave a feeling of control and tranquillity, as well as option for personal fulfilment. This is consistent with the search for finding a tailored life-style, as depicted in existing literature on privileged migration.

Summing up, for most interviews we observed an initial migration as part of the typical pursuing international career patterns of professional employment. For several, such patterns prolonged into changing jobs and switching to entrepreneurship in Romania, as a base country, not as a stop on the route. From this point of view, the interviewed EU mobile citizens missed no integration, and were an actual part of Romanian society. Again, integration was occurring at the top of society.

10.5.3   Navigational Integration: Access to Healthcare

In Romania, the majority of the population uses the public health system, even if the access to the voluntary health insurance extended during the last decades and is nowadays available for broader categories of people (e.g. some companies' benefits packages include private medical assurances) - (Vladescu et al., 2016, 66). However, the actual access to private health insurance and private health care is limited to a minority including mainly corporate employees from transnational companies active in banking, IT, and telecommunications, and defines an unequal healthcare landscape (Stan & Toma, 2019). Most of the interviewed immigrants have access to the upper layer of this uneven health care system. They use the private system of healthcare through self-paid or company-paid assurance packages, and consequently act in the manner their type of employment was supposed to predict for a Romanian employee with similar social positions.

In general, EU mobile citizens' experiences with the private health system were rather positive. They emphasize the medical staff proficiency, adequate medical equipment and the lack of linguistic barriers in accessing these services. Even more, some lack personal experience with the public healthcare sector, but have indirect knowledge upon it through interaction with Romanian co-workers and friends.

> *I have never been here in a public hospital. I just heard the stories (...) The doctors are good, very competent for the few things I had to do. They really handed perfectly my wife at [name of private clinic], really nice, the equipment is always good. The look is different than what you will see in... the public system. (AT1).*
>
> *[There is] a big gap between public and private. It is amazing. (...) It's not a question of education it's a question of infrastructure who's not following and give them the room and give them the appetite to stay because they are less paid in public hospital and they leave. (FR3).*

Their preference for private health system indicates low levels of confidence in the host country' public systems and the fear to access the mainstream public system. At discursive level, this is motivated by the poor medical infrastructure of the public system and a diffuse state of anxiety about using the public medical system. Among our interviewees, there were several who had to use to public health system (e.g., hospitals or emergency rooms) and they had mixed experiences which either altered in a positive way their views, or reinforced the negative attitudes towards the public health system. For example, a Spanish woman emphasized that she was very scarred about using the emergency room when her son had an accident at the playground. In her case, this was a first direct contact with the public system, but she gained confidence for using such services since then.

> *I needed sewing and I was in front of a private clinic and they sent us the public hospital for children and I was a scared that I heard a lot about [the public] health [system] (...)*
>
> *I was so scared ... I didn't know if, I take a plane and go to Spain .... just like that, just as fast ... and when I came in and saw it, it wasn't what I heard. It was very good for us (...).*
>
> *It was urgent and when I entered, I don't even know what it was like inside, it was still new, still new devices, still very good and then the ones I received were very fast [medical help] ... (ES1).*

Within the sample, there were no mentions of linguistic barriers in accessing the public health system and the interviewees were able to solve their medical issues using English, French or basic Romanian. In general, they did not feel discriminated against because there are foreigners, but one immigrant mentioned a privileged treatment compared to the local population when they accessed public health system.

> *I feel it was nice first but made me uncomfortable, because we were foreigner and look wealthy, they made us pass in front of lot of poor people and gypsies that they were waiting and that made me feel very uncomfortable as a person. I really had the feeling that they treated us....it was very nice in a way for sure for you but in the meantime shouldn't happen this, you are in a hospital. So that is with public hospitals.* (FR3).

To this general picture about the public health system, some immigrants also added aspects linked to the informal payments made by patients to the medical staff. These are presented as a standard component of the public health system. It can constitute a new incentive for preferring the private health system because for reducing anxiety linked to such informal payments which require some tacit knowledge (How to approach the staff? How much to give as informal payment? Is it legal? Is it dangerous?)

> *So, when you come from outside, your natural instinct is to paying each month quite a lot of money, so when you go to see the doctor, I mean...you go to see the doctor, it checks you, it tells you what's wrong, makes you a prescription, and you go and buy it. That's it. You understand me? You pay each month for that.... I understand people, I'm sure in the hospital they don't earn a lot of money, I understand that...it's...it's something you get used to it, you see this. You go to the hospital, normally you give the doctor some money, or you want to do an operation, you pay for the operation, even if you pay your money each month, it doesn't matter, you pay for the operation. So, it's strange, it's strange. (...).*
>
> *I think you get used to the system. I find it strange. OK, we're mainly private so we don't pay, but I find it strange to go to pay to the doctor, but you get used to it, I suppose.* (UK1).

Immigrants' integration to the host country embeds smooth access to medical services (Ager & Strang, 2008). In Romania, the use of the private health services is a functional mechanism which contribute to their general adaptation at the host country structure of opportunities, but this is highly dependent on immigrants' economic status, or it can be part of the package of benefits offered by the employer (which is also part of the status, given its embeddedness in the occupational choice). The qualitative approach allows us to see that this type of immigrants is fully aware about the host country health system, and they are able to accomplish their goals by combining private and public services if the case. It also allowed us to observe that they access the same type of services as their Romanian peers and base their judgements on information provided by the same network of peers.

Such navigational integration is similar to what richer/better educated Romanians living in Bucharest are doing: rely on private health care services and to navigate public health care if they have to. Simultaneously, this is contrary to the typical European model, even for expats, and (still) contrary to the habit of most Romanians that rely mainly on public health care system, and use private providers as last resort.

10.5.4   Social Integration: Volunteering, Interest in Politics, Informal Relations with Locals

The third type of integration is social. As a proxy, we look at experiences with volunteering, interest in politics, and connecting to locals as mechanisms for interacting with parts of the Romanian society. For our highly-skilled interviewees, such social interactions would be a valuable mean to interact and integrate in a wider society than the narrower in-group. Volunteering and participation in associations can be conceived as belonging to a community, and actively involving in solving its intimate problems.

One of the interviewees, a French woman in her 40 s, is intensively part of such activities. She reports engagement with an NGO and helping as volunteer in one of the poorest neighbourhoods in Bucharest. She offers time, knowledge and passion in fighting severe deprivation and poverty.

> *I know a bit Ferentari because I work with an NGO, I'm helping some people there. I know a bit the poor, really poor side of Bucharest because there is a friend of mine working with NGO helping kids and also helps the mother to learn a new job to be able to sustain their family and I go there, sometimes, when I have time to help.* (FR3).

However, the example of FR3 is unique within our sample. Apart from this case, only IT1 exhibit examples of involvement in associations and volunteering. For all others, such forms of social participation were not an option. Reasons remain less obvious but are unlikely to be related to the structure of opportunity or to personal characteristics. The structure of opportunity is indeed not very developed in Romania, a country with lower levels of participation, but the society, and in particular larger cities, were increasingly witnessing a blooming voluntary sector, in which the typical volunteer has the same profile as our highly-educated EU mobile citizens (Voicu et al., 2020). Therefore, lack of reported participation in volunteering and associative life is a potential indication for lower social integration.

This could be retrieved in low interest in local politics, which is also part of blending within the large society and not only in the immediate community of peers. Out of the eleven interviews, only AT1 reports sparse political interest in Romanian politics, while IT1 is quite active in this respect. However, interest in politics is low with respect to politics in the countries of origin as well. AT1 manifests a moderate interest in Austrian politics, CZ1 and IT1 know quite well the situation in their country of origin, PT1 has a low interest, while all the others reject, even with nihilism (in case of FR2) anything that relates to politics.

> *Interviewee: Have some feeds from Portuguese media so that I kind of know what is going on there, not that it really interests me but it permits some Portuguese news, If I am going the embassy and they say "A you know what app and write and blablabla and I don't know anything not likely so I keep this feed which I screen every day to you in country but just to add to what to talk when I meet them. They are not so many but ...*
> *Interviewer: You mean here in Bucharest.*
> *Interviewee: In Bucharest yeah ... I'm not really into politics story anything or like that so...I was discussing this morning with a friend, she was telling "Ah, you know about Bucharest highly new govern that was unified and about a guy.*

(...) So ...because... I wasn't assigned for these means and I really don't believe politicians can be friends so...for me it's completely indifferent things like that. (...)

Beyond these more formal ways to interact with Romania, there are the connections with locals. In this respect, only one interviewee (DE1) does not report at least a type of regular interaction with local people, for leisure, family relations, dining out, sports, etc. Romanian spouses play their roles, but the main agents for relationship are still the co-workers and the schoolmates of children. This leads again to a sort of integration in the same social strata, and little interaction outside it.

I have my wife that is Romanian first of all, I have a lot of Romanian friends (...) I made a group of football. There came all nationalities, we start to play, sometimes we are 6–7 players, sometimes we are up to 10, sometimes we are 20, there was a period when we were like 20 and they were Romanians, they were foreigners, they were from everywhere. (PT1).

Here?? I do not have many [friends', haha... We have met a lady, and we see each other, she and her husband are Romanians, their children are a little older than ours. Otherwise, we do not ... We stay together, teh four of us, we do not exit or meet people. [Our daughter] plays with a girl in kindergarten, and we were invited twice at Romanian kids' parties, and we have been also once in [an amusement park]. (ES1).

[Our kids] have very good friends from school. Their best friends are Romanian (PL1).

We have both Romanian and non-Romanian friends, probably more Romanian, because I don't work for foreigners generally, but with Romanians (UK1)

10.6   Conclusion

In this chapter, we have depicted the situation of intra-EU skilled migrants to Bucharest from the point of view of their integration in the local society. The findings place them in a selected non-migrant bubble that reunites local elites and foreigners. In fact, some of the interviewees explicitly stated that they are not part of a migrant bubble. With the potential limitation related to the low number of interviews, we have noticed the preferential access to private health care service, employment in managerial and top-level professional positions or as entrepreneurs, a limited formal social participation, compensated with informal contacts to Romanian society, and quite a high level of mastering and accepting local language, despite the preference for the nowadays lingua franca – English. EU citizenship was the background factor that boosted stability along with personal skills in easing the integration within the local community. Both contributed to the liquidity of the migration process through which the EU high-skilled migrants underwent.

Liquid migration implies unpredictability, temporality – sometimes expressed through circularity of movement, loser family ties – that stress the importance of social integration, a focus on employment, complemented with a migratory habitus that goes beyond the typical constraints given by material and social connections, and may stress lifestyle (Engbersen, 2018). We found all these characteristics reflected in the situation of our interviewees. They are in a fluid situation with respect to the desired length of staying, with the prospective settlement, with their family relations outside Romania, etc.

The integration is not done into the broader Romanian society, but in a thin selected stratum that reunites professionals. In many ways, the situation reminds of the segmented assimilation theory. However, the type of integration that we observe is somehow reversed: the EU mobile citizens are far from getting a stable position within the lower class, but they actually become part of the upper-middle or upper-class with the Romanian society. Their interactions with this class are quite powerful, and the exchanges are likely to be frequent and meaningful.

We explain the difference to the studies carried out elsewhere throughout the peculiar situation of the Bucharest-Ilfov region: a rich enclave in a poorer country. In the paper we did not report on the rather negative image that Romania had in the eyes of EU migrant citizens prior to coming to the country, and on the rather positive views at the time of interviews, but they are part of the definitory experiences that they have.

As compared to their potential situation in the home country, their high social status in Romania is a sign of relatively higher social mobility. This creates the context for the type of integration that we have described. It also comes with a general feeling of superiority as compared to the local society. It is worthy to mention that such representation is also common among the Romanian members of the stratum in which EU mobile citizens integrate, which often express feelings of disappointment with the wider Romanian society.

Nevertheless, with migration being liquid, the presence of EU migrants in the Romanian society can be temporary, and their integration simply fluid. Further research could consider stability of their presence within the society, and to which extent they manage to engage in exchanges that lead to contagion of values and lending norms and habits from the societies of origin to the host society, as well as borrowing and transmitting home such norms, values, and habits taken from the Romanian context.

The findings may also be important for policy makers. We go far beyond the typical debate on European integration policy that traditionally focused on third-country nationals that migrated into West-European countries (Engbersen, 2018). By considering the intra-European movement we consider a process that is actual, increases in size, and brings under the focus different needs and a debate that goes beyond citizenship. In fact, citizenship is the prerequisite that tend to divert attention from potential needs for intervention with respect to integration. The intra-EU high skilled migrants that we have studied are sui generis citizens with lower request for support. The local regulators should consider such integrated communities as part of their object for policy making: Expressing citizenship might be partially blocked by partial linguistic integration, while access to provision of social service is avoiding the public sector. When hazards occur, such actual citizens may face difficulties to cope with stressors, both in Romania and in their countries of birth. Tailored policies are needed to be prepared if the number of EU mobile citizens to Bucharest or in the wider Romania increases.

From a different perspective, representatives of other EU countries could consider such mobile citizens as potential factors to boost their interests among the upper-middle class of the Romanian society, that is within the influential stratum of the society. Citizenship becomes in this respect an asset that can be used for both the migrants, their communities of birth, and the societies in which they reside.

In this chapter we treated the EU high-skilled mobile citizens to Bucharest as a homogeneous group. The scope of the paper did not allow discussing gender-related differences, the role of age, West-East origin etc. Further research should explore such distinction, with the aim to increase knowledge related to this newer form of intra-European migration. Comparison to non-EU similar migrants can help understanding the role of citizenship in the process.

Data Sources

1. EUROSTAT

   - https://ec.europa.eu/eurostat/databrowser/view/tgs00005/default/map?lang=en
   - https://ec.europa.eu/eurostat/databrowser/view/tessi190/default/table?lang=en

2. General Inspectorate for Immigration in Romania
3. Work Inspection, Ministry of Labour and Social Protection (Romania)

References

Ager, A., & Strang, A. (2008). Understanding integration: A conceptual framework. *Journal of Refugee Studies, 21*(2), 166–191.

Andrejuk, K. (2017). Self-employed Migrants from EU member states in Poland: Differentiated professional trajectories and explanations of entrepreneurial success. *Journal of Ethnic and Migration Studies, 43*(4), 560–577.

Anghel, R. G., & Coşciug, A. (2018). Introduction to the special issue: Debating immigration in a country of emigration. *Social Change Review, 16*(1–2), 3–8.

Baker, S. E., & Edwards, R. (2012). How many qualitative interviews is enough? Expert voices and early career reflections on sampling and cases in qualitative research, *National Centre for Research Methods Review Paper*. Accessed on May 22, 2022 at https://eprints.ncrm.ac.uk/id/eprint/2273/4/how_many_interviews.pdf

Bauböck, R. (2007). Stakeholder citizenship and transnational political participation: A normative evaluation of external voting. *Fordham Law Review, 75*(5), 2393–2447.

Beaverstock, J. V. (2002). Transnational elites in global cities: British expatriates in Singapore's Financial District. *Geoforum, 33*(4), 525–538.

Becker, R., & Teney, C. (2020). Understanding high-skilled intra-European migration patterns: The case of European physicians in Germany. *Journal of Ethnic and Migration Studies, 46*(9), 1737–1755.

Benson, M., & O'Reilly, K. (2009). Migration and the search for a better way of life: A critical exploration of lifestyle migration. *The Sociological Review, 57*(4), 608–625.

Cederberg, M., & Villares-Varela, M. (2019). Ethnic entrepreneurship and the question of agency: The role of different forms of capital, and the relevance of social class. *Journal of Ethnic and Migration Studies, 45*(1), 115–132.

Coşciug, Anatolie, Andreea Vornicu, Bogdan Radu, Carmen Greab, Ovidiu Oltean, and Toma Burean. 2019. Indexul Integrării Imigranților În România - 2019 (The Index of Immigrants Integration in Romania - 2019). CRCM – Centrul Român de Cercetare a Migrației.

Croucher, S. (2009). Migrants of privilege: The political transnationalism of Americans in Mexico. *Identities. Global Studies in Culture and Power, 16*(4), 463–491.

Croucher, S. (2018). Rooted in relative privilege: US "expats" in Granada, Nicaragua. *Identities. Global Studies in Culture and Power, 25*(4), 436–455.

Dustmann, C. (1999). Temporary migration, human capital, and language fluency of migrants. *Scandinavian Journal of Economics, 101*(2), 297–314.

Engbersen, G. (2018). Liquid migration and its consequences for local integration policies. In P. Scholten & M. van Ostaijen (Eds.), *Between mobility and migration: The multi-level governance of intra-European movement* (pp. 63–76). Springer.

Favell, A. (2008). *Eurostars and Eurocities : Free movement and mobility in an integrating Europe.* Blackwell Publishers.

Fechtter, M. (2007). Living in a bubble: Expatriates' transnational spaces. In V. Amit (Ed.), *Going first class: New approaches to travel* (pp. 33–52). Berghahn Books.

Guest, G., Bunce, A., & Johnson, L. (2006). How many interviews are enough? An experiment with data saturation and variability. *Field Methods, 18*(1), 59–82.

Hagaman, A. K., & Wutich, A. (2017). How many interviews are enough to identify metathemes in multisited and cross-cultural research? Another perspective on guest, bunce, and Johnson's (2006) landmark study. *Field Methods, 29*(1), 23–41.

Harder, N., Figueroa, L., Gillum, R. M., Hangartner, D., Laitin, D. D., & Hainmueller, J. (2018). Multidimensional measure of immigrant integration. *Proceedings of the National Academy of Sciences of the United States of America, 115*(45), 11483–11488.

Hayes, M. (2014). "We gained a lot over what we would have had:" the geographic arbitrage of north American lifestyle migrants to Cuenca. *Ecuador, 40*(12), 1953–1971.

Hennink, M. M., Kaiser, B., & Marconi, V. C. (2017). Code saturation versus meaning saturation: How many interviews are enough? *Qualitative Health Research, 27*(4), 591–608.

Inglehart, R., & Welzel, C. (2005). *Modernization, cultural change, and democracy: The human development sequence.* Cambridge University Press.

Iredale, R. (2001). The migration of professionals: Theories and typologies. *International Migration, 39*(5), 7–26.

Jong, P. W., & de, and Helga de Valk. (2020). Intra-European migration decisions and welfare systems: The missing life course link. *Journal of Ethnic and Migration Studies, 46*(9), 1773–1791.

Kennedy, A. (2019). The politics of skilled immigration: Explaining the ups and downs of the US H-1B visa program. *International Migration Review, 53*(2), 346–370.

King, R. (2002). Towards a new map of European migration. *International Journal of Population Geography, 8*(2), 89–106.

Kolbe, M. (2021). When politics trumps economics: Contrasting high-skilled immigration policy-making in Germany and Austria. *International Migration Review, 55*(1), 31–57.

Kolbe, M., & Kayran, E. N. (2019). The limits of skill selective immigration policies: Welfare states and the commodification of labour immigrants. *Journal of European Social Policy, 29*(4), 478–497.

Kunz, S. (2016). Privileged Mobilities: Locating the expatriate in migration scholarship. *Geography Compass, 10*(3), 89–101.

Leinonen, J. (2012). Invisible immigrants, visible expats? Americans in Finnish discourses on immigration and internationalization. *Nordic Journal of Migration Research, 2*(3), 213–223.

Lutz, P. (2017). Two logics of policy intervention in immigrant integration: An institutionalist framework based on capabilities and aspirations. *Comparative Migration Studies, 5*(1), 1–18.

Marvel, M. R., Davis, J. L., & Sproul, C. R. (2016). Human capital and entrepreneurship research: A critical review and future directions. *Entrepreneurship Theory and Practice, 40*(3), 599–626.

Meier, L. (2014). Introduction: Local lives, work and social identities of migrant professionals in the City. In L. Meier (Ed.), *Migrant professionals in the City: Local encounters, identities, and inequalities: Local encounters, identities and inequalities* (pp. 1–20). Routledge.

Piekut, A. (2012). Visible and invisible ethnic "others" in Warsaw: Spaces of encounter and places of exclusion. In M. Grubbauer & J. Kusiak (Eds.), *Chasing Warsaw socio-material dynamics of urban change since 1990* (pp. 188–212). Campus Verlag.

Schinkel, W. (2017). *Imagined societies: A critique of immigrant integration in Western Europe.* Cambridge University Press.

Snel, E., Engbersen, G., & Leerkes, A. (2006). Transnational involvement and social integration. *Global Networks, 6*(3), 285–308.

Sobolewska, M., Galandini, S., & Lessard-Phillips, L. (2017). The public view of immigrant integration: Multidimensional and consensual. Evidence from survey experiments in the UK and the Netherlands. *Journal of Ethnic and Migration Studies, 43*(1), 58–79.

Stan, S., & Toma, V.-V. (2019). Accumulation by Dispossession and Public–Private Biomedical Pluralism in Romanian Health Care. *Medical Anthropology: Cross-Cultural Studies in Health and Illness, 38*(1), 85–99.

Triadafilopoulos, T., & Smith, C. D. (2013). Introduction. In T. Triadafilopoulos (Ed.), *Wanted and welcome? Policies for highly skilled immigrants in comparative perspective* (pp. 1–12). Springer.

Ucbasaran, D., Alsos, G. A., & Westhead, P. (2008). Habitual Entrepreneurs. *Foundations and Trends in Entrepreneurship, 4*(4), 309–450.

van Bochove, M., & Engbersen, G. (2015). Beyond cosmopolitanism and expat bubbles: Challenging dominant representations of knowledge workers and trailing spouses. *Population, Space and Place, 21*(4), 295–309.

Vertovec, S. (2009). *Transnationalism.* Routledge.

Vladescu, C., Scîntee, S. G., Olsavszky, V., Hernández-Quevedo, C., & Sagan, A. (2016). *Romania: Health system review. Health systems in transition.* LSE Research Online.

Voicu, B., & Vlase, I. (2014). High-skilled immigrants in times of crisis. A cross-European analysis. *International Journal of Intercultural Relations, 42*, 25–37.

Voicu, B., Alexe, I., Gostin, C., & Oneașcă, I. (2020). *Romania.* Country report on free movement rights and EU mobile citizens' inclusion.

von Koppenfels Amanda, K. (2014). *Migrants or expatriates?: Americans in Europe.* Palgrave Macmillan.

Waldinger, H. A., & Ward, R. (1990). *Ethnic entrepreneurs: Immigrant business in industrial societies.* Sage Publications Ltd.

Williams, A. M. (2007). Listen to me, learn with me: International migration and knowledge transfer. *British Journal of Industrial Relations, 45*(2), 361–382.

Wrigley, H. S. (2012). Dimensions of immigrant integration and civic engagement: Issues and exemplary programs. *New Directions for Adult and Continuing Education, 135*, 25–32.

Chapter 11
EU Citizenship: A Tool for Integration?

Sara Wallace Goodman

11.1 Introduction

European Union citizenship conveys important rights and opportunities to the almost 450 million citizens of EU Member States. European citizens are first and foremost citizens of their respective member states, but EU citizenship is designed to complement national citizenship, enabling individuals to move and live across the EU, participate in the political life of the EU, and exercise meaningful rights (e.g., diplomatic and consular protection in third countries). For instance, EU citizenship enables participation in local elections of an individual's their country of residence (independent of national citizenship), as well as vote for members of the European Parliament. Voting in these types of elections promises to increase the political legitimacy of the EU and, in principle, diminish the democratic deficit of this supranational institution. And through political participation that builds political legitimacy, EU citizens push this institution toward an "ever closer Union."

This is the aspirational view of citizenship—that citizenship is a vehicle for political integration. In practice, EU citizenship constitutes a rather idiosyncratic if uncertain role in the EU—Maarten Vink (2004, 25) even labels it "political kitsch". Electoral participation exhibits high variance across the member states and identification with "European identity" is weak, where the identity itself is described as "banal" (McNamara, 2015). In fact, in voting to "Brexit", a slim majority of British citizens expressed a willingness to forego EU benefits altogether, which they now experience in their deprivation of rights like free movement. And, most problematic, EU citizenship is deeply stratified, unequally experienced across individuals in the member states when it comes to family reunification, social rights and expulsion (Mantu et al., 2020). Can EU citizenship be a mechanism of incorporation given

S. W. Goodman (✉)
Department of Political Science, University of California, Irvine, CA, USA
e-mail: swgood@uci.edu

© The Author(s) 2023
R. Barbulescu et al. (eds.), *Revising the Integration-Citizenship Nexus in Europe*, IMISCOE Research Series, https://doi.org/10.1007/978-3-031-25726-1_11

these problems? Can EU citizenship compensate for political and social integration gaps created at national or subnational levels, detailed in previous chapters of this volume?

This chapter stands distinct in this volume in that it considers the nexus of citizenship and integration from a supernational perspective. A book claiming to re-examine the citizenship and integration nexus in Europe would simply be incomplete if it did not consider the layering of rights conveyed through supranational status. In studying the evolution and consequences of EU citizenship, I detail what kind of political integration is produced for the individual. I describe meaningful rights gained through EU citizenship, from mobility to social rights, and the ways in which these fill gaps in integration, particularly at the subnational level. In this analysis, this chapter also departs from previous chapters in taking a structural perspective, focusing not on the experiences of citizenship or individual-level observations but on policy as institutional opportunity structures.

This chapter also considers what I call reflective consequences: what the evolution and limitations of EU citizenship mean for the EU as a political organization. In other words, it simultaneously considers both directions: the consequences of EU citizenship for receiving individuals and the EU as the conferring regional organization. Initially, a shared community status – which would eventually be described by the term "citizen" – this European-wide status was designed to address the challenges of labor mobility in a shared economic area. It later evolved into an instrument for conferring social and political rights in a political union, establishing bonds of affinity and reducing the democratic deficit. In tracing changes in EU citizenship policy in this evolving regional organization, I show how the goalposts shift from economic to social to political rationales. Today, I argue, EU citizenship is *incomplete* as a democratic mechanism for conveying rights, *imbalanced* in acquisition rules across the member states, and *inconsistent* in establishing how EU political rights are practiced across member states. I illustrate the consequences of these "underdevelopments" in three critical policy areas, including Enlargement, national citizenship eligibility, and Brexit. To conclude, I argue that while EU citizenship yields some important short-term gains for individual integration – namely mobility and rights – there are long-term limitations to relying on EU citizenship to bridge the integration-citizenship gap. Moreover, an unevenly practiced EU citizenship raises some serious consequences for thinking about EU political authority and democratic legitimacy.

11.2   What Is EU Citizenship?

Like traditional *qua* national citizenship, EU citizenship is a status, a set of rights, and an identity. As a status, it permits individuals access to a burgundy-colored passport, intra-Union mobility, right to residence and myriad economic, civil and social rights. Those include the right to vote and run as a candidate in municipal and European Parliament elections in the member state of residence; the right to petition

Parliament, access documents, and appeal to the Ombudsman; diplomatic and consular protection and services in third countries, the right to address EU institutions in your language of choice; and, generally, the legal protection of EU law, from the Charter of Fundamental Rights to a variety of regulations and directives, like data privacy. Finally, it is an identity, though not a beloved[1] nor equally shared one (Matthijs & Merler, 2020), promoted through a common passport, flag, anthem, currency, and history. Any number of public opinion polls will illustrate how widely different the EU is valued across the member states (De Vries, 2018).

But citizenship is more than an individual status and identity—*who* is a national and *what* that person receives. Citizenship is fundamentally a transactional relationship between an individual and a state (Tilly, 1997). As part of this transaction, individuals get rights from the polity, but they also owe certain obligations. In exchange, the state has certain obligations to it's citizens but also claims rights. It is reciprocal in the truest sense. An individual requires citizenship for rights and protection, and a state requires citizenship, too, to delineate national boundaries and establish a constituency for administration (e.g., Weber, 1976) and, in democratic contexts, from who it derives its legitimacy (1959). While these understandings of citizenship tie an individual to a *national* state, there is nothing that limits the application of this concept to other types of polities, both above (international organizations) and below (subnational, city-state units). To wit, the codification of EU citizenship at Maastricht was referred to as a "constitutional moment" (Ackerman 1991, cited in Maas, 2007), not only meant to empower the individual through status but solidify the connection and legitimacy between EU institutions and its citizens.

Yet, because EU citizenship is a derivative of state assent—as the Treaty of Lisbon clarifies, "*Citizenship of the Union shall be additional to and not replace national citizenship*" – it only exists for individuals as moderated by and filtered through the member states. Simply put, this weakens the nature of the transactional tie. What do EU citizens get from *and owe* the EU, what does the EU owe and *get* from its citizens? First amended in the Amsterdam Treaty, and to pacify Danish opposition expressed in their failed Maastricht referendum, the language makes clear that EU citizenship is not a dual citizenship, but a subsidiary one.

During the heyday of European integration, many scholars were enthusiastic about the theoretical possibilities of post- or transnational citizenship (e.g., Soysal, 1994). Rainer Bauböck (1995), for instance, saw national citizenship as becoming a source of transnational citizenship and rights. David Jacobson (1997), on the other hand, expressed some concerns that postnational citizenship elevated a series of problems for international relations but celebrated the institiuationalization of human rights. Peter Schuck (1998), an American legal scholar, worried the trend devalued citizenship overall. But as EU integration marched on, and following a series of Treaty disappointments, from Amsterdam revisions to constitutional

---

[1]As Jacques Delors famously stated, perhaps prognosticated, "you cannot *fall in love* with the *single market*." https://www.cvce.eu/content/publication/2003/8/22/b9c06b95-db97-4774-a700-e8aea5172233/publishable_en.pdf

amendments, citizenship ultimately remained territorialized and complementary to national citizenship, part of a multilevel citizenship construction and not meant to be interchangeable (Bauböck, 2014).

11.3 The Evolution of an Incomplete, Imbalanced, and Inconsistent Citizenship

That EU citizenship is limited is not a novel observation.[2] But what are the consequences of this limited status? We can look at limited citizenship as a function of institutional *design*, namely the interchangeable assertiveness and restraint of the European Court of Justice (e.g. Kochenov, 2017) as well as member state preferences, in line with liberal intergovernmental accounts (Moravcsik, 1993).

"Limited by design" is not inherently problematic. Many have argued that its underdeveloped identity is purposeful, forwarding democratic defenses of the derivative nature of EU citizenship (Nicolaïdis, 2013; Bellamy, 2008). And no one would mistake EU citizenship as anything resembling a coherent identity, given the enduring variation in national practice, differences in status, and absence of collected social rights (e.g., collective protection against financial risk) (Weale, 2014). Moreover, group-making and identity formation is an ongoing process with no set endpoint or objective. When compared to other fledging forms generated by other regional unions, such as those in South and Central American or in sub-Saharan Africa, EU citizenship is the most advanced model of supranational citizenship (Maas, 2014, 409). But there are consequences, and it is a valuable exercise to hold up the image of what EU citizenship is *supposed* to be and do to what we can empirically observe.

According to Article 10 of the Treaty on European Union: "every citizen shall have the right to participate in the democratic life of the Union." Moreover, citizenship establishes a clear democratic mandate for EU institutions: "decisions shall be taken as openly and as closely as possible to the citizen" and "political parties at the European level contribute to forming European political awareness and to expressing the will of citizens of the Union". This establishes a benchmark for measuring the extent to which this ideal is obtained, where citizenship falls short, and what the policy consequences are of the gap in-between.

To assess the extent to which EU citizenship has reached this benchmark, we start at the beginning and trace the policy evolution itself. The story of EU citizenship is one of changing the goalpost, interest players (i.e., member states), and interests. As a result of these ongoing and changing dynamics, as new interests are introduced, others stall. Thus, we first detail a longitudinal account of how citizenship evolves to be *incomplete*.

---

[2] Vink (2005)'s book and Maas's (2007) penultimate book chapter share the same title: "Limits of European Citizenship."

EU citizenship is rooted in the Paris Treaty (1951), which established the European Coal and Steel Community and free movement for workers in those fields. This early establishment of workers' rights across borders of the member states set into motion a series of decisions that would layer on top of one another, accumulating in the concept of EU Citizenship alongside the codification of the political union at Maastricht in 1992. Indeed, if you search through the early treaty texts, you will not find a single reference to either "citizen" or "citizenship" before the Maastricht Treaty—and even this reference is nestled in a section dedicated to subsidiarity. But the idea of status for member state individuals *qua* workers takes root early and evolves.

Economic factors were not the sole drivers of this process. Maas (2007, 7) describes "the effort to entrench and expand a set of supranational rights, thereby creating European citizens" as reflecting "the will to create a community of people rather than simply a free market area." Nor was this progression incidental, or a byproduct of integration elsewhere. As early as the 1960s, the European Court of Justice (ECJ) established that "[The European Economic Community] is more than an agreement which merely creates mutual obligations between the contracting states. This view is confirmed by the preamble to the Treaty which refers not only to governments but to peoples. It is also confirmed more specifically by the establishment of institutions endowed with sovereign rights, the exercise of which affects members states *and also their citizens*" (quoted in Vink, 2005, 44–5).[3]

By the 1970s, the goal post started to move. Pushed by Belgium, Italy, and Spain, social policy (attaching social entitlements and rights of residence) appeared on the docket as a measure to protect workers. Yet while idea entrepreneurs were talking about "transform[ing] the free movement rights into an authentic common citizenship," strong opponents like Denmark and the UK checked these ambitions (Maas, 2007, 42–3). New members at the time (both ascended to EU membership in 1973), this disrupted a consensus among early member states, whose plan was to consolidate social rights in a singular status, merging categories of workers and rights in EU citizenship by incorporating the Social Protocol.

With the Single European Act (1986), which established free movement and flow of labor across intra-EU borders as a bridge to establishing a single market, the goal of EC worker's status started to change. Having realized one purpose (establish a status for labor mobility) and being effectively circumscribed in its second purpose (extend social rights) by new member states, status *cum* citizenship became a new tool for reducing the increasing chasm of democratic legitimacy between member state national citizens and EU institutions. As the European Parliament started to grow in prominence and power (Tsebelis, 1994), Eurocrats became concerned with

---

[3] The evolution of EU citizenship from an economic, market rights (free movement) to individual political (local voting) and social rights maps perfectly to T.H. Marshall's (1950) famed, postwar argument about working class Britons, "Social Citizenship." So are its flaws, including selective extension of rights, teleology, consolidation, and possibilities to reverse and revoke previous-won rights.

whether EU citizenship could mitigate the sizable democratic deficit (Follesdal & Hix, 2006).

Finally, while Maastricht may have been a "constitutional moment," the citizenship it produced that was far less ambitious than planned.[4] On the one hand, states like Spain were pushing "to make a qualitative jump which allows an area of essentially economic character to be transformed into an integrated area which would be at the direct service of the citizen" (Spanish proposal on European citizenship, quoted in Vink, 2001, 882). On the other, European citizenship was met by skepticism by other member states; Danish voters rejected the treaty in a national referendum; Belgian policymakers thought it did not go far enough, but also debated local voting rights (along with France and Luxembourg). Among the strongest of Maastricht supporters were those with citizens working across the EU in large numbers, e.g., Spain, Greece, Italy, and Portugal. Italy in particular was the largest sending state among the original EC members and the earliest and strongest advocate of free movement of workers. Some of the strongest supporters were also newer member states, who ratified the Treaty as they joined the EU. These views were not as vocal in the negotiation process, as they were not yet members. Thus, as a minimal policy, we can see how "Maastricht achieved less than some had hoped, but more than many had thought possible" (Maas, 2007, 59).

Another consequence of Maastricht is that, in failing to seize on the momentum of Europe's constitutional moment to "complete" EU citizenship, such as consolidating social rights, there lacked critical political momentum afterwards to move the project forward. Policy innovation after Maastricht can largely be characterized as sclerotic or plateauing. Maastricht took years to ratify across the member states, and Danish intransigence certainly impeded ongoing discussions. In one example, the Treaty of Amsterdam was meant to expand EU citizen rights, but instead, created a variety of policies circling—but not addressing—the issue, like employment and public health, and—as pertains directly to citizenship—only established the right to contact the EU in any language. Much of this was due to British and Danish opposition to elements of Maastricht. In fact, the very absence of rights-pursuing momentum—specifically that of consolidating social rights around a single status—is the source of its own incompleteness: "the attempt to add a veneer of common European rights over well-established national rights based on dissimilar ethical and moral conceptions…helps explain why EU citizenship did not develop faster or more fully, and why it could be weakened or even repealed" (Maas, 2007, 95). Failed referendums in France and the Netherlands on the constitutional Draft Treaty, the challenges of Enlargement, and the politically difficult issue of mass migration ultimately put the breaks on consolidating EU citizenship rights or moving citizenship status forward.[5] This type of incompleteness was portended by The Tindemans

---

[4] In addition to the consolidation of social rights, Maas (2007, 49) details goals like the Luxembourg Presidency's desire for a "citizen's obligation to display solidarity with other Union citizens."

[5] While policy was "stuck", a significant amount of legal integration took place, including decisions by the ECJ as the primary engine for interpreting EU citizenship. For instance, the ECJ's ruling in *Tjebbes* (Court of Justice, judgment of 12 March 2019, case C-221/17, *Tjebbes and*

Report of 1975, which argued that "An unfinished structure does not weather well: it must be completed, otherwise it collapses."[6] In sum, where EU citizenship establishes meaningful rights, its incompleteness leaves much to be desired. It remains an unfinished tool, providing status (and regularization for migrants of new member states) but unrealized potential in conveying other rights that are instrumental for filling immigrant integration gaps.

A second concern with EU citizenship as a mechanism of integration is its *imbalanced* application across the member states when it comes to conferring status and rights. Article 20 creates the link between member state and EU citizenship: "every person holding the nationality of a Member State shall be a citizen of the Union." This primarily excludes permanent residents, i.e., citizens with non-EU citizenship, who may enjoy other rights but can be barred from naturalization, which remains a sovereign prerogative of EU member states and thus from access to EU citizenship. Member states still retain full autonomy for defining naturalization procedures, and the EU has kept an arms-length on this matter, preserving national sovereignty in this area above all (de Groot & Luk, 2014). By member states retaining exclusion national competence in conferring citizenship, two different types of problems are created. First, EU citizenship procedures are not evenly applied across countries. Unlike in other federal systems (Weiler, 1999), EU citizenship has not produced "communitarianism" or even harmonization, and there is wide variation in national citizenship conferring practices (Goodman, 2010). This inconsistency can produce discriminatory practices cross-nationally, and rulings like Tjebbes (Court of Justice, judgment of 12 March 2019, *case* C-221/17) represent missed opportunities by the ECJ to address unevenness in national legislation (Swider, 2020).

States can use this exclusive right to pursue national priorities that may directly undercut other member states. For example, some member states use membership in the EU to sell citizenship through investor schemes. Countries like Malta profit from selling access to the EU while pushing the issues of immigration onto actual destinations. As member states also have not coordinated on immigration policy, individual member states decide which third country nationals (immigrants from outside of the EU) get access, and thus, begin a path to citizenship (or not). These practices make EU citizenship externally inconsistent, and subject to rife, economic discrimination. For their part, the EP and the Commission have opposed this practice since 2014, initiating infringement procedures against Malta and Cyprus. More

---

Others), ruled against the stripping EU citizens residing abroad of their citizenship based on non-renewal of their passport. This judgement was also evaluated by many as a bold expansion of the court's jurisdiction in matters of nationality law. See Stephen Coutts, "Bold and Thoughtful: The Court of Justice intervenes in nationality law Case C-221/17 Tjebbes." 25 March 2019. Available at https://europeanlawblog.eu/2019/03/25/bold-and-thoughtful-the-court-of-justice-intervenes-in-nationality-law-case-c-221-17-tjebbes/

[6] Available at https://www.cvce.eu/en/collections/unit-content/-/unit/02bb76df-d066-4c08-a58a-d4686a3e68ff/63f5fca7-54ec-4792-8723-1e626324f9e3/Resources#03f0d181-4838-4a86-a1b5-f143bb34cbd0

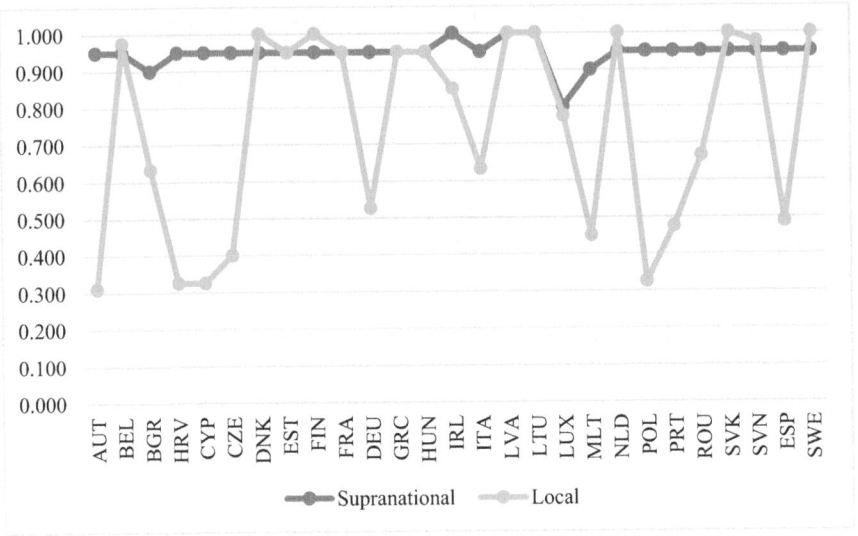

Fig. 11.1 Voting Rights for Second Country Nationals at the Supranational and Local Levels

recently, in response to Russia's War in Ukraine, the Commission announced their intention to end investor citizenship schemes of EU member states altogether.

Last, EU citizenship rights as practiced within states are themselves *inconsistent*. EU law establishes voting (and candidacy) rights for European Parliament elections for non-national EU citizens (also known as second-country nationals, where first country nationals are citizens of their country of residence). It also provides local voting rights for second-country nationals. Yet there is a wide gap between policy and practice across and within member states, with members states exercising significant discretion in interpreting eligibility and access restrictions. Fig. 11.1 presents voting rights for non-national EU citizens (i.e., SCNs), i.e., EU citizens resident in states other than that of their national citizenship, at both the European Parliament (supranational – SN) and local (LO) level. Data is from the GLOBALCIT Electoral Laws ("ELECLAW") database (2019),[7] which contains information on a range of issues and parameters of electoral inclusiveness, from voting to candidate rights.[8] Measures are scaled 0 to 1, where 1 is the most inclusive.

In principle, voting rights should not vary for EU citizens by country of residence. That they do in practice is evidence not only of unevenness of EU citizenship status across the member states, but incompleteness in harmonizing citizenship

---

[7] Policies are measured for 2015.

[8] These are voting rights for non-national EU citizens (VNCEU). The variable names are VNCEU-SN and VNCEU-LO. Both are composite indicators measuring the overall inclusiveness of voting rights of non-national EU citizens, combining basic eligibility and residence-based restrictions with access restrictions. For more, see (GLOBALCIT, 2019). National voting rights for non-national EU citizens is excluded from the Figure as there is no variation (all are scored at 0, or fully exclusive). The UK is also excluded from analysis as they are no longer a member of the EU.

practices.[9] In Fig. 11.1, we see that eligibility and access are basically equal for EU citizens when it comes to supranational elections, i.e., voting in European Parliament elections. Almost all states have a score at or approaching 1 (full inclusion). However, we see real variation when it comes to local voting rights. In addition to variation across states, we also observe democratic rights gaps between local and supranational voting rights within states (e.g., Austria, Poland).

A second type of gap—for the purposes of illustration—is when we compare local voting rights of second country national (SCN)—a right under EU law—to those of third country nationals (TCN), decided according to national discretion. We would expect less equality and inclusivity for TCNs, who lack EU citizenship status. On the other hand, if the argument is a democratic one – that individuals that live within a territory should have say in the rules by which they are governed – then gaps are a little more difficult to justify from a normative perspective.

Figure 11.2 presents degree of access to local voting rights for both EU citizens (SCNs) and non-EU citizens (TCNs).[10] Using the same scale of 0 to 1 (where 1 is the most inclusive), we see clear variation across member states. Along the x-axis, we see there is significant variation in local voting rights for EU citizens (SCNs)—this is the same variable from Fig. 11.1—and along the y-axis, further variation for

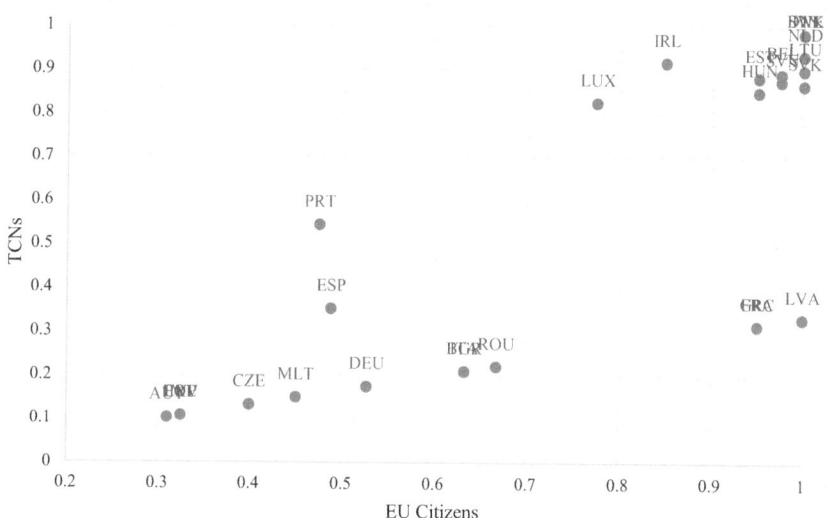

Fig. 11.2 Local Voting Rights for SCNs and TCNs

---

[9] While we would observe more within-case variation by comparing differing practices of access to federal elections across US states, the within-unit comparison and revealed variation presented here is still instructive.

[10] The x-axis (EU citizens) is the same variable from Figure 11.1 (VNCEU-LO), and the y-axis is local voting rights for non-citizen residents (VNC-LO).

TCNs. In the upper-right corner we see a cluster of around ten member states with inclusive practices for both SCNs and TCNs (including Finland, Denmark, Sweden, Netherlands, Estonia, Hungary, Slovakia, and Slovenia). Variation within category results from registration procedures and residence (e.g., Denmark requires 3 years residence for TCNs; Netherlands 5).

It is worth remarking on the generally bifurcated nature of the access to local voting rights for TCNs, where eleven member states are below .4 (i.e., trend toward exclusion). From a normative standpoint, this is problematic. TCNs may have lived in a country for years and due to strict nationality laws, some may be unable to naturalize. Maas (2008, 583) refers to the differential in rights between SCNs and TCNs as evidence that "EU citizenship's transformative potential remains unrealized," though the introduction of local voting rights for TCNs alongside SCNs in 2004 accession states (e.g., Estonia, Hungary, Lithuania, Slovenia, Slovakia) clearly constitute a "transformative effect" of EU membership. We also see a cluster of states where local voting rights are restricted for both SCN and TCN: Austria, Croatia, Cyprus and Poland.

The preceding discussion illustrates EU citizenship as incomplete, imbalanced across states, and inconsistent within states. This paints a mixed picture – one where real rights are obtained and meaningful integration can be facilitated, but also portends larger issues when considering coherence across the Union. The question that remains: What are the policy consequences of this type of a limited and uneven EU citizenship for Europe? What kind of authority can a democratic political entity claim if it is sustained by weak connection to those purportedly responsible for conferring legitimacy?

This next section turns form citizens to the polity as part of the analysis of "reflective consequences." I explore three policy issues to illustrate the consequences of what I term "underdevelopment" of EU citizenship: Enlargement, national citizenship eligibility, and Brexit (or what I describe as the problem of "suprastatelessness"). In each, EU citizenship is unable to address the problem at hand and, in many ways, generates more problems than it solves.

11.4 Consequences of Weak EU Citizenship: Some Examples

11.4.1 Enlargement

Enlargement presented two central challenges to EU citizenship. First, as already discussed, it introduced new negotiating partners into an evolving EU citizenship-making process, which necessarily disrupted an equilibrium with new goals and priorities. On top of substantive differences between Accession members and "older" member states, Enlargement also coincided with changes to voting procedure through the Treaty of Nice, whereby qualified majority voting was extended to free movement (and, thus, no longer required unanimity). This made it more likely for lowest common denominator solutions which could pass majority threshold. As Maas (2007, 79) notes, "those who hoped that European integration would shift from a focus on economic integration toward an increasing emphasis on individual rights were disappointed [with Enlargement]."

Second, the citizens of new member states—eager to exercise new opportunities for labor market mobility and worker rights—were difficult to integrate into existing labor market arrangements. Here, the issue is not that EU citizenship was incomplete, but it was almost too complete. It offered more to new member state citizens in terms of labor mobility and rights than existing members states were willing to give. With the 2004 Enlargement (which included eight countries of Central and Eastern Europe, including the Czech Republic, Hungary, and Poland, as well as former British colonies of Cyprus and Malta), there was trepidation among receiving, older members states in admitting migrants from new member states with high unemployment, e.g., Poland. Thus, as part of EU accession, a number of existing member states could establish transitional arrangements that limited labor movement. There was significant range in the amount of restrictions member states applied to new labor. On one end of the spectrum, Germany and Austria applied the full, seven-year protective period (lifting restrictions in 2011). On the other, in the 2004 enlargement round, only the UK, Sweden, and Ireland fully and immediately opened their labor markets to new EU citizens. British policymakers based their decision off the immediate labor market access granted to Spain and Portugal in 1986, which had a modest impact on the British labor market. Thus, they did not anticipate that over one million Polish workers would move to the UK and become a feature of the British service economy (Burrell, 2016). In the subsequent 2007 (Bulgaria and Romania) and 2013 (Croatia) rounds, the lineup of full versus limited access was different and, in the end, Ireland received more Polish workers per capita than the UK. Restrictions in response to 2007 weren't lifted until 2014[11] and, in the case of Austria's response to Croatian accession, restrictions were maintained until as recently as May 2019. Enlargement not only quickly revealed the limitations and conditionality of EU citizenship, it established a type of probationary status, perpetuating imbalance across the member states. This prevented further harmonization and consolidation of citizen rights—namely welfare rights—which would have been more difficult to distribute across the member states.

Moreover, Enlargement reveals how the *labor* benefits of EU citizenship ultimately do not depend on the relationship between the *citizen* of a state and the supranational but of the citizenship-conferring *member state* to the EU. Member states could only decide to delay access of new EU citizens to their labor markets—not any other benefits of EU membership like entry or residence—though access to employment and economic integration facilitates other forms of integration, including citizenship acquisition (Peters et al., 2018). Put another way, older member states in this case set the terms of economic integration. While one effect of the

---

[11] 2007 Enlargement (Bulgarian and Romania) citizens were prohibited from immediate work almost everywhere, except Finland and Sweden.

accession on May 1, 2004 was immediate regularization of thousands of migrants who held irregular status, these individuals continued to experience economic integration as outsiders despite newly-procured, formal EU citizenship status.

11.4.2 *Immigration and Eligibility for National Citizenship*

Citizenship is a discrete group, a type of club membership. A key challenge to EU authority is that it can only control who gets EU citizenship secondarily. We already discussed its derived status, and that EU citizens are made by gaining national citizenship of member states. But who becomes eligible to even begin the process of naturalization – that is, who is allowed to immigrate – is also a power for the member states alone. The EU has a common external border, but not a common immigration policy, notwithstanding the considerable regulatory power of the EU with regard to national policies of family migration and asylum. Put another way, the EU lacks immigration authority outside of decisions pertaining to the common market, with especially weak competence when it comes to harmonization of labor migration policies (e.g., EU blue card for highly skilled). This creates asymmetry of authority; national governments decide who enters and, ultimately, gets national and EU citizenship. This is the problem of imbalance or "horizontal equality" (Kochenov, 2017, xxviii), as it is these very individuals that ultimate convey legitimacy.

It is particularly visible when considering two types of citizenship acquisition: investment citizenship, or *jus pecuniae* (Dzankic, 2012), and inheritance citizenship, where citizenship is transmitted across generations to individuals who, unlike new immigrants, are born abroad yet permitted to skip integration measures. Most countries in the world maintain *jus sanguinis* provisions by which children inherit the citizenship of their parents without fulfilling integration requirements, like passing a language test or demonstrating citizenship knowledge. The concern here is the disparity between someone who inherits citizenship across several generations without residence versus an immigrant residing in a country that has to fulfil many requirements. Both investment and inheritance lay bare the imbalance of citizenship access *within* states, exacerbating EU citizenship access *across* member states.

Beginning with investment citizenship, as previously mentioned, three EU members states maintain explicit investor citizenship schemes—Bulgaria (since 2005), Cyprus (since 2007) and Malta (since 2013).[12] In the latter, the Malta Individual Investor Program aims to recruit high net worth investors and for upwards of €650,000,[13] applicants can buy Maltese citizenship and, therefore, the mobility to

---

[12] Many other states offer less systematic models, and several sell permanent residence statuses (e.g., Ireland, Italy, France, Spain).

[13] This is the base contribution. In addition, applicants need to make investments and purchase or rent residential property.

live, work, and travel in the EU.[14] In January 2019, the European Commission published its Report on Investor Citizenship Schemes, raising concern about the delinking of citizenship and residence, as well as the marketing of investment citizenship not as a national policy but a way to obtain the rights and privileges of EU citizenship.[15] It also suggested the sale of passports should be linked to conditionality criteria for new accession states. The Commission has no direct competence to regulate citizenship, yet this report aptly reflects how immigration—through investment citizenship as one example—poses new problems that existing institutions cannot solve. And, as described earlier, clamping down on investment citizenship became an acute priority in the wake of Russia's war on Ukraine, to prevent wealthy Russian oligarchs from buying refuge in the EU, so to speak.

Inheritance citizenship is a second case. Most states make provisions for children and grandchildren of citizens to inherit citizenship. But some countries maintain extraterritorial *jus sanguinis* rules that have generated huge potentials of EU born abroad based on ancestry, including Italy and Spain.[16] Some cases to illustrate the extreme difference in potential citizenship suffice. Greece and Germany, acquisition by cultural affinity requires demonstrating knowledge of the language or other conditions of naturalization, but oftentimes generational acquisition bypasses naturalization conditions, creating asymmetry between immigrants that jump through high hoops to obtain citizenship, compared to descendants living abroad that merely file paperwork and pay a fee. This type of internal inconsistency in citizenship assignment, as well as cross-national imbalance in assignment practices, ultimately undermines the coherence of an EU citizenship as an equitable membership category. States have near-total discretion to maintain whatever citizenship rules they like, but when an additional layer of EU rights is a consequence of that decision, there are clear and problematic democratic implications.

11.4.3 Brexit and Suprastatelessness

On June 23, 2016 British citizens voted to leave the EU (a slim but decisive majority of 51.9% to Leave versus 48.1 Remain). On January 31, 2020, they finally left. The interim period was defined by great uncertainty about the ability to "deliver Brexit," including what relationship the UK would have with the EU moving forward. This is when the status of EU citizens—both those living in the UK and British nationals using that status to live and work in Europe—became critical, affecting millions of

---

[14] Or, for $150,000, individuals can purchase citizenship of the small Pacific Island nation of Vanuatu and experience visa-free travel through Europe. https://www.bbc.com/news/business-49958628

[15] An additional concern was the role investor citizenship played in money laundering schemes. See https://ec.europa.eu/info/sites/info/files/com_2019_12_final_report.pdf

[16] For more, see Merve Erdilmen and Iseult Honohan, "Trends in birthright citizenship in EU 28, 2013–2020." EUI Technical Report. 2020. Available at https://cadmus.eui.eu/handle/1814/66646

people. EU citizens living in Britain lost protection, access, and status, and underwent years of uncertainty about their legal status, followed by bureaucratic hurdles for obtaining residency to continue living in a place they are already resident. The UK Settlement Scheme offers settled and pre-settled status for EU citizens and requires proof of identity and proof of continuous residence.

It is not surprising that EU citizenship did not grandfather-in protections for citizens of a state that chose to leave the EU. However, it is revealing is that EU citizenship status was not retained by British nationals living in the EU, a figure estimated at approximately 1.2 million citizens. Preserving its derived nature, EU citizenship and the rights it conveys, were stripped from British nationals living and working in the EU. Some of these rights were eventually "reacquired" but only after negotiations and individuals navigating dense, bureaucratic red tape. And, contrary to what many feared, in Brexit negotiations, the EU insisted and the UK agreed to preserve residence and labor market access rights for EU citizens in the UK and UK citizens in the EU. The implementation was far from perfect and required national legislation in EU member states, but the principle of maintaining as far as possible EU citizenship rights for those that would lose status was part of the consensus opinion.

Some British citizens used existing ties to take matters into their own hands. Around 500,000 British people applied for Irish citizenship during the first half of 2017. Uniquely, British Jews began to reapply for German citizenship in record numbers (eligible to "repatriate" if their families lost German citizenship between 1933 and 1945).[17]

But where opportunities to naturalize or hold dual citizenship are not possible, EU member states took different positions on their obligation. Several different models were initially floated to prevent rights deprivation for soon-to-be EU-less citizens, including the option model (e.g., Greenland), associate citizenship (van den Brink & Kochenov, 2019) and automatic naturalization (Huber, 2019). Italy, Germany, and the Netherlands were early guarantors that resident British citizens would have immediate access to residency permits. Eventually all EU states passed Brexit transition laws to this effect. The right to live and work in the EU for British nationals was guaranteed under the Withdrawal Agreement, but then directs the responsibility to each member state to set up a settlement scheme to register British citizens. The right to work and live across the EU ceased after the transition period, and citizens needed to apply to EU countries according to existing immigration rules.

There is an irony in these debates: after decades of building up an EU citizenship, it was not only thinkable but inevitable that some people will become immediately decoupled from that project in the case of a member state exiting. Citizenship rights – once won – are supposed to be difficult to unravel or take away, an teleological insight that dates back to T.H. Marshall (1950). International law protects individuals from statelessness, but there has yet to be an articulated legal argument

---

[17] https://www.jta.org/2018/10/19/global/germany-sees-dramatic-rise-citizenship-applications-british-jews

that transfers up to the supranational level. While some like Guy Verhofstadt, former Belgian Prime Minister and Member of European Parliament (MEP) since 2009, advocated for a type of "European associated citizenship," where EU member states granted British citizens living in Europe the full rights of EU citizens, this idea did not catch on more widely. EU status still proved valuable as British citizens living in member states sought permanent residence through citizenship. But this was bottom-up. We can remark on the absence of an aspirational vision in this critical moment and vast difference in political will compared to the EU's pre-Maastricht days.

11.5 Discussion

By simultaneously examining the consequences of EU citizenship on individuals *as well as* on the conferring organization, this paper provides a framework for thinking about what role citizenship might play in supporting immigrant integration at multiple levels, from the supranational to the national to the local level. This chapter reveals that while citizenship provides economic mobility and political integration at the sub- and supranational level for some—two important objectives that meaningfully fill the gaps left behind by national and local policies—it remains a status rife with inconsistencies.

Given these inconsistencies—and in keeping with the "reflective" analysis, we have one final question to address. We know what EU citizenship does and does not deliver for individuals, but what are the consequences on the rights-conferring polity, in terms of democratic legitimacy or even political authority? If citizenship establishes transactional ties between an individual and a democratic polity, what does it say about political legitimacy if that status is incomplete in rights attached to it, inconsistently accessed, and unevenly experienced? On the one hand, one can argue the EU does not even need a common citizenship. Citizenship may be a poor term for what exists—a series of privileges, from consular protection to mobility rights, without the expectations that individuals convey institutional legitimacy. On the other hand, the stated purpose of EU citizenship (TEU, Title II, Article 10) is to establish ties of democratic legitimacy, in both empowering EU citizens to vote European parliament elections and locally in municipal elections. The EU is a political union, where democratic legitimacy remains a central objective (Kohler-Koch & Rittberger, 2007) and where domestic dissensus is often the source for unravelling supranational goals (Hooghe & Marks, 2009). And given legitimacy and collective identity are inextricable (Benhabib, 1994), the encapsulation of these in citizenship has direct consequence for authority.

There are several reasons to think weak EU citizenship erodes legitimacy for the EU. First, the imbalanced and inconsistent nature of EU citizenship perpetuates a type of stratified citizenship. This is a serious problem for democratic systems. Domestic politics would not consider democracy legitimate in such contexts, as legitimacy is then only derived from those who are empowered (Caraway, 2004).

Why would we think otherwise for the legitimacy of the EU itself? Second, the incompleteness of EU citizenship widens the gap between the suprastate and the individual. One of the central purposes behind recent attempts at enhancing EU citizenship was to repair the democratic deficit, but stratified access to this right across the member states, not to mention low participation rates, does not achieve this goal. Third, there is increased skepticism of EU institutions and EU authority itself. Populist parties, Eurosceptics, and libertarian voices are recurring challenges to EU authority. Finally, in an observation similar to that made by Jones et al. (2016) regarding eurozone governance, it may be that EU citizenship achieved politically expedient goals in the short term, but undermine public support in the long term. That is, it is an example where overclaiming by pro-Europeans created outsized expectations and, ultimately, disenchantment.

A product of its own evolution, these inconsistencies reverberate across the member states to perpetuate an uneven status both across and within member states. Ultimately, this has not only for individuals but, ultimately, for the policy, both in terms of democratic legitimacy—where citizens that experience uneven rights and status are a threat to regime consolidation—and political authority, whereby the citizen-polity becomes tenuous. EU citizenship was initially designed to enable cross-border labor mobility. That eventually this became the very facet of citizenship that member states found contentious—even invasive of their sovereign, national prerogative to control borders (e.g., Brexit)—suggests citizenship is not the panacea democratic theorists, Eurocrats and Europhiles had hoped for. A sober reflection three decades after codification, and in the context of robust national populist support and democratic decline in EU member states, like Hungary and Poland, suggest the limitations of EU citizenship only skim the surface, and are unable to resolve or address deeper authority problems at hand.

With weak citizenship, a generous read of EU capacity is that it can proficiently and effectively regulate, but not meaningfully govern or represent. Self-limited authority and deliberately weak citizenship are necessarily modest—it prohibits fears of sovereignty encroachment and remains within bounds of appropriateness for suprastate organizations—but also short-sighted. There may be challenges in the future—even in the near present-day—in which citizens *need* EU authority and protection—immediate issues like status deprivation and consular services and safeguards against domestic authoritarian change (e.g., Hungary), but also imminent and ambiguous challenges like pandemics.

A more concerning conclusion might be that the EU is less dogmatic about democratic ideals over time (e.g., Kelemen, 2020), allowing momentum on EU citizenship to plateau due to indifference. The equilibrium is that the EU continues to operate as a regulatory authority. However, given the weak and incomplete nature of citizenship—and, thus, a shallow reservoir for deriving legitimacy—it struggles still to secure democratic, governing authority.

References

Bauböck, R. (1995). *Transnational citizenship : Membership and rights in international migration*. E. Elgar.

Bauböck, R. (2014). The three levels of citizenship within the European Union. *German Law Journal, 15*(5), 751–763.

Bellamy, R. (2008). Evaluating union citizenship: Belonging, rights and participation within the EU. *Citizenship Studies, 12*(6), 597–611.

Benhabib, S. (1994). Deliberative rationalality and models of democratic legitimacy. *Constellations, 1*(1), 26–52.

Burrell, K. (2016). *Polish migration to the UK in the'new'European Union*. Routledge.

Caraway, T. L. (2004). Inclusion and democratization: Class, gender, race, and the extension of suffrage. *Comparative Politics, 36*, 443–460.

de Groot, G.-R., & Luk, N. C. (2014). Twenty years of CJEU jurisprudence on citizenship. *German Law Journal, 15*(5), 821–834.

De Vries, C. E. (2018). *Euroscepticism and the future of European integration*. Oxford University Press.

Dzankic, Jelena. 2012. "The pros and cons of ius pecuniae: Investor citizenship in comparative perspective.".

Follesdal, A., & Hix, S. (2006). "why there is a democratic deficit in the EU: A response to Majone and Moravcsik." *JCMS. Journal of Common Market Studies, 44 (3):533-562*, 533–562.

GLOBALCIT. (2019). ELECLAW indicators. Version 5.1. edited by European University Institute. San Domenico di Fiesole.

Goodman, S. W. (2010). Naturalisation Policies in Europe: Exploring Patterns of Inclusion and Exclusion. In *EUDO Citizenship Comparative Reports*. Florence: EUDO Citizenship, Robert Schuman Centre for Advanced Studies, EUI.

Hooghe, L., & Marks, G. (2009). A postfunctionalist theory of European integration: From permissive consensus to constraining dissensus. *British Journal of Political Science, 39*(1), 1–23.

Huber, J. (2019). EU citizens in post-Brexit UK: The case for automatic naturalisation. *Journal of European Integration, 41*, 1–16.

Jacobson, D. (1997). *Rights across Borders: Immigration and the decline of citizenship*. Johns Hopkins University Press.

Jones, E., Daniel Kelemen, R., & Meunier, S. (2016). Failing forward? The euro crisis and the incomplete nature of European integration. *Comparative Political Studies, 49*(7), 1010–1034.

Kelemen, R. D. (2020). The European Union's authoritarian equilibrium. *Journal of European Public Policy, 27*(3), 481–499.

Kochenov, D. (Ed.). (2017). *EU citizenship and federalism*. Cambridge University Press.

Kohler-Koch, B., & Rittberger, B. (2007). *Debating the democratic legitimacy of the European Union*. Rowman & Littlefield.

Maas, W. (2007). *Creating European citizens*. Rowman & Littlefield.

Maas, W. (2008). Migrants, states, and EU citizenship's unfulfilled promise. *Citizenship Studies, 12*(6), 583–596.

Maas, W. (2014). European Union citizenship in retrospect and prospect. In *Routledge handbook of global citizenship studies*, (pp. 431–439). Routledge.

Mantu, S., Minderhoud, P., & Guild, E. (2020). *EU citizenship and free movement rights: Taking supranational citizenship*. BRILL.

Marshall, T. (1950). *Citizenship and social class and other essays*. Cambridge University Press.

Matthijs, M., & Merler, S. (2020). "mind the gap: Southern exit, northern voice and changing loyalties since the euro crisis." *JCMS. Journal of Common Market Studies, 58 (1):96-115*, 96–115.

McNamara, K. R. (2015). *The politics of everyday Europe: constructing authority in the European Union*. Oxford University Press.

Moravcsik, A. (1993). Preferences and power in the European Community: A liberal intergovernmentalist approach. *JCMS: Journal of Common Market Studies, 31 (4):473-524*, 473–524.

Nicolaïdis, K. (2013). European Demoicracy and its crisis. *JCMS: Journal of Common Market Studies, 51*(2), 351–369.

Peters, F., Vink, M., & Schmeets, H. (2018). Anticipating the citizenship premium: Before and after effects of immigrant naturalisation on employment. *Journal of Ethnic and Migration Studies, 44*(7), 1051–1080.

Schuck, P. H. (1998). Delgation and democracy: Comments on David Schoenbrod. *Cardozo Law Review, 20*, 775.

Soysal, Y. N. (1994). *Limits of citizenship : Migrants and postnational membership in Europe.* University of Chicago.

Swider, K. (2020). Legitimizing precarity of EU citizenship: Tjebbes. *Common Market Law Review, 57*(4), 1163–1182.

Tilly, C. (1997). A primer on citizenship. *Theory and Society, 26*(4), 599–602.

Tsebelis, G. (1994). The power of the European Parliament as a conditional agenda setter. *American Political Science Review, 88*(1), 128–142.

van den Brink, M., & Kochenov, D. (2019). Against associate EU citizenship. *JCMS: Journal of Common Market Studies, 57*, 1366–1382.

Vink, M. (2001). The limited Europeanization of domestic citizenship policy: Evidence from the Netherlands. *Journal of Common Market Studies, 39*(5), 875–896.

Vink, M. (2004). The unbearable lightness of European citizenship. *Citizenship, Social and Economics Education, 6*(1), 24–33.

Vink, M. P. (2005). *Limits of European citizenship : European integration and domestic immigration policies.* Palgrave Macmillan.

Weale, A. (2014). Citizenship in Europe and the logic of two-level political contracts. *German Law Journal, 15*(5), 867–881.

Weber, E. (1976). *Peasants into Frenchmen : The modernization of rural France, 1870–1914.* Stanford University Press.

Weiler, J. H. H. (1999). *The constitution of Europe:'Do the new clothes have an emperor?'and other essays on European integration.* Cambridge University Press.

Appendix

Chapter 3

Table S3.1 Descriptive statistics (1) full sample and household income groups (immigrants from the EU, incl. CH, IS and NO but excl. HR; 2007–2014)

		Overall	Below modal household income	Equal or above modal household income
Naturalised	Yes	34.45	36.24	29.02
	No	65.55	63.76	70.98
Gender	Male	39.28	39.52	38.55
	Female	60.72	60.48	61.45
Years since migration	3–9	26.97	27.05	26.71
	10–14	14.80	14.04	17.08
	15–19	11.58	11.46	11.96
	20–24	9.46	9.20	10.22
	25–29	7.76	7.33	9.06
	30–34	7.91	7.48	9.22
	35–39	7.38	7.44	7.21
	40+	14.15	16.00	8.54
Age at migration	18–30	64.09	64.59	62.58
	31–40	24.34	23.36	27.31
	41–50	8.11	8.31	7.53
	51+	3.46	3.75	2.58
Partner	No partner	27.38	31.42	15.16
	Foreign-born foreign partner	16.31	15.45	18.91
	Foreign-born Dutch partner	5.88	6.04	5.38

(continued)

Table S3.1 (continued)

		Overall	Below modal household income	Equal or above modal household income
	Native partner	50.43	47.09	60.56
Minor children	Yes	31.81	32.23	30.52
	No	68.19	67.77	69.48
Highest level of education	Low	13.06	15.82	4.72
	Middle	16.05	17.67	11.15
	High	15.36	12.85	22.97
	Unknown	55.52	53.66	61.15
Employment	Yes	55.16	49.31	72.89
	No	44.84	50.69	27.11
Household income	1–15,000	17.46	23.23	0
	15,001–20,000	20.33	27.04	0
	20,001–25,000	18.02	23.97	0
	25,001–30,000	14.05	18.69	0
	30,001+	30.14	7.08	100
		N = 203,962	N = 176,806	N = 77,796
		Obs = 1,230,925	Obs = 925,502	Obs = 305,423

Source: Statistics Netherlands

Table S3.2 Descriptive statistics (2) full sample and household income groups (immigrants from the EU, incl. CH, IS and NO but excl. HR; 2007–2014)

	Overall		Below modal household income		Equal or above modal household income	
	Mean	Std. deviation	Mean	Std. deviation	Mean	Std. deviation
Naturalised	0.3445	0.4752	0.3624	0.4807	0.2902	0.4539
Male	0.3928	0.4884	0.3952	0.4889	0.3855	0.4867
Years since migration	22.5230	14.5027	23.0355	14.9867	20.9700	12.8014
Age at migration	29.7617	8.9141	29.7239	9.1536	29.8761	8.1445
No partner	0.2738	0.4459	0.3142	0.4642	0.1516	0.3586
Foreign-born foreign partner	0.1631	0.3694	0.1545	0.3614	0.1891	0.3916
Foreign-born Dutch partner	0.0588	0.2352	0.0604	0.2383	0.0538	0.2257
Native partner	0.5043	0.5000	0.4709	0.4992	0.6056	0.4887
Minor children	0.3181	0.4657	0.3223	0.4674	0.3052	0.4605

(continued)

Table S3.2 (continued)

	Overall		Below modal household income		Equal or above modal household income	
Low education	0.1306	0.3370	0.1582	0.3649	0.0472	0.2121
Middle education	0.1605	0.3671	0.1767	0.3814	0.1115	0.3148
High education	0.1536	0.3606	0.1285	0.3347	0.2297	0.4207
Unknown education	0.5552	0.4969	0.5366	0.4987	0.6115	0.4874
Employment	0.5516	0.4973	0.4931	0.5000	0.7289	0.4445
Household income	28,004.99	34,307.33	20,056.50	6,642.64	52,090.77	61,953.88
	N = 203,962		N = 176,806		N = 77,796	
	Obs = 1,230,925		Obs = 925,502		Obs = 305,423	

Source: Statistics Netherlands

Table S3.3 Linear fixed-effects regression on the heterogeneous effect of the increase in application fees for naturalisation in the Netherlands in 2010 on naturalisation rates (immigrants from the EU, incl. CH, IS and NO but excl. HR; 2007–2014)[a]

	F.E. regression			F.E. regression – below modal household income			F.E. regression – equal or above modal household income		
	B		Std. error	B		Std. error	B		Std. error
2010–2014	−0.069	***	0.001	−0.072	***	0.001	−0.056	***	0.002
2007–2009	ref.		ref.	ref.		ref.	ref.		ref.
***: p < 0.001	N = 203,962			N = 176,806			N = 77,796		
	Obs = 1,230,925			Obs = 925,502			Obs = 305,423		
	R^2 = 0.3418			R^2 = 0.3468			R^2 = 0.3344		

Source: Statistics Netherlands

[a]Results include controls for gender, years since migration, years since migration squared, age at migration, age at migration squared, partner status, having minor children, employment, household income, highest level of education, dual citizenship toleration, municipality fixed-effects, origin country fixed-effects, and the annual employment rate and vote share for far-right parties. Standard errors clustered by individuals

Table S3.4 Linear difference-in-differences regression on the effect of the increase in application fees for naturalisation in the Netherlands in 2010 on naturalisation rates among immigrants from below modal income households relative to immigrants from above modal income households (immigrants from the EU, incl. CH, IS and NO but excl. HR; 2007–2014)[a]

	Main model			Parallel trend assumption		
	B		Std. error	B		Std. error
post * < modal household income	−0.015	***	0.002			
2007 * < modal household income				ref.		ref.
2008 * < modal household income				−0.002		0.002
2009 * < modal household income				−0.001		0.002
2010 * < modal household income				−0.007	**	0.002
2011 * < modal household income				−0.008	**	0.003
2012 * < modal household income				−0.014	***	0.003
2013 * < modal household income				−0.024	***	0.003
2014 * < modal household income				−0.031	***	0.003
**: $p < 0.01$	N = 203,962			N = 203,962		
***: $p < 0.001$	Obs = 1,230,925			Obs = 1,230,925		
	$R^2 = 0.3411$			$R^2 = 0.3411$		

Source: Statistics Netherlands
[a]Results include controls for gender, years since migration, years since migration squared, age at migration, age at migration squared, partner status, having minor children, employment, household income, highest level of education, dual citizenship toleration, municipality fixed-effects, origin country fixed-effects and year fixed-effects. Standard errors clustered by individuals

Table S3.5 Linear fixed-effects regression on the heterogeneous effect of the increase in application fees for naturalisation in the Netherlands in 2010 on naturalisation rates, including coefficients for covariates (immigrants from the EU, incl. CH, IS and NO but excl. HR)[a]

		B		Std. error
Post * < modal household income		−0.015	***	0.002
Post		−0.041	***	0.001
< modal household income		0.016	***	0.002
Gender	Male	0.119	***	0.002
	Female	ref.		ref.
Years since migration		0.021	***	0.000
Years since migration ^ 2		−0.000	***	0.000
Age at migration		−0.011	***	0.001
Age at migration ^ 2		0.000	***	0.000
Partner	No partner	ref.		ref.
	Foreign-born foreign partner	−0.209	***	0.002
	Foreign-born naturalised partner	0.121	***	0.006
	Native partner	−0.006		0.005
Minor children	Yes	0.006	**	0.002
	No	ref.		ref.
Paid employment	Yes	−0.001		0.002
	No	ref.		ref.
Household income		0.000	*	0.000

(continued)

Table S3.5 (continued)

		B		Std. error
Highest level of education	High	ref.		ref.
	Middle	−0.005		0.004
	Low	−0.021	***	0.004
	Unknown	−0.020	***	0.003
Dual citizenship toleration	Yes	0.007		0.005
	No	ref.		ref.
*: p < 0.05		N = 203,962		
**: p < 0.01		Obs = 1,230,925		
***: p < 0.001		R^2 = 0.3411		

Source: Statistics Netherlands
[a]Includes municipality fixed-effects and origin country fixed-effects. Standard errors clustered by individuals

Chapter 4

Table S4.1 Top non-UK nationalities in the UK, 2019

Nationality	Born in UK	Born in country of nationality	Other country of birth
Poland	125,000	771,000	5,000
Romania	34,000	400,000	16,000
India	18,000	336,000	11,000
Ireland	–	294,000	26,000
Italy	22,000	203,000	79,000
Portugal	22,000	154,000	75,000
Pakistan	20,000	182,000	5,000
France	19,000	147,000	25,000
Lithuania	22,000	162,000	5,000
Spain	13,000	132,000	43,000
Germany	9,000	109,000	26,000
United States	5,000	88,000	46,000
Bulgaria	7,000	110,000	4,000
China	5,000	82,000	25,000
Hungary	7,000	88,000	14,000
Latvia	11,000	85,000	3,000
Nigeria	8,000	88,000	2,000
Netherlands	10,000	54,000	24,000
Australia	4,000	76,000	6,000
South Africa	3,000	80,000	3,000
EU citizens	**333,000**	**2,967,000**	**415,000**
Non-EU citizens	**141,000**	**2,184,000**	**205,000**

Source: ONS Population by country of birth and nationality (January 2019–December 2019), table 2.6

Chapter 6

Table S6.1 SNRPs included in this article (Overview of the selected parties and their electoral performance from 1990–2018)

South Tyrol legislative term/seats in regional parliament / party (year of foundation)	1993–1998	1998–2003	2003–2008	2008–2013	2013–2018	2018–
Südtiroler Volkspartei/SVP (1958)	19	21	21	18	17	15
Die Freiheitlichen/dF (1992)	2	1	2	5	6	2
Union für Südtirol/UfS (1992)	2	2	2	1	1 (BU)	0
Südtiroler Freiheit/SF (2007)	split from UfS in 2007			2	3	2
total seats of ethno-regionalist parties (total assembly = 35)	*23*	*24*	*25*	*26*	*27*	*19*
Percentage of regionalist parties in the assembly	*65.7%*	*68.5%*	*71.4%*	*74.2%*	*77%*	*54%*

Corsica legislative term/seats in regional parliament / party (year of foundation)	1992–1998	1998–2004 (1999–2004, the elections of 1998 have been annulled and repeated 1999)	2004–2010	2010–2015	2017–
Corsica Nazione/CN (1987)	9	8	transformed into PN in 2001		
Presenza Nazionale/PN (2001)			8 (in coalition with CHJAMA – PNC – CN/ INDEP – ANC – VERDI – PSI)		41 Pe a Corsica (Coalition of all regionalist parties)
Corsica Libera/CL		merged with CN, *Rinnovu* and *A Mossa Naziunale*		4	
Femu A Corsica/FeC		merger of UPC, *A Scelta Nova* and *A Mossa Naziunale*		11	

	1990–1994	1994–1998	1998–2001	2001–2005	2005–2009	2009–2013	2012–2016	2016–
total seats of ethno-regionalist parties (total assembly = 51)	13 — 4 seats were gained by the MPA (*Movimientu per l'Autodeterminazionel* Movement for Self-determination)	8	8			15	41	
Percentage of regionalist parties in the assembly	25.5%	15.7%	15.7%			29.4%	65%	

Basque Country

legislative term/ seats in regional parliament **party (year of foundation)**	1990–1994	1994–1998	1998–2001	2001–2005	2005–2009	2009–2013	2012–2016	2016–
Partido Nacionalista Vasco/PNV (1895)	22	22	21	33	29	30	27	27
Herri Batasuna/HB (1978)	13	11	renamed EH					
Euskal Herritarrok/EH (1998)			14	renamed B				
Bildu/B (2001)				7	banned in 2003		21 Coalition Bildu	21 (Bildu)
Euskal Herrialdeetako Alderdi Komunista/EHAK (2002)					9			
Aralar Party (2000)					1	4		
Euskadiko Ezuerra/EE (split from EE for 1990 elections, and a part of it merged after 1990 elections with Partido Socialista de Euskadi (PSE), another again with EA)	1							
Eusko Alkartasuna/EA (1987)	9	8	6			1		
total seats of ethno-regionalist parties (total assembly = 75)	45	41	41	40	39	35	48	48
Percentage of regionalist parties in the assembly	60%	54.5%	54.5%	53.3%	52%	46.7%	64%	64%

(continued)

Table S6.1 (continued)

Scotland	1999–2003	2003–2007	2007–2011	2011–2015	2016–
legislative term/seats in regional parliament* the prior electoral performance of the SNP at the UK parliament: **1992: 3/651 seats** **1997: 6/651 seats**					
party (year of foundation)					
Scottish National Party/SNP (1934)	35	27	47	69	63
SG (1999)	1	7	2	1	6
total seats of ethno-regionalist parties (total assembly = 129)	*36*	*34*	*49*	*70*	*69*
Percentage of regionalist parties in the assembly	*27.9%*	*26.4%*	*38%*	*54.3%*	*53.5%*

Wales	1999–2003	2003–2007	2007–2011	2011–2015	2016–
legislative term/seats in regional parliament* the prior electoral performance of the SNP at the UK parliament: **1992: 4/651 seats** **1997: 4/651 seats**					
party (year of foundation)* the prior electoral performance at the UK parliament is not listed					
Plaid Cymru/PC (1925)	17	17	15	11	12
total seats of ethno-regionalist parties (total assembly = 60)	*17*	*17*	*15*	*11*	*12*
Percentage of regionalist parties in the assembly	*28.3%*	*28.3%*	*25%*	*18.3%*	*20%*

Data: homepages of the regional governments

Table S6.2 Overview of ideological positions of the elected SNRPs in the five minority nations (electoral systems indicated in brackets in the row heading)

	Non-secessionist parties		Ambiguous parties	Secessionist parties	
	moderately autonomist	assertive autonomist		strongly committed to secession	extremist (by violent means)
South Tyrol *(personalized proportional representation)*		SVP (centre-right)		UfS (right); dF (right); SF (right)	
Basque Country *(closed list proportional representation)*		PNV (1990–2000; centre-right) Bildu (centre-right)	PNV (2000s; centre-right)	EE (left); EA (centre-left); Aralar (radical-left)	HB-B (radical-left)
Scotland *(mixed member proportional representation system)*				SNP (centre-left)	
Wales *(mixed member proportional representation system)*		PC (left)			
Corsica *(personalized proportional representation)*		FeC (left) Pe A Corsica (left)		CL (left); Coalition of CHJAMA – PNC – CN/ INDEP – ANC – VERDI – PSI (left); MPA (left)	

Table S6.3 Overview of minority regions

	Total population (census 2011)	Members of minority – use of language/self-identification	% share of migrants 2011 and main migrant groups
Basque Country	2,179,815	~25% Basque as first language	139,369 6.4% Romania, Morocco, Colombia
Corsica	314,486	10% use Corsican on a regular basis	27,481 8.7% Maghreb, Portugal, Italy
South Tyrol	505,067	69.4% identify as German speakers, 26% Italian, 4.5% Ladin	44,362 8.7% Albania, Germany, Morocco, Pakistan
Scotland	5,295,403	84% identify as Scottish	347,045 6.5% South Asia, Romania, Poland
Wales	3,063,456	19% speak Welsh on a regular basis	167,871 5.5% South Asia, Romania, Poland

The manufacturer's authorised representative in the EU is Springer
Nature Customer Service Centre GmbH, Europaplatz 3, 69115 Heidelberg,
Germany. If you have any concerns regarding our products, please
contact ProductSafety@springernature.com

Printed and bound by CPI Group (UK) Ltd, Croydon, CR0 4YY

29/04/2026
02099526-0001